Quantitative Models in

Recent advances in data c   nable
marketing researchers to st   e of
transactions and purchases, i   cific
characteristics and marketing

 This book presents the mos   practically relevant quantitative models for marketing research. Each model is presented in detail with a self-contained discussion, which includes: a demonstration of the mechanics of the model, empirical analysis, real-world examples, and interpretation of results and findings. The reader of the book will learn how to apply the techniques, as well as understand the latest methodological developments in the academic literature.

 Pathways are offered in the book for students and practitioners with differing statistical and mathematical skill levels, although a basic knowledge of elementary numerical techniques is assumed.

PHILIP HANS FRANSES is Professor of Applied Econometrics affiliated with the Econometric Institute and Professor of Marketing Research affiliated with the Department of Marketing and Organization, both at Erasmus University Rotterdam. He has written successful textbooks in time series analysis.

RICHARD PAAP is Postdoctoral Researcher with the Rotterdam Institute for Business Economic Studies at Erasmus University Rotterdam. His research interests cover applied (macro-)econometrics, Bayesian statistics, time series analysis, and marketing research.

Quantitative Models in Marketing Research

Philip Hans Franses

and

Richard Paap

CAMBRIDGE
UNIVERSITY PRESS

CAMBRIDGE UNIVERSITY PRESS
Cambridge, New York, Melbourne, Madrid, Cape Town, Singapore,
São Paulo, Delhi, Dubai, Tokyo, Mexico City

Cambridge University Press
The Edinburgh Building, Cambridge CB2 8RU, UK

Published in the United States of America by Cambridge University Press, New York

www.cambridge.org
Information on this title: www.cambridge.org/9780521143653

First published 2001
Fifth printing 2007
First paperback printing 2010

A catalogue record for this publication is available from the British Library

Library of Congress Cataloguing in Publication data

Franses, Philip Hans, 1963–
    Quantitative models in marketing research / by Philip Hans Franses
    and Richard Paap.
        p.   cm.
    Includes bibliographical references and index.
    ISBN 0-521-80166-4
    1. Marketing research–Mathematical models. I. Paap, Richard. II. Title.

HF5415.2 .F714 2001
658.8′3′015118–dc21   2001025424

ISBN 978-0-521-80166-9 Hardback
ISBN 978-0-521-14365-3 Paperback

Cambridge University Press has no responsibility for the persistence or
accuracy of URLs for external or third-party Internet Web sites referred to in
this publication, and does not guarantee that any content on such Web sites is,
or will remain, accurate or appropriate.

Contents

Figures

Tables

Preface

In marketing research one sometimes considers rather advanced quantitative (econometric) models for revealed preference data (such as sales and brand choice). Owing to an increased availability of empirical data, market researchers can choose between a variety of models, such as regression models, choice models and duration models. In this book we summarize several relevant models and deal with these in a fairly systematic manner. It is our hope that academics and practitioners find this book useful as a reference guide, that students learn to grasp the basic principles, and, in general, that the reader finds it useful for a better understanding of the academic literature on marketing research.

Several individuals affiliated with the marketing group at the School of Economics, Erasmus University Rotterdam, helped us with the data and presentation. We thank Dennis Fok and Jedid-Jah Jonker for making some of the data accessible to us. The original data were provided by ROBECO and the Astmafonds and we thank these institutions for their kind assistance. Paul de Boer, Charles Bos, Bas Donkers, Rutger van Oest, Peter Verhoef and an anonymous reviewer went through the entire manuscript and made many useful comments. Finally, we thank the Rotterdam Institute for Business Economic Studies (RIBES) and the Econometric Institute for providing a stimulating research environment and the Netherlands Organization for Scientific Research (NWO) for its financial support.

PHILIP HANS FRANSES
RICHARD PAAP
Rotterdam, November 2000

1 Introduction and outline of the book

Recent advances in data collection and data storage techniques enable marketing researchers to study the characteristics of many actual transactions and purchases, that is, revealed preference data. Owing to the large number of observations and the wealth of available information, a detailed analysis of these data is possible. This analysis usually addresses the effects of marketing instruments and the effects of household-specific characteristics on the transaction. Quantitative models are useful tools for this analysis. In this book we review several such models for revealed preference data. In this chapter we give a general introduction and provide brief introductions to the various chapters.

1.1 Introduction

It is the aim of this book to present various important and practically relevant quantitative models, which can be used in present-day marketing research. The reader of this book should become able to apply these methods in practice, as we provide the data which we use in the various illustrations and we also add the relevant computer code for EViews if it is not already included in version 3.1. Other statistical packages that include estimation routines for some of the reviewed models are, for example, LIMDEP, SPSS and SAS. Next, the reader should come to understand (the flavor of) the latest methodological developments as these are put forward in articles in, for example, *Marketing Science*, the *Journal of Marketing Research*, the *Journal of Consumer Research* and the *International Journal of Research in Marketing*. For that matter, we also discuss interesting new developments in the relevant sections.

The contents of this book originate from lecture notes prepared for undergraduate and graduate students in Marketing Research and in Econometrics. Indeed, it is our intention that this book can be used at different teaching levels. With that aim, all chapters have the same format, and we indicate which sections correspond with which teaching level. In section 1.2, we will provide more details. For all readers, however, it is necessary to have a basic knowledge of elementary regression techniques and of some matrix algebra. Most introductory texts on quantitative methods include such material, but as a courtesy we bring together some important topics in an Appendix at the end of this book.

There are a few other books dealing with sets of quantitative models similar to the ones we consider. Examples are Maddala (1983), Ben-Akiva and Lerman (1985), Cramer (1991) and Long (1997). The present book differs from these textbooks in at least three respects. The first is that we discuss the models and their specific application in marketing research concerning revealed preference data. Hence, we pay substantial attention to the interpretation and evaluation of the models in the light of the specific applications. The second difference is that we incorporate recent important developments, such as modeling unobserved heterogeneity and sample selection, which have already become quite standard in academic marketing research studies (as may be noticed from many relevant articles in, for example, the *Journal of Marketing Research* and *Marketing Science*). The third difference concerns the presentation of the material, as will become clear in section 1.2 below. At times the technical level is high, but we believe it is needed in order to make the book reasonably self-contained.

1.1.1 On marketing research

A useful definition of marketing research, given in the excellent introductory textbook by Lehmann et al. (1998, p. 1), is that "[m]arketing research is the collection, processing, and analysis of information on topics relevant to marketing. It begins with problem definition and ends with a report and action recommendations." In the present book we focus only on the part that concerns the analysis of information. Additionally, we address only the type of analysis that requires the application of statistical and econometric methods, which we summarize under the heading of quantitative models. The data concern revealed preference data such as sales and brand choice. In other words, we consider models for quantitative data, where we pay specific attention to those models that are useful for marketing research. We do not consider models for stated preference data or other types of survey data, and hence we abstain from, for example, LISREL-type models and various multivariate techniques. For a recent treatment of combining revealed and stated preference data, see Hensher et al. (1999). Finally, we assume that the data have already been collected and that the research question has been clearly defined.

The reasons we focus on revealed preference data, instead of on stated preference data, are as follows. First, there are already several textbooks on LISREL-type models (see, for example, Jöreskog and Sörbom, 1993) and on multivariate statistical techniques (see, for example, Johnson and Wichern, 1998). Second, even though marketing research often involves the collection and analysis of stated preference data, we observe an increasing availability of revealed preference data.

Typical research questions in marketing research concern the effects of marketing instruments and household-specific characteristics on various marketing performance measures. Examples of these measures are sales, market shares, brand choice and interpurchase times. Given knowledge of these effects, one can decide to use marketing instruments in a selective manner and to address only apparently relevant subsamples of the available population of households. The latter is usually called segmentation.

Recent advances in data collection and data storage techniques, which result in large data bases with a substantial amount of information, seem to have changed the nature of marketing research. Using loyalty cards and scanners, supermarket chains can track all purchases by individual house-holds (and even collect information on the brands and products that were not purchased). Insurance companies, investment firms and charity institutions keep track of all observable activities by their clients or donors. These developments have made it possible to analyze not only what individuals themselves state they do or would do (that is, stated preference), but also what individuals actually do (revealed preference). This paves the way for greater insights into what really drives loyalty to an insurance company or into the optimal design for a supermarket, to mention just a few possible issues. In the end, this could strengthen the relationship between firms and customers.

The large amount of accurately measured marketing research data implies that simple graphical tools and elementary modeling techniques in most cases simply do not suffice for dealing with present-day problems in marketing. In general, if one wants to get the most out of the available data bases, one most likely needs to resort to more advanced techniques. An additional reason is that more detailed data allow more detailed questions to be answered. In many cases, more advanced techniques involve quantitative models, which enable the marketing researcher to examine various correlations between marketing response variables and explanatory variables measuring, for example, household-specific characteristics, demographic variables and marketing-mix variables.

In sum, in this book we focus on quantitative models for revealed preference data in marketing research. For conciseness, we do not discuss the various issues related to solving business problems, as this would require an entirely different book. The models we consider are to be viewed as helpful practical tools when analyzing marketing data, and this analysis can be part of a more comprehensive approach to solving business problems.

1.1.2   Data

Marketing performance measures can appear in a variety of formats. And, as we will demonstrate in this book, these differing formats often need different models in order to perform a useful analysis of these measures.

To illustrate varying formats, consider "sales" to be an obvious marketing performance measure. If "sales" concerns the number of items purchased, the resultant observations can amount to a limited range of count data, such as 1, 2, 3, ... However, if "sales" refers to the monetary value in dollars (or cents) of the total number of items purchased, we may consider it as a continuous variable. Because the evaluation of a company's sales may depend on all other sales, one may instead want to consider market shares. These variables are bounded between 0 and 1 by construction.

Sales and market shares concern variables which are observed over time. Typically one analyzes weekly sales and market shares. Many other marketing research data, however, take only discrete (categorical) values or are only partially observed. The individual response to a direct mailing can take a value of 1 if there is a response, and 0 if the individual does not respond. In that case one has encountered a binomial dependent variable. If households can choose between three or more brands, say brands A, B, C and D, one has encountered a multinomial dependent variable. It may then be of interest to examine whether or not marketing-mix instruments have an effect on brand choice. If the brands have a known quality or preference ranking that is common to all households, the multinomial dependent variable is said to be ordered; if not, it is unordered. Another example of an ordered categorical variable concerns questionnaire items, for which individuals indicate to what extent they disagree, are indifferent, or agree with a certain statement.

Marketing research data can also be only partially observed. An example concerns donations to charity, for which individuals have received a direct mailing. Several of these individuals do not respond, and hence donate nothing, while others do respond and at the same time donate some amount. The interest usually lies in investigating the distinguishing characteristics of the individuals who donate a lot and those who donate a lesser amount, while taking into account that individuals with perhaps similar characteristics donate nothing. These data are called censored data. If one knows the amount donated by an individual only if it exceeds, say, $10, the corresponding data are called truncated data.

Censoring is also a property of duration data. This type of observation usually concerns the time that elapses between two events. Examples in marketing research are interpurchase times and the duration of a relationship between a firm and its customers. These observations are usually collected for panels of individuals, observed over a span of time. At the time of the first observations, it is unlikely that all households buy a product or brand at the same time, and hence it is likely that some durations (or relationships) are already ongoing. Such interpurchase times can be useful in order to understand, for example, whether or not promotions accelerate purchasing behavior. For direct marketing, one might model the time between sending out the direct mailing and the response, which perhaps can be reduced by additional nationwide advertising. In addition, insurance companies may benefit from lengthy relationships with their customers.

1.1.3   Models

As might be expected from the above summary, it is highly unlikely that all these different types of data could be squeezed into one single model framework. Sales can perhaps be modeled by single-equation linear regression models and market shares by multiple-equation regression models (because market shares are interconnected), whereas binomial and multinomial data require models that take into account that the dependent variable is not continuous. In fact, the models for these choice data usually consider, for example, the probability of a response to a direct mailing and the probability that a brand is selected out of a set of possible brands. Censored data require models that take into account the probability that, for example, households do not donate to charity. Finally, models for duration data take into account that the time that has elapsed since the last event has an effect on the probability that the next event will happen.

It is the purpose of this book to review quantitative models for various typical marketing research data. The standard Linear Regression model is one example, while the Multinomial Logit model, the Binomial Logit model, the Nested Logit model, the Censored Regression model and the Proportional Hazard model are other examples. Even though these models have different names and take account of the properties of the variable to be explained, the underlying econometric principles are the same. One can summarize these principles under the heading of an econometric modeling cycle. This cycle involves an understanding of the representation of the model (what does the model actually do? what can the model predict? how can one interpret the parameters?), estimation of the unknown parameters, evaluation of the model (does the model summarize the data in an adequate way? are there ways to improve the model?), and the extension of the model, if required.

We follow this rather schematic approach, because it is our impression that studies in the academic marketing research literature are sometimes not very explicit about the decision to use a particular model, how the parameters were estimated, and how the model results should be interpreted. Additionally, there are now various statistical packages which include estimation routines for such models as the Nested Logit model and the Ordered Probit model (to name just a few of the more exotic ones), and it frequently turns out that it is not easy to interpret the output of these statistical packages and to verify the adequacy of the procedures followed. In many cases this output contains a wealth of statistical information, and it is not always clear what this all means and what one should do if statistics take particular values. By making explicit several of the modeling steps, we aim to bridge this potential gap between theory and practice.

1.2   Outline of the book

This book aims to describe some of the main features of various potentially useful quantitative models for marketing research data. Following a chapter on the data used throughout this book, there are six chapters, each dealing with one type of dependent variable. These chapters are subdivided into sections on (1) representation and interpretation, (2) the estimation of the model parameters, (3) model diagnostics and inference, (4) a detailed illustration and (5) advanced topics.

All models and methods are illustrated using actual data sets that are or have been effectively used in empirical marketing research studies in the academic literature. The data are available through relevant websites. In chapter 2, we discuss the data and also some of the research questions. To sharpen the focus, we will take the data as the main illustration throughout each chapter. This means that, for example, the chapter on a multinomial dependent variable (chapter 5) assumes that such a model is useful for modeling brand choice. Needless to say, such a model may also be useful for other applications. Additionally, to reduce confusion, we will consider the behavior of a household, and assume that it makes the decisions. Of course this can be replaced by individuals, customers or other entities, if needed.

1.2.1   *How to use this book*

The contents of the book are organized in such a way that it can be used for teaching at various levels or for personal use given different levels of training.

The first of the five sections in each of chapters 3 to 8 contains the representation of the relevant model, the interpretation of the parameters, and sometimes the interpretation of the full model (by focusing, for example, on elasticities). The fourth section contains a detailed illustration, whose content one should be able to grasp given an understanding of the content of the first section. These two sections can be used for undergraduate as well as for graduate teaching at a not too technical level. In fact, we ourselves have tried out these sections on undergraduate students in marketing at Erasmus University Rotterdam (and, so far, we have not lost our jobs).

Sections 2 and 3 usually contain more technical material because they deal with parameter estimation, diagnostics, forecasting and model selection. Section 2 always concerns parameter estimation, and usually we focus on the Maximum Likelihood method. We provide ample details of this method as we believe it is useful for a better understanding of the principles under-lying the diagnostic tests in section 3. Furthermore, many computer packages do not provide diagnostics and, using the formulas in section 2, one can compute them oneself. Finally, if one wants to program the estima-tion routines oneself, one can readily use the material. In many cases one can replicate our estimation results using the relevant standard routines in EViews (version 3.1). In some cases these routines do not exist, and in that case we give the relevant EViews code at the end of the relevant chap-ters. In addition to sections 1 and 4, one could consider using sections 2 and 3 to teach more advanced undergraduate students, who have a training in econometrics or advanced quantitative methods, or graduate students in marketing or econometrics.

Finally, section 5 of each chapter contains advanced material, which may not be useful for teaching. These sections may be better suited to advanced graduate students and academics. Academics may want to use the entire book as a reference source.

1.2.2 Outline of chapter contents

The outline of the various chapters is as follows. In chapter 2 we start off with detailed graphical and tabulated summaries of the data. We consider weekly sales, a binomial variable indicating the choice between two brands, an unordered multinomial variable concerning the choice between four brands, an ordered multinomial variable for household-specific risk profiles, a censored variable measuring the amount of money donated to charity and, finally, interpurchase times in relation to liquid detergent.

In chapter 3 we give a concise treatment of the standard Linear Regression model, which can be useful for a continuous dependent variable. We assume some knowledge of basic matrix algebra and of elementary

statistics. We discuss the representation of the model and the interpretation
of its parameters. We also discuss Ordinary Least Squares (OLS) and
Maximum Likelihood (ML) estimation methods. The latter method is discussed because it will be used in most chapters, although the concepts underlying the OLS method return in chapters 7 and 8. We choose to follow the
convention that the standard Linear Regression model assumes that the data
are normally distributed with a constant variance but with a mean that
obtains different values depending on the explanatory variables. Along similar lines, we will introduce models for binomial, multinomial and duration
dependent variables in subsequent chapters. The advanced topics section in
chapter 3 deals with the attraction model for market shares. This model
ensures that market shares sum to unity and that they lie within the range
$[0, 1]$.

The next chapter deals with a binomial dependent variable. We discuss the
binomial Logit and Probit models. These models assume a nonlinear relation
between the explanatory variables and the variable to be explained.
Therefore, we pay considerable attention to parameter interpretation and
model interpretation. We discuss the ML estimation method and we provide
some relevant model diagnostics and evaluation criteria. As with the standard Linear Regression model, the diagnostics are based on the residuals
from the model. Because these residuals can be defined in various ways for
these models, we discuss this issue at some length. The advanced topics
section is dedicated to the inclusion of unobserved parameter heterogeneity
in the model and to the effects of sample selection for the Logit model.

In chapter 5 we expand on the material of chapter 4 by focusing on an
unordered multinomial dependent variable. Quite a number of models can
be considered, for example the Multinomial Logit model, the Multinomial
Probit model, the Nested Logit model and the Conditional Logit model. We
pay substantial attention to outlining the key differences between the various
models in particular because these are frequently used in empirical marketing
research.

In chapter 6 we focus on the Logit model and the Probit model for an
ordered multinomial dependent variable. Examples of ordered multinomial
data typically appear in questionnaires. The example in chapter 6 concerns
customers of a financial investment firm who have been assigned to three
categories depending on their risk profiles. It is the aim of the empirical
analysis to investigate which customer-specific characteristics can explain
this classification. In the advanced topics section, we discuss various other
models for ordered categorical data.

Chapter 7 deals with censored and truncated dependent variables, that is,
with variables that are partly continuous and partly take some fixed value
(such as 0 or 100) or are partly unknown. We mainly focus on the Truncated

Regression model and on the two types of Tobit model, the Type-1 and Type-2 Tobit models. We show what happens if one neglects the fact that the data are only partially observed. We discuss estimation methods in substantial detail. The illustration concerns a model for money donated to charity for a large sample of individuals. In the advanced topics section we discuss other types of models for data censored in some way.

Finally, in chapter 8 we deal with a duration dependent variable. This variable has the specific property that its value can be made dependent on the time that has elapsed since the previous event. For some marketing research applications this seems a natural way to go, because it may become increasingly likely that households will buy, for example, detergent if it is already a while since they purchased it. We provide a discussion of the Accelerated Lifetime model and the Proportional Hazard model, and outline their most important differences. The advanced topics section contains a discussion of unobserved heterogeneity. It should be stressed here that the technical level both of chapter 8 and of chapter 5 is high.

Before we turn to the various models, we first look at some marketing research data.

2 Features of marketing research data

The purpose of quantitative models is to summarize marketing research data such that useful conclusions can be drawn. Typically the conclusions concern the impact of explanatory variables on a relevant marketing variable, where we focus only on revealed preference data. To be more precise, the variable to be explained in these models usually is what we call a marketing performance measure, such as sales, market shares or brand choice. The set of explanatory variables often contains marketing-mix variables and household-specific characteristics.

This chapter starts by outlining why it can be useful to consider quantitative models in the first place. Next, we review a variety of performance measures, thereby illustrating that these measures appear in various formats. The focus on these formats is particularly relevant because the marketing measures appear on the left-hand side of a regression model. Were they to be found on the right-hand side, often no or only minor modifications would be needed. Hence there is also a need for different models. The data which will be used in subsequent chapters are presented in tables and graphs, thereby highlighting their most salient features. Finally, we indicate that we limit our focus in at least two directions, the first concerning other types of data, the other concerning the models themselves.

2.1 Quantitative models

The first and obvious question we need to address is whether one needs quantitative models in the first place. Indeed, as is apparent from the table of contents and also from a casual glance at the mathematical formulas in subsequent chapters, the analysis of marketing data using a quantitative model is not necessarily a very straightforward exercise. In fact, for some models one needs to build up substantial empirical skills in order for these models to become useful tools in new applications.

Why then, if quantitative models are more complicated than just looking at graphs and perhaps calculating a few correlations, should one use these models? The answer is not trivial, and it will often depend on the particular application and corresponding marketing question at hand. If one has two sets of weekly observations on sales of a particular brand, one for a store with promotions in all weeks and one for a store with no promotions at all, one may contemplate comparing the two sales series in a histogram and perhaps test whether the average sales figures are significantly different using a simple test. However, if the number of variables that can be correlated with the sales figures increases – for example, the stores differ in type of customers, in advertising efforts or in format – this simple test somehow needs to be adapted to take account of these other variables. In present-day marketing research, one tends to have information on numerous variables that can affect sales, market shares and brand choice. To analyze these observations in a range of bivariate studies would imply the construction of hundreds of tests, which would all be more or less dependent on each other. Hence, one may reject one relationship between two variables simply because one omitted a third variable. To overcome these problems, the simplest strategy is to include all relevant variables in a single quantitative model. Then the effect of a certain explanatory variable is corrected automatically for the effects of other variables.

A second argument for using a quantitative model concerns the notion of correlation itself. In most practical cases, one considers the linear correlation between variables, where it is implicitly assumed that these variables are continuous. However, as will become apparent in the next section and in subsequent chapters, many interesting marketing variables are not continuous but discrete (for example, brand choice). Hence, it is unclear how one should define a correlation. Additionally, for some marketing variables, such as donations to charity or interpurchase times, it is unlikely that a useful correlation between these variables and potential explanatory variables is linear. Indeed, we will show in various chapters that the nature of many marketing variables makes the linear concept of correlation less useful.

In sum, for a small number of observations on just a few variables, one may want to rely on simple graphical or statistical techniques. However, when complexity increases, in terms of numbers of observations and of variables, it may be much more convenient to summarize the data using a quantitative model. Within such a framework it is easier to highlight correlation structures. Additionally, one can examine whether or not these correlation structures are statistically relevant, while taking account of all other correlations.

A quantitative model often serves three purposes, that is, description, forecasting and decision-making. Description usually refers to an investigation of which explanatory variables have a statistically significant effect on the dependent variable, conditional on the notion that the model does fit the data well. For example, one may wonder whether display or feature promotion has a positive effect on sales. Once a descriptive model has been constructed, one may use it for out-of-sample forecasting. This means extrapolating the model into the future or to other households and generating forecasts of the dependent variable given observations on the explanatory variables. In some cases, one may need to forecast these explanatory variables as well. Finally, with these forecasts, one may decide that the outcomes are in some way inconvenient, and one may examine which combinations of the explanatory variables would generate, say, more sales or shorter time intervals between purchases. In this book, we will not touch upon such decision-making, and we sometimes discuss forecasting issues only briefly. In fact, we will mainly address the descriptive purpose of a quantitative model.

In order for the model to be useful it is important that the model fits the data well. If it does not, one may easily generate biased forecasts and draw inappropriate conclusions concerning decision rules. A nice feature of the models we discuss in this book, in contrast to rules of thumb or more exploratory techniques, is that the empirical results can be used to infer if the constructed model needs to be improved. Hence, in principle, one can continue with the model-building process until a satisfactory model has been found. Needless to say, this does not always work out in practice, but one can still to some extent learn from previous mistakes.

Finally, we must stress that we believe that quantitative models are useful only if they are considered and applied by those who have the relevant skills and understanding. We do appreciate that marketing managers, who are forced to make decisions on perhaps a day-to-day basis, are not the most likely users of these models. We believe that this should not be seen as a problem, because managers can make decisions on the basis of advice generated by others, for example by marketing researchers. Indeed, the construction of a useful quantitative model may take some time, and there is no guarantee that the model will work. Hence, we would argue that the models to be discussed in this book should be seen as potentially helpful tools, which are particularly useful when they are analyzed by the relevant specialists. Upon translation of these models into management support systems, the models could eventually be very useful to managers (see, for example, Leeflang et al., 2000).

2.2 Marketing performance measures

In this section we review various marketing performance measures, such as sales, brand choice and interpurchase times, and we illustrate these with the data we actually consider in subsequent chapters. Note that the examples are not meant to indicate that simple tools of analysis would not work, as suggested above. Instead, the main message to take from this chapter is that marketing data appear in a variety of formats. Because these variables are the dependent variables, we need to resort to different model types for each variable. Sequentially, we deal with variables that are continuous (such as sales), binomial (such as the choice between two brands), unordered multinomial (a choice between more than two brands), ordered multinomial (attitude rankings), and truncated or censored continuous (donations to charity) and that concern durations (the time between two purchases). The reader will notice that several of the data sets we use were collected quite a while ago. We believe, however, that these data are roughly prototypical of what one would be able to collect nowadays in similar situations. The advantage is that we can now make these data available for free. In fact, all data used in this book can be downloaded from http://www.few.eur.nl/few/people/paap.

2.2.1 A continuous variable

Sales and market shares are usually considered to be continuous variables, especially if these relate to frequently purchased consumer goods. Sales are often measured in terms of dollars (or some other currency), although one might also be interested in the number of units sold. Market shares are calculated in order to facilitate the evaluation of brand sales with respect to category sales. Sales data are bounded below by 0, and market shares data lie between 0 and 1. All brand market shares within a product category sum to 1. This establishes that sales data can be captured by a standard regression model, possibly after transforming sales by taking the natural logarithm to induce symmetry. Market shares, in contrast, require a more complicated model because one needs to analyze all market shares at the same time (see, for example, Cooper and Nakanishi, 1988, and Cooper, 1993).

In chapter 3 we will discuss various aspects of the standard Linear Regression model. We will illustrate the model for weekly sales of Heinz tomato ketchup, measured in US dollars. We have 124 weekly observations, collected between 1985 and 1988 in one supermarket in Sioux Falls, South Dakota. The data were collected by A.C. Nielsen. In figure 2.1 we give a time series graph of the available sales data (this means that the observations are arranged according to the week of observation). From this graph it is immediately obvious that there are many peaks, which correspond with high sales weeks. Naturally it is of interest to examine if these peaks correspond with promotions, and this is what will be pursued in chapter 3.

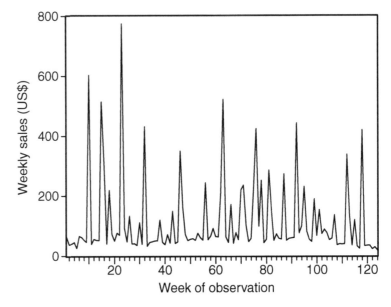

Figure 2.1   Weekly sales of Heinz tomato ketchup

In figure 2.2 we present the same sales data, but in a histogram. This graph shows that the distribution of the data is not symmetric. High sales figures are observed rather infrequently, whereas there are about thirty to forty weeks with sales of about US$50–100. It is now quite common to transform

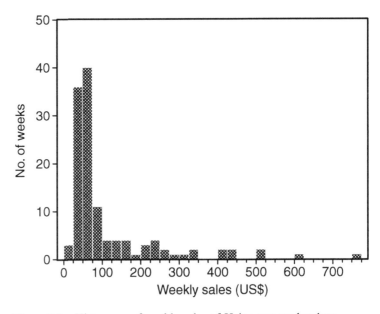

Figure 2.2   Histogram of weekly sales of Heinz tomato ketchup

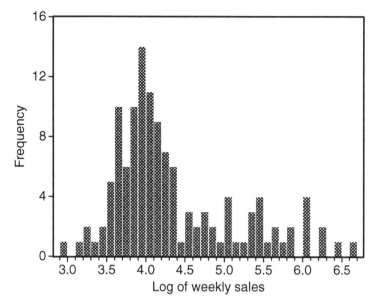

Figure 2.3   Histogram of the log of weekly sales of Heinz tomato ketchup

such a sales variable by applying the natural logarithmic transformation (log). The resultant log sales appear in figure 2.3, and it is clear that the distribution of the data has become more symmetric. Additionally, the distribution seems to obey an approximate bell-shaped curve. Hence, except for a few large observations, the data may perhaps be summarized by an approximately normal distribution. It is exactly this distribution that underlies the standard Linear Regression model, and in chapter 3 we will take it as a starting point for discussion. For further reference, we collect a few important distributions in section A.2 of the Appendix at the end of this book.

In table 2.1 we summarize some characteristics of the dependent variable and explanatory variables concerning this case of weekly sales of Heinz tomato ketchup. The average price paid per item was US$1.16. In more than 25% of the weeks, this brand was on display, while in less than 10% of the weeks there was a coupon promotion. In only about 6% of the weeks, these promotions were held simultaneously. In chapter 3, we will examine whether or not these variables have any explanatory power for log sales while using a standard Linear Regression model.

2.2.2   A binomial variable

Another frequently encountered type of dependent variable in marketing research is a variable that takes only two values. As examples, these values may concern the choice between brand A and brand B (see Malhotra,

Table 2.1 *Characteristics of the dependent variable and explanatory variables: weekly sales of Heinz tomato ketchup*

Variables	Mean
Sales (US$)	114.47
Price (US$)	1.16
% display only[a]	26.61
% coupon only[b]	9.68
% display and coupon[c]	5.65

Notes:
[a]Percentage of weeks in which the brand was on display only.
[b]Percentage of weeks in which the brand had a coupon promotion only.
[c]Percentage of weeks in which the brand was both on display and had a coupon promotion.

1984) or between two suppliers (see Doney and Cannon, 1997), and the value may equal 1 in the case where someone responds to a direct mailing while it equals 0 when someone does not (see Bult, 1993, among others). It is the purpose of the relevant quantitative model to correlate such a binomial variable with explanatory variables. Before going into the details, which will be much better outlined in chapter 4, it suffices here to state that a standard Linear Regression model is unlikely to work well for a binomial dependent variable. In fact, an elegant solution will turn out to be that we do not consider the binomial variable itself as the dependent variable, but merely consider the probability that this variable takes one of the two possible outcomes. In other words, we do not consider the choice for brand A, but we focus on the probability that brand A is preferred. Because this probability is not observed, and in fact only the actual choice is observed, the relevant quantitative models are a bit more complicated than the standard Linear Regression model in chapter 3.

As an illustration, consider the summary in table 2.2, concerning the choice between Heinz and Hunts tomato ketchup. The data originate from a panel of 300 households in Springfield, Missouri, and were collected by A.C. Nielsen using an optical scanner. The data involve the purchases made during a period of about two years. In total, there are 2,798 observations. In 2,491 cases (89.03%), the households purchased Heinz, and in 10.97% of cases they preferred Hunts see also figure 2.4, which shows a histogram of the choices. On average it seems that Heinz and Hunts were about equally expensive, but, of course, this is only an average and it may well be that on specific purchase occasions there were substantial price differences.

Table 2.2 *Characteristics of the dependent*
variable and explanatory variables: the choice
between Heinz and Hunts tomato ketchup

Variables	Heinz	Hunts
Choice percentage	89.03	10.97
Average price (US$ × 100/oz.)	3.48	3.36
% display only[a]	15.98	3.54
% feature only[b]	12.47	3.65
% feature and display[c]	3.75	0.93

Notes:
[a]Percentage of purchase occasions when a brand was
on display only.
[b]Percentage of purchase occasions when a brand was
featured only.
[c]Percentage of purchase occasions when a brand was
both on display and featured.

Furthermore, table 2.2 contains information on promotional activities such
as display and feature. It can be seen that Heinz was promoted much more
often than Hunts. Additionally, in only 3.75% of the cases we observe
combined promotional activities for Heinz (0.93% for Hunts). In chapter
4 we will investigate whether or not these variables have any explanatory
value for the probability of choosing Heinz instead of Hunts.

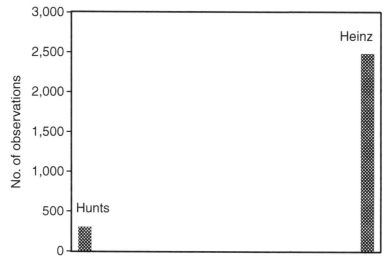

Figure 2.4   Histogram of the choice between Heinz and Hunts tomato
ketchup

2.2.3   An unordered multinomial variable

In many real-world situations individual households can choose between more than two brands, or in general, face more than two choice categories. For example, one may choose between four brands of saltine crackers, as will be the running example in this subsection and in chapter 5, or between three modes of public transport (such as a bus, a train or the subway). In this case there is no natural ordering in the choice options, that is, it does not matter if one chooses between brands A, B, C and D or between B, A, D and C. Such a dependent variable is called an unordered multinomial variable. This variable naturally extends the binomial variable in the previous subsection. In a sense, the resultant quantitative models to be discussed in chapter 5 also quite naturally extend those in chapter 4. Examples in the marketing research literature of applications of these models can be found in Guadagni and Little (1983), Chintagunta et al. (1991), Gönül and Srinivasan (1993), Jain et al. (1994) and Allenby and Rossi (1999), among many others.

To illustrate various variants of models for an unordered multinomial dependent variable, we consider an optical scanner panel data set on purchases of four brands of saltine crackers in the Rome (Georgia) market, collected by Information Resources Incorporated. The data set contains information on all 3,292 purchases of crackers made by 136 households over about two years. The brands were Nabisco, Sunshine, Keebler and a collection of private labels. In figure 2.5 we present a histogram of the actual

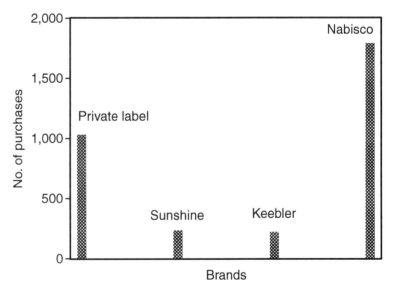

Figure 2.5   Histogram of the choice between four brands of saltine crackers

Table 2.3 *Characteristics of the dependent variable and explanatory variables: the choice between four brands of saltine crackers*

Variables	Private label	Sunshine	Keebler	Nabisco
Choice percentage	31.44	7.26	6.68	54.44
Average price (US$)	0.68	0.96	1.13	1.08
% display only[a]	6.32	10.72	8.02	29.16
% feature only[b]	1.15	1.61	1.64	3.80
% feature and display[c]	3.55	2.16	2.61	4.86

Notes:
[a]Percentage of purchase occasions when the brand was on display only.
[b]Percentage of purchase occasions when the brand was featured only.
[c]Percentage of purchase occasions when the brand was both on display and featured.

purchases, where it is known that each time only one brand was purchased. Nabisco is clearly the market leader (54%), with private label a good second (31%). It is obvious that the choice between four brands results in discrete observations on the dependent variable. Hence again the standard Linear Regression model of chapter 3 is unlikely to capture this structure. Similarly to the binomial dependent variable, it appears that useful quantitative models for an unordered multinomial variable address the probability that one of the brands is purchased and correlate this probability with various explanatory variables.

In the present data set of multinomial brand choice, we also have the actual price of the purchased brand and the shelf price of other brands. Additionally, we know whether there was a display and/or newspaper feature of the four brands at the time of purchase. Table 2.3 shows some data characteristics. "Average price" denotes the mean of the price of a brand over the 3,292 purchases; the Keebler crackers were the most expensive. "Display" refers to the fraction of purchase occasions that a brand was on display and "feature" refers to the fraction of occasions that a brand was featured. The market leader, Nabisco, was relatively often on display (29%) and featured (3.8%). In chapter 5, we will examine whether or not these variables have any explanatory value for the eventually observed brand choice.

2.2.4   An ordered multinomial variable

Sometimes in marketing research one obtains measurements on a multinomial and discrete variable where the sequence of categories is fixed.

An example concerns the choice between brands where these brands have a widely accepted ordering in terms of quality. Another example is provided by questionnaires, where individuals are asked to indicate whether they disagree with, are neutral about, or agree with a certain statement. Reshuffling the discrete outcomes of such a multinomial variable would destroy the relation between adjacent outcome categories, and hence important information gets lost.

In chapter 6 we present quantitative models for an ordered multinomial dependent variable. We illustrate these models for a variable with three categories that measures the risk profile of individuals, where this profile is assigned by a financial investment firm on the basis of certain criteria (which are beyond our control). In figure 2.6 we depict the three categories, which are low-, middle- and high-risk profile. It is easy to imagine that individuals who accept only low risk in financial markets are those who most likely have only savings accounts, while those who are willing to incur high risk most likely are active on the stock market. In total we have information on 2,000 individuals, of whom 329 are in the low-risk category and 1,140 have the intermediate profile.

In order to examine whether or not the classification of individuals into risk profiles matches with some of their characteristics, we aim to correlate the ordered multinomial variable with the variables in table 2.4 and to explore their potential explanatory value. Because the data are confidential, we can label our explanatory variables only with rather neutral terminology.

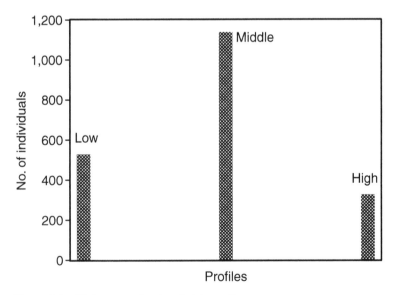

Figure 2.6   Histogram of ordered risk profiles

Table 2.4 *Characteristics of the dependent variable and explanatory variables: ordered risk profiles*

Variables	Total[a]	Risk profile		
		Low[b]	Middle[b]	High[b]
Relative category frequency	100.00	26.55	57.00	16.45
Funds of type 2	2.34	1.25	2.12	4.85
Transactions of type 1	0.89	1.04	0.86	0.72
Transactions of type 3	1.46	0.31	0.60	6.28
Wealth (NLG 10,000)	0.65	0.50	0.53	1.34

Notes:
[a]Average values of the explanatory variables in the full sample.
[b]Average values of the explanatory variables for low-, middle- and high-risk profile categories.

In this table, we provide some summary statistics averaged for all 2,000 individuals. The fund and transaction variables concern counts, while the wealth variable is measured in Dutch guilders (NLG). For some of these variables we can see that the average value increases (or decreases) with the risk profile, thus being suggestive of their potential explanatory value.

2.2.5 A limited continuous variable

A typical data set in direct mailing using, say, catalogs involves two types of information. The first concerns the response of a household to such a mailing. This response is then a binomial dependent variable, like the one to be discussed in chapter 4. The second concerns the number of items purchased or the amount of money spent, and this is usually considered to be a continuous variable, like the one to be discussed in chapter 3. However, this continuous variable is observed only for those households that respond. For a household that does not respond, the variable equals 0. Put another way, the households that did not purchase from the catalogs might have purchased some things once they had responded, but the market researcher does not have information on these observations. Hence, the continuous variable is censored because one does not have all information.

In chapter 7 we discuss two approaches to modeling this type of data. The first approach considers a single-equation model, which treats the non-response or zero observations as special cases. The second approach considers separate equations for the decision to respond and for the amount of money spent given that a household has decided to respond. Intuitively, the second approach is more flexible. For example, it may describe that higher age makes an individual less likely to respond, but, given the decision to respond, we may expect older individuals to spend more (because they tend to have higher incomes).

To illustrate the relevant models for data censored, in some way, we consider a data set containing observations for 4,268 individuals concerning donations to charity. From figure 2.7 one can observe that over 2,500 individuals who received a mailing from charity did not respond. In figure 2.8, we graph the amount of money donated to charity (in Dutch guilders). Clearly, most individuals donate about 10–20 guilders, although there are a few individuals who donate more than 200 guilders. In line with the above discussion on censoring, one might think that, given the histogram of figure 2.8, one is observing only about half of the (perhaps normal) distribution of donated money. Indeed, negative amounts are not observed. One might say that those individuals who would have wanted to donate a negative amount of money decided not to respond in the first place.

In table 2.5, we present some summary statistics, where we again consider the average values across the two response (no/yes) categories. Obviously, the average amount donated by those who did not respond is zero. In chapter 7 we aim to correlate the censored variable with observed characteristics of the individuals concerning their past donating behavior. These variables are usually summarized under the headings Recency, Frequency and

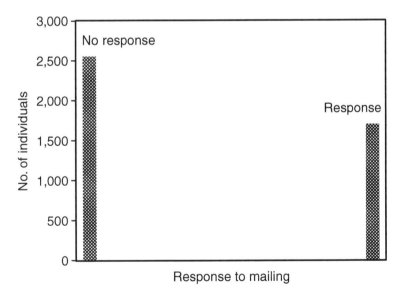

Figure 2.7   Histogram of the response to a charity mailing

Table 2.5 *Characteristics of the dependent variable and explanatory variables: donations to charity*

Variables	Total[a]	No response[b]	Response[b]
Relative response frequency	100.00	60.00	40.00
Gift (NLG)	7.44	0.00	18.61
Responded to previous mailing	33.48	20.73	52.61
Weeks since last response	59.05	72.09	39.47
Percentage responded mailings	48.43	39.27	62.19
No. of mailings per year	2.05	1.99	2.14
Gift last response	19.74	17.04	23.81
Average donation in the past	18.24	16.83	20.36

Notes:
[a]Average values of the explanatory variables in the full sample.
[b]Average values of the explanatory variables for no response and response observations, respectively.

Monetary Value (RFM). For example, from the second panel of table 2.5, we observe that, on average, those who responded to the previous mailing are likely to donate again (52.61% versus 20.73%), and those who took a long time to donate the last time are unlikely to donate now (72.09% versus

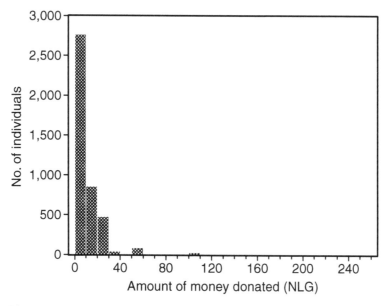

Figure 2.8   Histogram of the amount of money donated to charity

39.47%). Similar kinds of intuitively plausible indications can be obtained from the last two panels in table 2.5 concerning the pairs of Frequency and Monetary Value variables. Notice, however, that this table is not informative as to whether these RFM variables also have explanatory value for the amount of money donated. We could have divided the gift size into categories and made similar tables, but this can be done in an infinite number of ways. Hence, here we have perhaps a clear example of the relevance of constructing and analyzing a quantitative model, instead of just looking at various table entries.

2.2.6   A duration variable

The final type of dependent variable one typically encounters in marketing research is one that measures the time that elapses between two events. Examples are the time an individual takes to respond to a direct mailing, given knowledge of the time the mailing was received, the time between two consecutive purchases of a certain product or brand, and the time between switching to another supplier. Some recent marketing studies using duration data are Jain and Vilcassim (1991), Gupta (1991), Helsen and Schmittlein (1993), Bolton (1998), Allenby et al. (1999) and Gönül et al. (2000), among many others. Vilcassim and Jain (1991) even consider interpurchase times in combination with brand switching, and Chintagunta and Prasad (1998) consider interpurchase times together with brand choice.

Duration variables have a special place in the literature owing to their characteristics. In many cases variables which measure time between events are censored. This is perhaps best understood by recognizing that we sometimes do not observe the first event or the timing of the event just prior to the available observation period. Furthermore, in some cases the event has not ended at the end of the observation period. In these cases, we know only that the duration exceeds some threshold. If, however, the event starts and ends within the observation period, the duration variable is fully observed and hence uncensored. In practice, one usually has a combination of censored and uncensored observations. A second characteristic of duration variables is that they represent a time interval and not a single point in time. Therefore, if we want to relate duration to explanatory variables, we may have to take into account that the values of these explanatory variables may change during the duration. For example, prices are likely to change in the period between two consecutive purchases and hence the interpurchase time will depend on the sequence of prices during the duration. Models for duration variables therefore focus not on the duration but on the probability that the duration will end at some moment given that it lasted until then. For example, these models consider the probability that a product will be purchased this week, given that it has not been acquired since the previous purchase. In chapter 8 we will discuss the salient aspects of two types of duration models.

For illustration, in chapter 8 we use data from an A.C. Nielsen household scanner panel data set on sequential purchases of liquid laundry detergents in Sioux Falls, South Dakota. The observations originate from the purchase behavior of 400 households with 2,657 purchases starting in the first week of July 1986 and ending on July 16, 1988. Only those households are selected that purchased the (at that time) top six national brands, that is, Tide, Eraplus and Solo (all three marketed by Procter & Gamble) and Wisk, Surf and All (all three marketed by Lever Brothers), which accounted for 81% of the total market for national brands. In figure 2.9, we depict the empirical distribution of the interpurchase times, measured in days between two purchases. Most households seem to buy liquid detergent again after 25–50 days, although there are also households that can wait for more than a year. Obviously, these individuals may have switched to another product category.

For each purchase occasion, we know the time since the last purchase of liquid detergents, the price (cents/oz.) of the purchased brands and whether the purchased brand was featured or displayed (see table 2.6). Furthermore, we know the household size, the volume purchased on the previous purchase occasion, and expenditures on non-detergent products. The averages of the explanatory variables reported in the table are taken over the 2,657 inter-

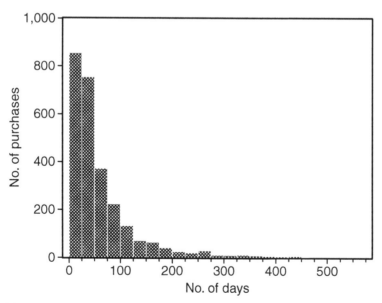

Figure 2.9   Histogram of the number of days between two liquid detergent
              purchases

Table 2.6 *Characteristics of the dependent
variable and explanatory variables: the time
between liquid detergent purchases*

Variables	Mean
Interpurchase time (days)	62.52
Household size	3.06
Non-detergent expenditures (US$)	39.89
Volume previous purchase occasion	77.39
Price (US$ ×100/oz.)	4.94
% display only[a]	2.71
% feature only[b]	6.89
% display and feature[c]	13.25

Notes:
[a]Percentage of purchase occasions when the brand was
on display only.
[b]Percentage of purchase occasions when the brand was
featured only.
[c]Percentage of purchase occasions when the brand was
on both display and featured.

purchase times. In the models to be dealt with in chapter 8, we aim to correlate the duration dependent variable with these variables in order to examine if household-specific variables have more effect on interpurchase times than marketing variables do.

2.2.7 Summary

To conclude this section on the various types of dependent variables, we provide a brief summary of the various variables and the names of the corresponding models to be discussed in the next six chapters. In table 2.7 we list the various variables and connect them with the as yet perhaps unfamiliar names of models. These names mainly deal with assumed distribution functions, such as the logistic distribution (hence logit) and the normal distribution. The table may be useful for reference purposes once one has gone through the entire book, or at least through the reader-specific relevant chapters and sections.

2.3 What do we exclude from this book?

We conclude this chapter with a brief summary of what we have decided to exclude from this book. These omissions concern data and mod-

Table 2.7 *Characteristics of a dependent variable and the names of relevant models to be discussed in chapters 3 to 8*

Dependent variable	Name of model	Chapter
Continuous	Standard Linear Regression model	3
Binomial	Binomial Logit/Probit model	4
Unordered multinomial	Multinomial Logit/Probit model	5
	Conditional Logit/Probit model	5
	Nested Logit model	5
Ordered multinomial	Ordered Logit/Probit model	6
Truncated, censored	Truncated Regression model	7
	Censored Regression (Tobit) model	7
Duration	Proportional Hazard model	8
	Accelerated Lifetime model	8

els, mainly for revealed preference data. As regards data, we leave out extensive treatments of models for count data, when there are only a few counts (such as 1 to 4 items purchased). The corresponding models are less fashionable in marketing research. Additionally, we do not explicitly consider data on diffusion processes, such as the penetration of new products or brands. A peculiarity of these data is that they are continuous on the one hand, but bounded from below and above on the other hand. There is a large literature on models for these data (see, for example, Mahajan et al., 1993).

As regards models, there are a few omissions. First of all, we mainly consider single-equation regression-based models. More precisely, we assume a single and observed dependent variable, which may be correlated with a set of observed explanatory variables. Hence, we exclude multivariate models, in which two or more variables are correlated with explanatory variables at the same time. Furthermore, we exclude an explicit treatment of panel models, where one takes account of the possibility that one observes all households during the same period and similar measurements for each household are made. Additionally, as mentioned earlier, we do not consider models that use multivariate statistical techniques such as discriminant analysis, factor models, cluster analysis, principal components and multidimensional scaling, among others. Of course, this does not imply that we believe these techniques to be less useful for marketing research.

Within our chosen framework of single-equation regression models, there are also at least two omissions. Ideally one would want to combine some of the models that will be discussed in subsequent chapters. For example, one might want to combine a model for no/yes donation to charity with a model for the time it takes for a household to respond together with a model for the amount donated. The combination of these models amounts to allowing for the presence of correlation across the model equations. Additionally, it is very likely that managers would want to know more about the dynamic (long-run and short-run) effects of their application of marketing-mix strategies (see Dekimpe and Hanssens, 1995). However, the tools for these types of analysis for other than continuous time series data have only very recently been developed (see, for some first attempts, Erdem and Keane, 1996, and Paap and Franses, 2000, and the advanced topics section of chapter 5). Generally, at present, these tools are not sufficiently developed to warrant inclusion in the current edition of this book.

3   A continuous dependent variable

In this chapter we review a few principles of econometric modeling, and illustrate these for the case of a continuous dependent variable. We assume basic knowledge of matrix algebra and of basic statistics and mathematics (differential algebra and integral calculus). As a courtesy to the reader, we include some of the principles on matrices in the Appendix (section A.1). This chapter serves to review a few issues which should be useful for later chapters. In section 3.1 we discuss the representation of the standard Linear Regression model. In section 3.2 we discuss Ordinary Least Squares and Maximum Likelihood estimation in substantial detail. Even though the Maximum Likelihood method is not illustrated in detail, its basic aspects will be outlined as we need it in later chapters. In section 3.3, diagnostic measures for outliers, residual autocorrelation and heteroskedasticity are considered. Model selection concerns the selection of relevant variables and the comparison of non-nested models using certain model selection criteria. Forecasting deals with within-sample or out-of-sample prediction. In section 3.4 we illustrate several issues for a regression model that correlates sales with price and promotional activities. Finally, in section 3.5 we discuss extensions to multiple-equation models, thereby mainly focusing on modeling market shares.

This chapter is not at all intended to give a detailed account of econometric methods and econometric analysis. Much more detail can, for example, be found in Greene (2000), Verbeek (2000) and Wooldridge (2000). In fact, this chapter mainly aims to set some notation and to highlight some important topics in econometric modeling. In later chapters we will frequently make use of these concepts.

3.1   The standard Linear Regression model

In empirical marketing research one often aims to correlate a random variable Y_t with one (or more) explanatory variables such as x_t, where the index t denotes that these variables are measured over time, that is, $t = 1, 2, \ldots, T$. This type of observation is usually called time series observation. One may also encounter cross-sectional data, which concern, for example, individuals $i = 1, 2, \ldots, N$, or a combination of both types of data. Typical store-level scanners generate data on Y_t, which might be the weekly sales (in dollars) of a certain product or brand, and on x_t, denoting for example the average actual price in that particular week.

When Y_t is a continuous variable such as dollar sales, and when it seems reasonable to assume that it is independent of changes in price, one may consider summarizing these sales by

$$Y_t \sim N(\mu, \sigma^2), \tag{3.1}$$

that is, the random variable sales is normally distributed with mean μ and variance σ^2. For further reference, in the Appendix (section A.2) we collect various aspects of this and other distributions. In figure 3.1 we depict an example of such a normal distribution, where we set μ at 1 and σ^2 at 1. In practice, the values of μ and σ^2 are unknown, but they could be estimated from the data.

In many cases, however, one may expect that marketing instruments such as prices, advertising and promotions do have an impact on sales. In the case of a single price variable, x_t, one can then choose to replace (3.1) by

$$Y_t \sim N(\beta_0 + \beta_1 x_t, \sigma^2), \tag{3.2}$$

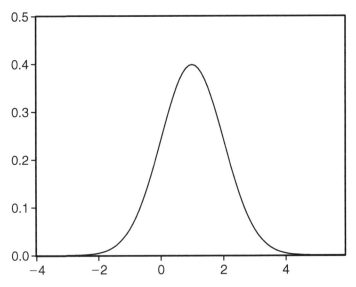

Figure 3.1   Density function of a normal distribution with $\mu = \sigma^2 = 1$

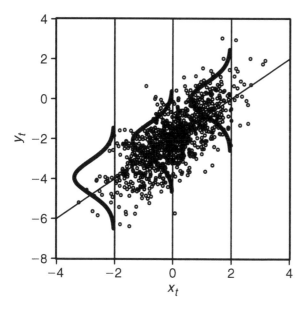

Figure 3.2   Scatter diagram of y_t against x_t

where the value of the mean μ is now made dependent on the value of the explanatory variable, or, in other words, where the conditional mean of Y_t is now a linear function of β_0 and $\beta_1 x_t$, with β_0 and β_1 being unknown parameters. In figure 3.2, we depict a set of simulated y_t and x_t, generated by

$$x_t = 0.0001t + \varepsilon_{1,t} \quad \text{with } \varepsilon_{1,t} \sim N(0, 1)$$
$$y_t = -2 + x_t + \varepsilon_{2,t} \quad \text{with } \varepsilon_{2,t} \sim N(0, 1), \tag{3.3}$$

where t is $1, 2, \ldots, T$. In this graph, we also depict three density functions of a normal distribution for three observations on Y_t. This visualizes that each observation on y_t equals $\beta_0 + \beta_1 x_t$ plus a random error term, which in turn is a drawing from a normal distribution. Notice that in many cases it is unlikely that the conditional mean of Y_t is equal to $\beta_1 x_t$ only, as in that case the line in figure 3.2 would always go through the origin, and hence one should better always retain an intercept parameter β_0.

In case there is more than one variable having an effect on Y_t, one may consider

$$Y_t \sim N(\beta_0 + \beta_1 x_{1,t} + \cdots + \beta_K x_{K,t}, \sigma^2), \tag{3.4}$$

where $x_{1,t}$ to $x_{K,t}$ denote the K potentially useful explanatory variables. In case of sales, variable $x_{1,t}$ can for example be price, variable $x_{2,t}$ can be advertising and variable $x_{3,t}$ can be a variable measuring promotion. To simplify notation (see also section A.1 in the Appendix), one usually defines the $(K+1) \times 1$ vector of parameters β, containing the $K+1$ unknown parameters β_0, β_1 to β_K, and the $1 \times (K+1)$ vector X_t, containing the known variables 1, $x_{1,t}$ to $x_{K,t}$. With this notation, (3.4) can be summarized as

$$Y_t \sim N(X_t\beta, \sigma^2). \tag{3.5}$$

Usually one encounters this model in the form

$$Y_t = X_t\beta + \varepsilon_t, \tag{3.6}$$

where ε_t is an unobserved stochastic variable assumed to be distributed as normal with mean zero and variance σ^2, or in short,

$$\varepsilon_t \sim N(0, \sigma^2). \tag{3.7}$$

This ε_t is often called an error or disturbance. The model with components (3.6) and (3.7) is called the standard Linear Regression model, and it will be the focus of this chapter.

The Linear Regression model can be used to examine the contemporaneous correlations between the dependent variable Y_t and the explanatory variables summarized in X_t. If one wants to examine correlations with previously observed variables, such as in the week before, one can consider replacing X_t by, for example, X_{t-1}. A parameter β_k measures the partial effect of a variable $x_{k,t}$ on Y_t, $k \in \{1, 2, \ldots, K\}$, assuming that this variable is uncorrelated with the other explanatory variables and ε_t. This can be seen from the partial derivative

$$\frac{\partial Y_t}{\partial x_{k,t}} = \beta_k. \tag{3.8}$$

Note that if $x_{k,t}$ is not uncorrelated with some other variable $x_{l,t}$, this partial effect will also depend on the partial derivative of $x_{l,t}$ to $x_{k,t}$, and the corresponding β_l parameter. Given (3.8), the elasticity of $x_{k,t}$ for y_t is now given by $\beta_k x_{k,t}/y_t$. If one wants a model with time-invariant elasticities with value β, one should consider the regression model

$$\log Y_t \sim N(\beta_0 + \beta_1 \log x_{1,t} + \cdots + \beta_K \log x_{K,t}, \sigma^2), \tag{3.9}$$

where log denotes the natural logarithmic transformation, because in that case

$$\frac{\partial Y_t}{\partial x_{k,t}} = \beta_k \frac{y_t}{x_{k,t}}. \tag{3.10}$$

Of course, this logarithmic transformation can be applied only to positive-valued observations. For example, when a 0/1 dummy variable is included to measure promotions, this transformation cannot be applied. In that case, one simply considers the 0/1 dummy variable. The elasticity of such a dummy variable then equals $\exp(\beta_k) - 1$.

Often one is interested in quantifying the effects of explanatory variables on the variable to be explained. Usually, one knows which variable should be explained, but in many cases it is unknown which explanatory variables are relevant, that is, which variables appear on the right-hand side of (3.6). For example, it may be that sales are correlated with price and advertising, but that they are not correlated with display or feature promotion. In fact, it is quite common that this is exactly what one aims to find out with the model. In order to answer the question about which variables are relevant, one needs to have estimates of the unknown parameters, and one also needs to know whether these unknown parameters are perhaps equal to zero. Two familiar estimation methods for the unknown parameters will be discussed in the next section.

Several estimation methods require that the maintained model is not misspecified. Unfortunately, most models constructed as a first attempt are misspecified. Misspecification usually concerns the notion that the maintained assumptions for the unobserved error variable ε_t in (3.7) are violated or that the functional form (which is obviously linear in the standard Linear Regression model) is inappropriate. For example, the error variable may have a variance which varies with a certain variable, that is, σ^2 is not constant but is σ_t^2, or the errors at time t are correlated with those at $t-1$, for example, $\varepsilon_t = \rho \varepsilon_{t-1} + u_t$. In the last case, it would have been better to include y_{t-1} and perhaps also X_{t-1} in (3.5). Additionally, with regard to the functional form, it may be that one should include quadratic terms such as $x_{k,t}^2$ instead of the linear variables.

Unfortunately, usually one can find out whether a model is misspecified only once the parameters for a first-guess model have been estimated. This is because one can only estimate the error variable given these estimates, that is

$$\hat{\varepsilon}_t = y_t - X_t \hat{\beta}, \tag{3.11}$$

where a hat indicates an estimated value. The estimated error variables are called residuals. Hence, a typical empirical modeling strategy is, first, to put forward a tentative model, second, to estimate the values of the unknown parameters, third, to investigate the quality of the model by applying a variety of diagnostic measures for the model and for the estimated error variable, fourth, to re-specify the model if so indicated by these diagnostics until the model has become satisfactory, and, finally, to interpret the values of the parameters. Admittedly, a successful application of this strategy requires quite some skill and experience, and there seem to be no straightforward guidelines to be followed.

3.2   Estimation

In this section we briefly discuss parameter estimation in the standard Linear Regression model. We first discuss the Ordinary Least Squares (OLS) method, and then we discuss the Maximum Likelihood (ML) method. In doing so, we rely on some basic results in matrix algebra, summarized in the Appendix (section A.1). The ML method will also be used in later chapters as it is particularly useful for nonlinear models. For the standard Linear Regression model it turns out that the OLS and ML methods give the same results. As indicated earlier, the reader who is interested in this and the next section is assumed to have some prior econometric knowledge.

3.2.1   Estimation by Ordinary Least Squares

Consider again the standard Linear Regression model

$$Y_t = X_t\beta + \varepsilon_t, \quad \text{with } \varepsilon_t \sim N(0, \sigma^2). \tag{3.12}$$

The least-squares method aims at finding that value of β for which $\sum_{t=1}^{T} \varepsilon_t^2 = \sum_{t=1}^{T}(y_t - X_t\beta)^2$ gets minimized. To obtain the OLS estimator we differentiate $\sum_{t=1}^{T} \varepsilon_t^2$ with respect to β and solve the following first-order conditions for β

$$\frac{\partial \sum_{t=1}^{T}(y_t - X_t\beta)^2}{\partial \beta} = \sum_{t=1}^{T} X_t'(y_t - X_t\beta) = 0, \tag{3.13}$$

which yields

$$\hat{\beta} = \left(\sum_{t=1}^{T} X_t'X_t\right)^{-1} \sum_{t=1}^{T} X_t'y_t. \tag{3.14}$$

Under the assumption that the variables in X_t are uncorrelated with the error variable ε_t, in addition to the assumption that the model is appropriately specified, the OLS estimator is what is called consistent. Loosely speaking, this means that when one increases the sample size T, that is, if one collects more observations on y_t and X_t, one will estimate the underlying β with increasing precision.

In order to examine if one or more of the elements of β are equal to zero or not, one can use

$$\hat{\beta} \overset{a}{\sim} N\left(\beta, \hat{\sigma}^2\left(\sum_{t=1}^{T} X_t'X_t\right)^{-1}\right), \tag{3.15}$$

where $\overset{a}{\sim}$ denotes "distributed asymptotically as", and where

$$\hat{\sigma}^2 = \frac{1}{T - (K+1)} \sum_{t=1}^{T} (y_t - X_t\hat{\beta})^2 = \frac{1}{T - (K+1)} \sum_{t=1}^{T} \hat{\varepsilon}_t^2 \qquad (3.16)$$

is a consistent estimator of σ^2. An important requirement for this result is that the matrix $(\sum_{t=1}^{T} X_t'X_t)/T$ approximates a constant value as T increases. Using (3.15), one can construct confidence intervals for the $K+1$ parameters in β. Typical confidence intervals cover 95% or 90% of the asymptotic distribution of $\hat{\beta}$. If these intervals include the value of zero, one says that the underlying but unknown parameter is not significantly different from zero at the 5% or 10% significance level, respectively. This investigation is usually performed using a so-called z-test statistic, which is defined as

$$z_{\hat{\beta}_k} = \frac{\hat{\beta}_k - 0}{\sqrt{\hat{\sigma}^2 \left(\left(\sum_{t=1}^{T} X_t'X_t \right)^{-1} \right)_{k,k}}}, \qquad (3.17)$$

where the subscript (k, k) denotes the matrix element in the k'th row and k'th column. Given the adequacy of the model and given the validity of the null hypothesis that $\beta_k = 0$, it holds that

$$z_{\hat{\beta}_k} \overset{a}{\sim} N(0, 1). \qquad (3.18)$$

When $z_{\hat{\beta}_k}$ takes a value outside the region $[-1.96, 1.96]$, it is said that the corresponding parameter is significantly different from 0 at the 5% level (see section A.3 in the Appendix for some critical values). In a similar manner, one can test whether β_k equals, for example, β_k^*. In that case one has to replace the denominator of (3.17) by $\hat{\beta}_k - \beta_k^*$. Under the null hypothesis that $\beta_k = \beta_k^*$ the z-statistic is again asymptotically normally distributed.

3.2.2   Estimation by Maximum Likelihood

An estimation method based on least-squares is easy to apply, and it is particularly useful for the standard Linear Regression model. However, for more complicated models, such as those that will be discussed in subsequent chapters, it may not always lead to the best possible parameter estimates. In that case, it would be better to use the Maximum Likelihood (ML) method.

In order to apply the ML method, one should write a model in terms of the joint probability density function $p(y|X; \theta)$ for the observed variables y given X, where θ summarizes the model parameters β and σ^2, and where p

denotes probability. For given values of θ, $p(\cdot|\cdot; \theta)$ is a probability density function for y conditional on X. Given $(y|X)$, the likelihood function is defined as

$$L(\theta) = p(y|X; \theta). \tag{3.19}$$

This likelihood function measures the probability of observing the data $(y|X)$ for different values of θ. The ML estimator $\hat{\theta}$ is defined as the value of θ that maximizes the function $L(\theta)$ over a set of relevant parameter values of θ. Obviously, the ML method is optimal in the sense that it yields the value of $\hat{\theta}$ that gives the maximum likely correlation between y and X, given X. Usually, one considers the logarithm of the likelihood function, which is called the log-likelihood function

$$l(\theta) = \log(L(\theta)). \tag{3.20}$$

Because the natural logarithm is a monotonically increasing transformation, the maxima of (3.19) and (3.20) are naturally obtained for the same values of θ.

To obtain the value of θ that maximizes the likelihood function, one first differentiates the log-likelihood function (3.20) with respect to θ. Next, one solves the first-order conditions given by

$$\frac{\partial l(\theta)}{\partial \theta} = 0 \tag{3.21}$$

for θ resulting in the ML estimate denoted by $\hat{\theta}$. In general it is usually not possible to find an analytical solution to (3.21). In that case, one has to use numerical optimization techniques to find the ML estimate. In this book we opt for the Newton–Raphson method because the special structure of the log-likelihood function of many of the models reviewed in the following chapters results in efficient optimization, but other optimization methods such as the BHHH method of Berndt et al. (1974) can be used instead (see, for example, Judge et al., 1985, Appendix B, for an overview). The Newton–Raphson method is based on meeting the first-order condition for a maximum in an iterative manner. Denote the gradient $G(\theta)$ and Hessian matrix $H(\theta)$ by

$$\begin{aligned} G(\theta) &= \frac{\partial l(\theta)}{\partial \theta} \\ H(\theta) &= \frac{\partial^2 l(\theta)}{\partial \theta \partial \theta'}, \end{aligned} \tag{3.22}$$

then around a given value θ_h the first-order condition for the optimization problem can be linearized, resulting in $G(\theta_h) + H(\theta_h)(\theta - \theta_h) = 0$. Solving this for θ gives the sequence of estimates

$$\theta_{h+1} = \theta_h - H(\theta_h)^{-1}G(\theta_h).$$ (3.23)

Under certain regularity conditions, which concern the log-likelihood function, these iterations converge to a local maximum of (3.20). Whether a global maximum is found depends on the form of the function and on the procedure to determine the initial estimates θ_0. In practice it can thus be useful to vary the initial estimates and to compare the corresponding log-likelihood values. ML estimators have asymptotically optimal statistical properties under fairly mild conditions. Apart from regularity conditions on the log-likelihood function, the main condition is that the model is adequately specified.

In many cases, it holds true that

$$\sqrt{T}(\hat{\theta} - \theta) \overset{a}{\sim} N(0, \hat{\mathcal{I}}^{-1}),$$ (3.24)

where $\hat{\mathcal{I}}$ is the so-called information matrix evaluated at $\hat{\theta}$, that is,

$$\hat{\mathcal{I}} = -E\left[\frac{\partial^2 l(\theta)}{\partial\theta\partial\theta'}\right]\Bigg|_{\theta=\hat{\theta}},$$ (3.25)

where E denotes the expectation operator.

To illustrate the ML estimation method, consider again the standard Linear Regression model given in (3.12). The log-likelihood function for this model is given by

$$L(\beta, \sigma^2) = \prod_{t=1}^{T} \frac{1}{\sigma\sqrt{2\pi}}\exp(-\frac{1}{2\sigma^2}(y_t - X_t\beta)^2)$$ (3.26)

such that the log-likelihood reads

$$l(\beta, \sigma^2) = \sum_{t=1}^{T}\left(-\frac{1}{2}\log 2\pi - \log\sigma - \frac{1}{2\sigma^2}(y_t - X_t\beta)^2\right),$$ (3.27)

where we have used some of the results summarized in section A.2 of the Appendix. The ML estimates are obtained from the first-order conditions

$$\frac{\partial l(\beta, \sigma^2)}{\partial\beta} = \sum_{t=1}^{T}\frac{1}{\sigma^2}X_t'(y_t - X_t\beta) = 0$$

$$\frac{\partial l(\beta, \sigma^2)}{\partial\sigma^2} = \sum_{t=1}^{T}\left(-\frac{1}{2\sigma^2} + \frac{1}{2\sigma^4}(y_t - X_t\beta)^2\right) = 0.$$ (3.28)

Solving this results in

$$\hat{\beta} = \left(\sum_{t=1}^{T} X_t' X_t \right)^{-1} \sum_{t=1}^{T} X_t' y_t$$

$$\hat{\sigma}^2 = \frac{1}{T} \sum_{t=1}^{T} (y_t - X_t \hat{\beta})^2 = \frac{1}{T} \sum_{t=1}^{T} \hat{\varepsilon}_t^2. \qquad (3.29)$$

This shows that the ML estimator for β is equal to the OLS estimator in (3.14), but that the ML estimator for σ^2 differs slightly from its OLS counterpart in (3.16).

The second-order derivatives of the log-likelihood function, which are needed in order to construct confidence intervals for the estimated parameters (see (3.24)), are given by

$$\frac{\partial^2 l(\beta, \sigma^2)}{\partial \beta \partial \beta'} = -\frac{1}{\sigma^2} \sum_{t=1}^{T} X_t' X_t$$

$$\frac{\partial^2 l(\beta, \sigma^2)}{\partial \beta \partial \sigma^2} = -\frac{1}{\sigma^4} \sum_{t=1}^{T} X_t' (y_t - X_t \beta) \qquad (3.30)$$

$$\frac{\partial^2 l(\beta, \sigma^2)}{\partial \sigma^2 \partial \sigma^2} = \sum_{t=1}^{T} \left(\frac{1}{2\sigma^4} - \frac{1}{\sigma^6} (y_t - X_t \beta)^2 \right).$$

Upon substituting the ML estimates in (3.24) and (3.25), one can derive that

$$\hat{\beta} \overset{a}{\sim} N \left(\beta, \hat{\sigma}^2 \left(\sum_{t=1}^{T} X_t' X_t \right)^{-1} \right), \qquad (3.31)$$

which, owing to (3.29), is similar to the expression obtained for the OLS method.

3.3   Diagnostics, model selection and forecasting

Once the parameters have been estimated, it is important to check the adequacy of the model. If a model is incorrectly specified, there may be a problem with the interpretation of the parameters. Also, it is likely that the included parameters and their corresponding standard errors are calculated incorrectly. Hence, it is better not to try to interpret and use a possibly misspecified model, but first to check the adequacy of the model.

There are various ways to derive tests for the adequacy of a maintained model. One way is to consider a general specification test, where the maintained model is the null hypothesis and the alternative model assumes that any of the underlying assumptions are violated. Although these general tests can be useful as a one-time check, they are less useful if the aim is to obtain clearer indications as to how one might modify a possibly misspecified model. In this section, we mainly discuss more specific diagnostic tests.

3.3.1 Diagnostics

There are various ways to derive tests for the adequacy of a maintained model. One builds on the Lagrange Multiplier (LM) principle. In some cases the so-called Gauss–Newton regression is useful (see Davidson and MacKinnon, 1993). Whatever the principle, a useful procedure is the following. The model parameters are estimated and the residuals are saved. Next, an alternative model is examined, which often leads to the suggestion that certain variables were deleted from the initial model in the first place. Tests based on auxiliary regressions, which involve the original variables and the omitted variables, can suggest whether the maintained model should be rejected for the alternative model. If so, one assumes the validity of the alternative model, and one starts again with parameter estimation and diagnostics.

The null hypothesis in this testing strategy, at least in this chapter, is the standard Linear Regression model, that is,

$$Y_t = X_t\beta + \varepsilon_t, \tag{3.32}$$

where ε_t obeys

$$\varepsilon_t \sim N(0, \sigma^2). \tag{3.33}$$

A first and important test in the case of time series variables (but not for cross-sectional data) concerns the absence of correlation between ε_t and ε_{t-1}, that is, the same variable lagged one period. Hence, there should be no autocorrelation in the error variable. If there is such correlation, this can also be visualized by plotting estimated ε_t against ε_{t-1} in a two-dimensional scatter diagram. Under the alternative hypothesis, one may postulate that

$$\varepsilon_t = \rho\varepsilon_{t-1} + v_t, \tag{3.34}$$

which is called a first-order autoregression (AR(1)) for ε_t. By writing $\rho Y_{t-1} = X_{t-1}\beta\rho + \rho\varepsilon_{t-1}$, and subtracting this from (3.32), the regression model under this alternative hypothesis is now given by

$$Y_t = \rho Y_{t-1} + X_t\beta - X_{t-1}\beta\rho + v_t. \tag{3.35}$$

It should be noticed that an unrestricted model with Y_{t-1} and X_{t-1} would contain $1 + (K+1) + K = 2(K+1)$ parameters because there is only one intercept, whereas, owing to the common ρ parameter, (3.35) has only $1 + (K + 1) = K + 2$ unrestricted parameters.

One obvious way to examine if the error variable ε_t is an AR(1) variable is to add y_{t-1} and X_{t-1} to the initial regression model and to examine their joint significance. Another way is to consider the auxiliary test regression

$$\hat{\varepsilon}_t = X_t \gamma + \eta \hat{\varepsilon}_{t-1} + w_t. \tag{3.36}$$

If the error variable is appropriately specified, this regression model should not be able to describe the estimated errors well. A simple test is now given by testing the significance of $\hat{\varepsilon}_{t-1}$ in (3.36). This can be done straightforwardly using the appropriate z-score statistic (see (3.17)). Consequently, a test for residual autocorrelation at lags 1 to p can be performed by considering

$$\hat{\varepsilon}_t = X_t \gamma + \eta_1 \hat{\varepsilon}_{t-1} + \cdots + \eta_p \hat{\varepsilon}_{t-p} + w_t, \tag{3.37}$$

and by examining the joint significance of $\hat{\varepsilon}_{t-1}$ to $\hat{\varepsilon}_{t-p}$ with what is called an F-test. This F-test is computed as

$$F = \left(\frac{RSS_0 - RSS_1}{p} \right) \Big/ \left(\frac{RSS_1}{T - (K + 1) - p} \right), \tag{3.38}$$

where RSS_0 denotes the residual sum of squares under the null hypothesis (which is here that the added lagged residual variables are irrelevant), and RSS_1 is the residual sum of squares under the alternative hypothesis. Under the null hypothesis, this test has an $F(p, T - (K + 1) - p)$ distribution (see section A.3 in the Appendix for some critical values).

An important assumption for the standard Linear Regression model is that the variance of the errors has a constant value σ^2 (called homoskedastic). It may however be that this variance is not constant, but varies with the explanatory variables (some form of heteroskedasticity), that is, for example,

$$\sigma_t^2 = \alpha_0 + \alpha_1 x_{1,t}^2 + \cdots + \alpha_K x_{K,t}^2. \tag{3.39}$$

Again, one can use graphical techniques to provide a first impression of potential heteroskedasticity. To examine this possibility, a White-type (1980) test for heteroskedasticity can then be calculated from the auxiliary regression

$$\hat{\varepsilon}_t^2 = v_0 + v_1 x_{1,t} + \cdots + v_K x_{K,t} + \gamma_1 x_{1,t}^2 + \cdots + \gamma_K x_{K,t}^2 + w_t, \tag{3.40}$$

The actual test statistic is the joint F-test for the significance of final K variables in (3.40). Notice that, when some of the explanatory variables are 0/1 dummy variables, the squares of these are the same variables again, and hence it is pointless to include these squares.

Finally, the standard Linear Regression model assumes that all observations are equally important when estimating the parameters. In other words, there are no outliers or otherwise influential observations. Usually, an outlier is defined as an observation that is located far away from the estimated regression line. Unfortunately, such an outlier may itself have a non-negligible effect on the location of that regression line. Hence, in practice, it is important to check for the presence of outliers. An indication may be an implausibly large value of an estimated error. Indeed, when its value is more than three or four times larger than the estimated standard deviation of the residuals, it may be considered an outlier.

A first and simple indication of the potential presence of outliers can be given by a test for the approximate normality of the residuals. When the error variable in the standard Linear Regression model is distributed as normal with mean 0 and variance σ^2, then the skewness (the standardized third moment) is equal to zero and the kurtosis (the standardized fourth moment) is equal to 3. A simple test for normality can now be based on the normalized residuals $\hat{\varepsilon}_t / \hat{\sigma}$ using the statistics

$$\frac{1}{\sqrt{6T}} \sum_{t=1}^{T} \left(\frac{\hat{\varepsilon}_t}{\hat{\sigma}} \right)^3 \tag{3.41}$$

and

$$\frac{1}{\sqrt{24T}} \sum_{t=1}^{T} \left(\left(\frac{\hat{\varepsilon}_t}{\hat{\sigma}} \right)^4 - 3 \right). \tag{3.42}$$

Under the null hypothesis, each of these two test statistics is asymptotically distributed as standard normal. Their squares are asymptotically distributed as $\chi^2(1)$, and the sum of these two as $\chi^2(2)$. This last $\chi^2(2)$-normality test (Jarque–Bera test) is often applied in practice (see Bowman and Shenton, 1975, and Bera and Jarque, 1982). Section A.3 in the Appendix provides relevant critical values.

3.3.2 Model selection

Supposing the parameters have been estimated, and the model diagnostics do not indicate serious misspecification, then one may examine the fit of the model. Additionally, one can examine if certain explanatory variables can be deleted.

A simple measure, which is the R^2, considers the amount of variation in y_t that is explained by the model and compares it with the variation in y_t itself. Usually, one considers the definition

$$R^2 = 1 - \frac{\sum_{t=1}^{T} \hat{\varepsilon}_t^2}{\sum_{t=1}^{T}(y_t - \bar{y}_t)^2}, \tag{3.43}$$

where $\bar{y}_t$ denotes the average value of y_t. When $R^2 = 1$, the fit of the model is perfect; when $R^2 = 0$, there is no fit at all. A nice property of R^2 is that it can be used as a single measure to evaluate a model and the included variables, provided the model contains an intercept.

If there is more than a single model available, one can also use the so-called Akaike information criterion, proposed by Akaike (1969), which is calculated as

$$\text{AIC} = \frac{1}{T}(-2l(\hat{\theta}) + 2n), \tag{3.44}$$

or the Schwarz (or Bayesian) information criterion of Schwarz (1978)

$$\text{BIC} = \frac{1}{T}(-2l(\hat{\theta}) + n \log T), \tag{3.45}$$

where $l(\hat{\theta})$ denotes the maximum of the log-likelihood function obtained for the included parameters θ, and where n denotes the total number of parameters in the model. Alternative models including fewer or other explanatory variables have different values for $\hat{\theta}$ and hence different $l(\hat{\theta})$, and perhaps also a different number of variables. The advantage of AIC and BIC is that they allow for a comparison of models with different elements in X_t, that is, non-nested models. Additionally, AIC and BIC provide a balance between the fit and the number of parameters.

One may also consider the Likelihood Ratio test or the Wald test to see if one or more variables can be deleted. Suppose that the general model under the alternative hypothesis is the standard Linear Regression model, and suppose that the null hypothesis imposes g independent restrictions on the parameters. We denote the ML estimator for θ under the null hypothesis by $\hat{\theta}_0$ and the ML estimator under the alternative hypothesis by $\hat{\theta}_A$. The Likelihood Ratio (LR) test is now defined as

$$\text{LR} = -2 \log \frac{L(\hat{\theta}_0)}{L(\hat{\theta}_A)} = -2(l(\hat{\theta}_0) - l(\hat{\theta}_A)). \tag{3.46}$$

Under the null hypothesis it holds that

$$\text{LR} \overset{a}{\sim} \chi^2(g). \tag{3.47}$$

The null hypothesis is rejected if the value of LR is sufficiently large, compared with the critical values of the relevant $\chi^2(g)$ distribution (see section A.3 in the Appendix).

The LR test requires two optimizations: ML under the null hypothesis and ML under the alternative hypothesis. The Wald test, in contrast, is based on the unrestricted model only. Note that the z-score in (3.18) is a Wald test for a single parameter restriction. Now we discuss the Wald test for more than one parameter restriction. This test concerns the extent to which the restrictions are satisfied by the unrestricted estimator $\hat{\beta}$ itself, comparing it with its confidence region. Under the null hypothesis one has $r\beta = 0$, where the r is a $g \times (K+1)$ to indicate g specific parameter restrictions. The Wald test is now computed as

$$W = (r\hat{\beta} - 0)'[r\hat{\mathcal{I}}(\hat{\beta})^{-1}r']^{-1}(r\hat{\beta} - 0), \qquad (3.48)$$

and it is asymptotically distributed as $\chi^2(g)$. Note that the Wald test requires the computation only of the unrestricted ML estimator, and not the one under the null hypothesis. Hence, this is a useful test if the restricted model is difficult to estimate. On the other hand, a disadvantage is that the numerical outcome of the test may depend on the way the restrictions are formulated, because similar restrictions may lead to the different Wald test values. Likelihood Ratio tests or Lagrange Multiplier type tests are therefore often preferred. The advantage of LM-type tests is that they need parameter estimates only under the null hypothesis, which makes these tests very useful for diagnostic checking. In fact, the tests for residual serial correlation and heteroskedasticity in section 3.3.1 are LM-type tests.

3.3.3 Forecasting

One possible use of a regression model concerns forecasting. The evaluation of out-of-sample forecasting accuracy can also be used to compare the relative merits of alternative models. Consider again

$$Y_t = X_t\beta + \varepsilon_t. \qquad (3.49)$$

Then, given the familiar assumptions on ε_t, the best forecast for ε_t for $t+1$ is equal to zero. Hence, to forecast y_t for time $t+1$, one should rely on

$$\hat{y}_{t+1} = \hat{X}_{t+1}\hat{\beta}. \qquad (3.50)$$

If $\hat{\beta}$ is assumed to be valid in the future (or, in general, for the observations not considered for estimating the parameters), the only information that is needed to forecast y_t concerns $\hat{X}_{t+1}$. In principle, one then needs a model for X_t to forecast X_{t+1}. In practice, however, one usually divides the sample of T observations into T_1 and T_2, with $T_1 + T_2 = T$. The model is constructed and its parameters are estimated for T_1 observations. The out-of-sample forecast fit is evaluated for the T_2 observations. Forecasting then assumes knowledge of X_{t+1}, and the forecasts are given by

$$\hat{y}_{T_1+j} = X_{T_1+j}\hat{\beta}, \qquad (3.51)$$

with $j = 1, 2, \ldots, T_2$. The forecast error is

$$e_{T_1+j} = y_{T_1+j} - \hat{y}_{T_1+j}. \tag{3.52}$$

The (root of the) mean of the T_2 squared forecast errors ((R)MSE) is often used to compare the forecasts generated by different models.

A useful class of models for forecasting involves time series models (see, for example, Franses, 1998). An example is the autoregression of order 1, that is,

$$Y_t = \rho Y_{t-1} + \varepsilon_t. \tag{3.53}$$

Here, the forecast of y_{T_1+1} is equal to $\hat{\rho} y_{T_1}$. Obviously, this forecast includes values that are known (y_{T_1}) or estimated (ρ) at time T_1. In fact, $\hat{y}_{T_1+2} = \hat{\rho} \hat{y}_{T_1+1}$, where $\hat{y}_{T_1+1}$ is the forecast for $T_1 + 1$. Hence, time series models can be particularly useful for multiple-step-ahead forecasting.

3.4　Modeling sales

In this section we illustrate various concepts discussed above for a set of scanner data including the sales of Heinz tomato ketchup (S_t), the average price actually paid (P_t), coupon promotion only (CP_t), major display promotion only (DP_t), and combined promotion (TP_t). The data are observed over 124 weeks. The source of the data and some visual characteristics have already been discussed in section 2.2.1. In the models below, we will consider sales and prices after taking natural logarithms. In figure 3.3 we give a scatter diagram of $\log S_t$ versus $\log P_t$. Clearly there is no evident correlation between these two variables. Interestingly, if we look at the scatter diagram of $\log S_t$ versus $\log P_t - \log P_{t-1}$ in figure 3.4, that is, of the differences, then we notice a more pronounced negative correlation.

For illustration, we first start with a regression model where current log sales are correlated with current log prices and the three dummy variables for promotion. OLS estimation results in

$$\begin{aligned}
\log S_t = {}& 3.936 - 0.117 \ \log P_t + 1.852 \ TP_t \\
& (0.106) \quad (0.545) \qquad\qquad (0.216) \\
& + 1.394 \ CP_t + 0.741 \ DP_t + \hat{\varepsilon}_t, \\
& \ (0.170) \qquad\quad (0.116)
\end{aligned} \tag{3.54}$$

where estimated standard errors are given in parentheses. As discussed in section 2.1, these standard errors are calculated as

$$SE_{\hat{\beta}_k} = \sqrt{\hat{\sigma}^2((X'X)^{-1})_{k,k}}, \tag{3.55}$$

where $\hat{\sigma}^2$ denotes the OLS estimator of σ^2 (see (3.16)).

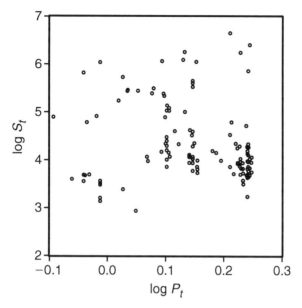

Figure 3.3　Scatter diagram of $\log S_t$ against $\log P_t$

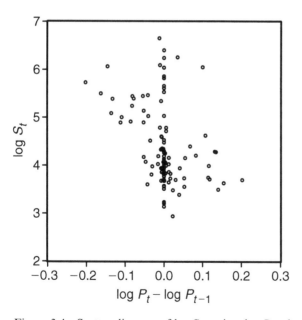

Figure 3.4　Scatter diagram of $\log S_t$ against $\log P_t - \log P_{t-1}$

Before establishing the relevance and usefulness of the estimated parameters, it is important to diagnose the quality of the model. The LM-
based tests for residual autocorrelation at lag 1 and at lags 1–5 (see section
3.3.1) obtain the values of 0.034 and 2.655, respectively. The latter value is
significant at the 5% level. The $\chi^2(2)$-test for normality of the residuals is
0.958, which is not significant at the 5% level. The White test for heteroskedasticity obtains a value of 8.919, and this is clearly significant at the 1%
level. Taking these diagnostics together, it is evident that this first attempt
leads to a misspecified model, that is, there is autocorrelation in the residuals
and there is evidence of heteroskedasticity. Perhaps this misspecification
explains the unexpected insignificance of the price variable.

In a second attempt, we first decide to take care of the dynamic structure
of the model. We enlarge it by including first-order lags of all the explanatory
variables and by adding the one-week lagged logs of the sales. The OLS
estimation results for this model are

$$\log S_t = \begin{array}{l} 3.307 + 0.120 \ \log S_{t-1} - 3.923 \ \log P_t + 4.792 \ \log P_{t-1} \\ (0.348) \quad (0.086) \qquad\qquad (0.898) \qquad\qquad (0.089) \end{array}$$

$$\begin{array}{l} + 1.684 \ TP_t + 0.241 \ TP_{t-1} + 1.395 \ CP_t \\ \ (0.188) \qquad\ (0.257) \qquad\quad\ (0.147) \end{array}$$

$$\begin{array}{l} - 0.425 \ CP_{t-1} + 0.325 \ DP_t + 0.407 \ DP_{t-1} + \hat{\varepsilon}_t, \qquad (3.56) \\ \ (0.187) \qquad\quad\ (0.119) \qquad\ (0.127) \end{array}$$

where the parameters -3.923 for $\log P_t$ and $4.792 \ \log P_{t-1}$ suggest an effect
of about -4 for $\log P_t - \log P_{t-1}$ (see also figure 3.4). The LM tests for
residual autocorrelation at lag 1 and at lags 1–5 obtain the values of 0.492
and 0.570, respectively, and these are not significant. However, the $\chi^2(2)$-test
for normality of the residuals now obtains the significant value of 12.105.
The White test for heteroskedasticity obtains a value of 2.820, which is
considerably smaller than before, though still significant. Taking these diagnostics together, it seems that there are perhaps some outliers, and maybe
these are also causing heteroskedasticity, but that, on the whole, the model
seems not too bad.

This seems to be confirmed by the R^2 value for this model, which is
0.685. The effect of having two promotions at the same time is 1.684,
while the effect of having these promotions in different weeks is
$1.395 - 0.425 + 0.325 + 0.407 = 1.702$, which is about equal to the joint
effect. Interestingly, a display promotion in the previous week still has a
positive effect on the sales in the current week (0.407), whereas a coupon
promotion in the previous week establishes a so-called postpromotion dip
(-0.425) (see van Heerde et al., 2000, for a similar model).

3.5   Advanced topics

In the previous sections we considered single-equation econometric models, that is, we considered correlating y_t with X_t. In some cases however, one may want to consider more than one equation. For example, it may well be that the price level is determined by past values of sales. In that case, one may want to extend earlier models by including a second equation for the log of the actual price. If this model then includes current sales as an explanatory variable, one may end up with a simultaneous-equations model. A simple example of such a model is

$$\log S_t = \mu_1 + \rho_1 \log S_{t-1} + \beta_1 \log P_t + \varepsilon_{1,t}$$
$$\log P_t = \mu_2 + \rho_2 \log P_{t-1} + \beta_2 \log S_t + \varepsilon_{2,t}.$$
(3.57)

When a simultaneous-equations model contains lagged explanatory variables, it can often be written as what is called a Vector AutoRegression (VAR). This is the multiple-equation extension of the AR model mentioned in section 3.3 (see Lütkepohl, 1993).

Multiple-equation models also emerge in marketing research when the focus is on modeling market shares instead of on sales (see Cooper and Nakanishi, 1988). This is because market shares sum to unity. Additionally, as market shares lie between 0 and 1, a more specific model may be needed. A particularly useful model is the attraction model. Let $A_{j,t}$ denote the attraction of brand j at time t, $t = 1, \ldots, T$, and suppose that it is given by

$$A_{j,t} = \exp(\mu_j + \varepsilon_{j,t}) \prod_{k=1}^{K} x_{k,j,t}^{\beta_{k,j}} \qquad \text{for } j = 1, \ldots, J,$$
(3.58)

where $x_{k,j,t}$ denotes the k'th explanatory variable (such as price, distribution, advertising) for brand j at time t and where $\beta_{k,j}$ is the corresponding coefficient. The parameter μ_j is a brand-specific constant, and the error term $(\varepsilon_{1,t}, \ldots, \varepsilon_{J,t})'$ is multivariate normally distributed with zero mean and Σ as covariance matrix. For the attraction to be positive, $x_{k,j,t}$ has to be positive, and hence rates of changes are often not allowed. The variable $x_{k,j,t}$ may, for instance, be the price of brand j. Note that for dummy variables (for example, promotion) one should include $\exp(x_{k,j,t})$ in order to prevent $A_{j,t}$ becoming zero.

Given the attractions, the market share of brand j at time t is now defined as

$$M_{j,t} = \frac{A_{j,t}}{\sum_{l=1}^{J} A_{l,t}} \qquad \text{for } j = 1, \ldots, J.$$
(3.59)

This assumes that the attraction of the product category is the sum of the attractions of all brands and that $A_{j,t} = A_{l,t}$ implies that $M_{j,t} = M_{l,t}$. Combining (3.58) with (3.59) gives

$$M_{j,t} = \frac{\exp(\mu_j + \varepsilon_{j,t}) \prod_{k=1}^{K} x_{k,j,t}^{\beta_{k,j}}}{\sum_{l}^{J} \exp(\mu_l + \varepsilon_{l,t}) \prod_{k=1}^{K} x_{k,l,t}^{\beta_{k,l}}} \quad \text{for } i = j, \dots, J. \tag{3.60}$$

To enable parameter estimation, one can linearize this model by, first, taking brand J as the benchmark such that

$$\frac{M_{j,t}}{M_{J,t}} = \frac{\exp(\mu_j + \varepsilon_{j,t}) \prod_{k=1}^{K} x_{k,j,t}^{\beta_{k,j}}}{\exp(\mu_J + \varepsilon_{J,t}) \prod_{k=1}^{K} x_{k,J,t}^{\beta_{k,J}}}, \tag{3.61}$$

and, second, taking natural logarithms on both sides, which results in the $(J-1)$ equations

$$\log M_{j,t} = \log M_{J,t} + (\mu_j - \mu_J) + \sum_{k=1}^{K}(\beta_{k,j} - \beta_{k,J}) \log x_{k,j,t} \tag{3.62}$$
$$+ \varepsilon_{j,t} - \varepsilon_{J,t},$$

for $j = 1, \dots, J-1$. Note that one of the μ_j parameters $j = 1, \dots, J$ is not identified because one can only estimate $\mu_j - \mu_J$. Also, for similar reasons, one of the $\beta_{k,j}$ parameters is not identified for each k. In fact, only the parameters $\mu_j^* = \mu_j - \mu_J$ and $\beta_{k,j}^* = \beta_{k,j} - \beta_{k,J}$ are identified. In sum, the attraction model assumes $J-1$ model equations, thereby providing an example of how multiple-equation models can appear in marketing research. The market share attraction model bears some similarities to the so-called multinomial choice models in chapter 5. Before we turn to these models, we first deal with binomial choice in the next chapter.

4 A binomial dependent variable

In this chapter we focus on the Logit model and the Probit model for binary choice, yielding a binomial dependent variable. In section 4.1 we discuss the model representations and ways to arrive at these specifications. We show that parameter interpretation is not straightforward because the parameters enter the model in a nonlinear way. We give alternative approaches to interpreting the parameters and hence the models. In section 4.2 we discuss ML estimation in substantial detail. In section 4.3, diagnostic measures, model selection and forecasting are considered. Model selection concerns the choice of regressors and the comparison of non-nested models. Forecasting deals with within-sample or out-of-sample prediction. In section 4.4 we illustrate the models for a data set on the choice between two brands of tomato ketchup. Finally, in section 4.5 we discuss issues such as unobserved heterogeneity, dynamics and sample selection.

4.1 Representation and interpretation

In chapter 3 we discussed the standard Linear Regression model, where a continuously measured variable such as sales was correlated with, for example, price and promotion variables. These promotion variables typically appear as 0/1 dummy explanatory variables in regression models. As long as such dummy variables are on the right-hand side of the regression model, standard modeling and estimation techniques can be used. However, when 0/1 dummy variables appear on the left-hand side, the analysis changes and alternative models and inference methods need to be considered. In this chapter the focus is on models for dependent variables that concern such binomial data. Examples of binomial dependent variables are the choice between two brands made by a household on the basis of, for example, brand-specific characteristics, and the decision whether or not to donate to charity. In this chapter we assume that the data correspond to a single cross-section, that is, a sample of N individuals has been observed during a single time period and it is assumed that they correspond to one and the same population. In the advanced topics section of this chapter, we abandon this assumption and consider other but related types of data.

4.1.1 Modeling a binomial dependent variable

Consider the linear model

$$Y_i = \beta_0 + \beta_1 x_i + \varepsilon_i, \tag{4.1}$$

for individuals $i = 1, 2, \ldots, N$, where β_0 and β_1 are unknown parameters. Suppose that the random variable Y_i can take a value only of 0 or 1. For example, Y_i is 1 when a household buys brand A and 0 when it buys B, where x_i is, say, the price difference between brands A and B. Intuitively it seems obvious that the assumption that the distribution of ε_i is normal, with mean zero and variance σ^2, that is,

$$Y_i \sim N(\beta_0 + \beta_1 x_i, \sigma^2), \tag{4.2}$$

is not plausible. One can imagine that it is quite unlikely that this model maps possibly continuous values of x_i exactly on a variable, Y_i, which can take only two values. This is of course caused by the fact that Y_i itself is not a continuous variable.

To visualize the above argument, consider the observations on x_i and y_i when they are created using the following Data Generating Process (DGP), that is,

$$\begin{aligned} x_i &= 0.0001i + \varepsilon_{1,i} \quad \text{with } \varepsilon_{1,i} \sim N(0, 1) \\ y_i^* &= -2 + x_i + \varepsilon_{2,i} \quad \text{with } \varepsilon_{2,i} \sim N(0, 1), \end{aligned} \tag{4.3}$$

where $i = 1, 2, \ldots, N = 1{,}000$. Note that the same kind of DGP was used in chapter 3. Additionally, in order to obtain binomial data, we apply the rule $Y_i = 1$ if $y_i^* > 0$ and $Y_i = 0$ if $y_i^* \leq 0$. In figure 4.1, we depict a scatter diagram of this binomial variable y_i against x_i. This diagram also shows the fit of an OLS regression of y_i on an intercept and x_i. This graph clearly shows that the assumption of a standard linear regression for binomial data is unlikely to be useful.

The solution to the above problem amounts to simply assuming another distribution for the random variable Y_i. Recall that for the standard Linear Regression model for a continuous dependent variable we started with

$$Y_i \sim N(\mu, \sigma^2). \tag{4.4}$$

In the case of binomial data, it would now be better to opt for

$$Y_i \sim BIN(1, \pi), \tag{4.5}$$

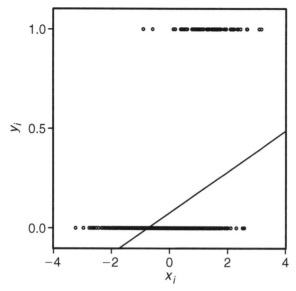

Figure 4.1   Scatter diagram of y_i against x_i, and the OLS regression line of y_i
on x_i and a constant

where BIN denotes the Bernoulli distribution with a single unknown parameter π (see section A.2 in the Appendix for more details of this distribution). A familiar application of this distribution concerns tossing a fair coin.
In that case, the probability π of obtaining heads or tails is 0.5.

When modeling marketing data concerning, for example, brand choice or
the response to a direct mailing, it is unlikely that the probability π is known
or that it is constant across individuals. It makes more sense to extend (4.5)
by making π dependent on x_i, that is, by considering

$$Y_i \sim \mathrm{BIN}(1, F(\beta_0 + \beta_1 x_i)), \tag{4.6}$$

where the function F has the property that it maps $\beta_0 + \beta_1 x_i$ onto the interval (0,1). Hence, instead of considering the precise value of Y_i, one now
focuses on the probability that, for example, $Y_i = 1$, given the outcome of
$\beta_0 + \beta_1 x_i$. In short, for a binomial dependent variable, the variable of interest is

$$\Pr[Y_i = 1 | X_i] = 1 - \Pr[Y_i = 0 | X_i], \tag{4.7}$$

where Pr denotes probability, where X_i collects the intercept and the variable
x_i (and perhaps other variables), and where we use the capital letter Y_i to
denote a random variable with realization y_i, which takes values conditional
on the values of x_i.

As an alternative to this more statistical argument, there are two other ways to assign an interpretation to the fact that the focus now turns towards modeling a probability instead of an observed value. The first, which will also appear to be useful in chapter 6 where we discuss ordered categorical data, starts with an unobserved (also called latent) but continuous variable y_i^*, which in the case of a single explanatory variable is assumed to be described by

$$y_i^* = \beta_0 + \beta_1 x_i + \varepsilon_i. \tag{4.8}$$

For the moment we leave the distribution of ε_i unspecified. This latent variable can, for example, amount to some measure for the difference between unobserved preferences for brand A and for brand B, for each individual i. Next, this latent continuous variable gets mapped onto the binomial variable y_i by the rule:

$$\begin{aligned} Y_i &= 1 \quad \text{if } y_i^* > 0 \\ Y_i &= 0 \quad \text{if } y_i^* \leq 0. \end{aligned} \tag{4.9}$$

This rule says that, when the difference between the preferences for brands A and B is positive, one would choose brand A and this would be denoted as $Y_i = 1$. The model is then used to correlate these differences in preferences with explanatory variables, such as, for example, the difference in price.

Note that the threshold value for y_i^* in (4.9) is equal to zero. This restriction is imposed for identification purposes. If the threshold were τ, the intercept parameter in (4.8) would change from β_0 to $\beta_0 - \tau$. In other words, τ and β_0 are not identified at the same time. It is common practice to solve this by assuming that τ is equal to zero. In chapter 6 we will see that in other cases it can be more convenient to set the intercept parameter equal to zero.

In figure 4.2, we provide a scatter diagram of y_i^* against x_i, when the data are again generated according to (4.3). For illustration, we depict the density function for three observations on y_i^* for different x_i, where we now assume that the error term is distributed as standard normal. The shaded areas correspond with the probability that $y_i^* > 0$, and hence that one assigns these latent observations to $Y_i = 1$. Clearly, for large values of x_i, the probability that $Y_i = 1$ is very close to 1, whereas for small values of x_i this probability is 0.

A second and related look at a model for a binomial dependent variable amounts to considering utility functions of individuals. Suppose an individual i assigns utility $u_{A,i}$ to brand A based on a perceived property x_i, where this variable measures the observed price difference between brands A and B, and that he/she assigns utility $u_{B,i}$ to brand B. Furthermore, suppose that these utilities are linear functions of x_i, that is,

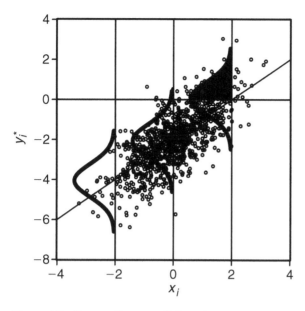

Figure 4.2   Scatter diagram of y_i^* against x_i

$$u_{A,i} = \alpha_A + \beta_A x_i + \varepsilon_{A,i}$$
$$u_{B,i} = \alpha_B + \beta_B x_i + \varepsilon_{B,i}. \qquad (4.10)$$

One may now define that an individual buys brand A if the utility of A exceeds that of B, that is,

$$\Pr[Y_i = 1|X_i] = \Pr[u_{A,i} > u_{B,i}|X_i]$$
$$= \Pr[\alpha_A - \alpha_B + (\beta_A - \beta_B)x_i > \varepsilon_{A,i} - \varepsilon_{B,i}|X_i] \qquad (4.11)$$
$$= \Pr[\varepsilon_i \leq \beta_0 + \beta_1 x_i|X_i],$$

where ε_i equals $\varepsilon_{A,i} - \varepsilon_{B,i}$, β_0 equals $\alpha_A - \alpha_B$ and β_1 is $\beta_A - \beta_B$. This shows that one cannot identify the individual parameters in (4.11); one can identify only the difference between the parameters. Hence, one way to look at the parameters β_0 and β_1 is to see these as measuring the effect of x_i on the choice for brand A relative to brand B. The next step now concerns the specification of the distribution of ε_i.

4.1.2   The Logit and Probit models

The discussion up to now has left the distribution of ε_i unspecified. In this subsection we will consider two commonly applied cumulative distribution functions. So far we have considered only a single explanatory variable, and in particular examples below we will continue to do so.

However, in the subsequent discussion we will generally assume the avail-ability of $K + 1$ explanatory variables, where the first variable concerns the intercept. As in chapter 3, we summarize these variables in the $1 \times (K + 1)$ vector X_i, and we summarize the $K + 1$ unknown parameters β_0 to β_K in a $(K + 1) \times 1$ parameter vector β.

The discussion in the previous subsection indicates that a model that correlates a binomial dependent variable with explanatory variables can be constructed as

$$\begin{aligned} \Pr[Y_i = 1|X_i] &= \Pr[y_i^* > 0|X_i] \\ &= \Pr[X_i\beta + \varepsilon_i > 0|X_i] \\ &= \Pr[\varepsilon_i > -X_i\beta|X_i] \\ &= \Pr[\varepsilon_i \leq X_i\beta|X_i]. \end{aligned} \qquad (4.12)$$

The last line of this set of equations states that the probability of observing $Y_i = 1$ given X_i is equal to the cumulative distribution function of ε_i, eval-uated at $X_i\beta$. In shorthand notation, this is

$$\Pr[Y_i = 1|X_i] = F(X_i\beta), \qquad (4.13)$$

where $F(X_i\beta)$ denotes the cumulative distribution function of ε_i evaluated in $X_i\beta$. For further use, we denote the corresponding density function evaluated in $X_i\beta$ as $f(X_i\beta)$.

There are many possible choices for F, but in practice one usually con-siders either the normal or the logistic distribution function. In the first case, that is

$$F(X_i\beta) = \Phi(X_i\beta) = \int_{-\infty}^{X_i\beta} \frac{1}{\sqrt{2\pi}} \exp\left(-\frac{z^2}{2}\right) dz, \qquad (4.14)$$

the resultant model is called the Probit model, where the symbol Φ is com-monly used for standard normal distribution. For further use, the corre-sponding standard normal density function evaluated in $X_i\beta$ is denoted as $\phi(X_i\beta)$. The second case takes

$$F(X_i\beta) = \Lambda(X_i\beta) = \frac{\exp(X_i\beta)}{1 + \exp(X_i\beta)}, \qquad (4.15)$$

which is the cumulative distribution function according to the standardized logistic distribution (see section A.2 in the Appendix). In this case, the resul-tant model is called the Logit model. In some applications, the Logit model is written as

$$\Pr[Y_i = 1|X_i] = 1 - \Lambda(-X_i\beta), \qquad (4.16)$$

which is of course equivalent to (4.15).

It should be noted that the two cumulative distribution functions above are already standardized. The reason for doing this can perhaps best be understood by reconsidering $y_i^* = X_i\beta + \varepsilon_i$. If y_i^* were multiplied by a factor k, this would not change the classification y_i^* into positive or negative values upon using (4.9). In other words, the variance of ε_i is not identified, and therefore ε_i can be standardized. This variance is equal to 1 in the Probit model and equal to $\frac{1}{3}\pi^2$ in the Logit model.

The standardized logistic and normal cumulative distribution functions behave approximately similarly in the vicinity of their mean values. Only in the tails can one observe that the distributions have different patterns. In other words, if one has a small number of, say, $y_i = 1$ observations, which automatically implies that one considers the left-hand tail of the distribution because the probability of having $y_i = 1$ is apparently small, it may matter which model one considers for empirical analysis. On the other hand, if the fraction of $y_i = 1$ observations approaches $\frac{1}{2}$, one can use

$$\varepsilon_i^{\text{Logit}} \approx \sqrt{\frac{1}{3}\pi^2}\varepsilon_i^{\text{Probit}},$$

although Amemiya (1981) argues that the factor 1.65 might be better. This appropriate relationship also implies that the estimated parameters of the Logit and Probit models have a similar relation.

4.1.3 Model interpretation

The effects of the explanatory variables on the dependent binomial variable are not linear, because they get channeled through a cumulative distribution function. For example, the cumulative logistic distribution function in (4.15) has the component $X_i\beta$ in the numerator and in the denominator. Hence, for a positive parameter β_k, it is not immediately clear what the effect is of a change in the corresponding variable x_k.

To illustrate the interpretation of the models for a binary dependent variable, it is most convenient to focus on the Logit model, and also to restrict attention to a single explanatory variable. Hence, we confine the discussion to

$$\Lambda(\beta_0 + \beta_1 x_i) = \frac{\exp(\beta_0 + \beta_1 x_i)}{1 + \exp(\beta_0 + \beta_1 x_i)}$$

$$= \frac{\exp\left(\beta_1\left(\frac{\beta_0}{\beta_1} + x_i\right)\right)}{1 + \exp\left(\beta_1\frac{\beta_0}{\beta_1} + x_i\right)} . \tag{4.17}$$

This expression shows that the inflection point of the logistic curve occurs at $x_i = -\beta_0/\beta_1$, and that then $\Lambda(\beta_0 + \beta_1 x_i) = \frac{1}{2}$. When x_i is larger than $-\beta_0/\beta_1$, the function value approaches 1, and when x_i is smaller than $-\beta_0/\beta_1$, the function value approaches 0.

In figure 4.3, we depict three examples of cumulative logistic distribution functions

$$\Lambda(\beta_0 + \beta_1 x_i) = \frac{\exp(\beta_0 + \beta_1 x_i)}{1 + \exp(\beta_0 + \beta_1 x_i)}, \tag{4.18}$$

where x_i ranges between -4 and 6, and where β_0 can be -2 or -4 and β_1 can be 1 or 2. When we compare the graph of the case $\beta_0 = -2$ and $\beta_1 = 1$ with that where $\beta_1 = 2$, we observe that a large value of β_1 makes the curve steeper. Hence, the parameter β_1 changes the steepness of the logistic function. In contrast, if we fix β_1 at 1 and compare the curves with $\beta_0 = -2$ and $\beta_0 = -4$, we notice that the curve shifts to the right when β_0 is more negative

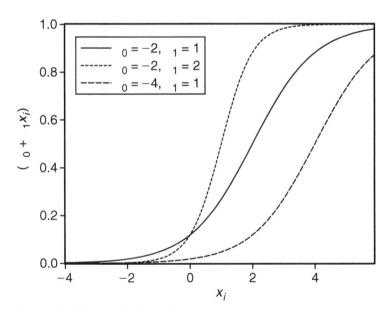

Figure 4.3   Graph of $\Lambda(\beta_0 + \beta_1 x_i)$ against x_i

but that its shape stays the same. Hence, changes in the intercept parameter only make the curve shift to the left or the right, depending on whether the change is positive or negative. Notice that when the curve shifts to the right, the number of observations with a probability $\Pr[Y_i = 1|X_i] > 0.5$ decreases. In other words, large negative values of the intercept β_0 given the range of x_i values would correspond with data with few $y_i = 1$ observations.

The nonlinear effect of x_i can also be understood from

$$\frac{\partial\Lambda(\beta_0 + \beta_1 x_i)}{\partial x_i} = \Lambda(\beta_0 + \beta_1 x_i)[1 - \Lambda(\beta_0 + \beta_1 x_i)]\beta_1. \tag{4.19}$$

This shows that the effect of a change in x_i depends not only on the value of β_1 but also on the value taken by the logistic function.

The effects of the variables and parameters in a Logit model (and similarly in a Probit model) can also be understood by considering the odds ratio, which is defined by

$$\frac{\Pr[Y_i = 1|X_i]}{\Pr[Y_i = 0|X_i]}. \tag{4.20}$$

For the Logit model with one variable, it is easy to see using (4.15) that this odds ratio equals

$$\frac{\Lambda(\beta_0 + \beta_1 x_i)}{1 - \Lambda(\beta_0 + \beta_1 x_i)} = \exp(\beta_0 + \beta_1 x_i). \tag{4.21}$$

Because this ratio can take large values owing to the exponential function, it is common practice to consider the log odds ratio, that is,

$$\log\left(\frac{\Lambda(\beta_0 + \beta_1 x_i)}{1 - \Lambda(\beta_0 + \beta_1 x_i)}\right) = \beta_0 + \beta_1 x_i. \tag{4.22}$$

When $\beta_1 = 0$, the log odds ratio equals β_0. If additionally $\beta_0 = 0$, this is seen to correspond to an equal number of observations $y_i = 1$ and $y_i = 0$. When this is not the case, but the β_0 parameter is anyhow set equal to 0, then the $\beta_1 x_i$ component of the model has to model the effect of x_i and the intercept at the same time. In practice it is therefore better not to delete the β_0 parameter, even though it may seem to be insignificant.

If there are two or more explanatory variables, one may also assign an interpretation to the differences between the various parameters. For example, consider the case with two explanatory variables in a Logit model, that is,

$$\Lambda(\beta_0 + \beta_1 x_{1,i} + \beta_2 x_{2,i}) = \frac{\exp(\beta_0 + \beta_1 x_{1,i} + \beta_2 x_{2,i})}{1 + \exp(\beta_0 + \beta_1 x_{1,i} + \beta_2 x_{2,i})}. \tag{4.23}$$

For this model, one can derive that

$$\frac{\dfrac{\partial \Pr[Y_i = 1|X_i]}{\partial x_{1,i}}}{\dfrac{\partial \Pr[Y_i = 1|X_i]}{\partial x_{2,i}}} = \frac{\beta_1}{\beta_2}, \tag{4.24}$$

where the partial derivative of $\Pr[Y_i = 1|X_i]$ with respect to $x_{k,i}$ equals

$$\frac{\partial \Pr[Y_i = 1|X_i]}{\partial x_{k,i}} = \Pr[Y_i = 1|X_i](1 - \Pr[Y_i = 1|X_i])\beta_k \quad k = 1, 2. \tag{4.25}$$

Hence, the ratio of the parameter values gives a measure of the relative effect of the two variables on the probability that $Y_i = 1$.

Finally, one can consider the so-called quasi-elasticity of an explanatory variable. For a Logit model with again a single explanatory variable, this quasi-elasticity is defined as

$$\frac{\partial \Pr[Y_i = 1|X_i]}{\partial x_i} x_i = \Pr[Y_i = 1|X_i](1 - \Pr[Y_i = 1|X_i])\beta_1 x_i, \tag{4.26}$$

which shows that this elasticity also depends on the value of x_i. A change in the value of x_i has an effect on $\Pr[Y_i = 1|X_i]$ and hence an opposite effect on $\Pr[Y_i = 0|X_i]$. Indeed, it is rather straightforward to derive that

$$\frac{\partial \Pr[Y_i = 1|X_i]}{\partial x_i} x_i + \frac{\partial \Pr[Y_i = 0|X_i]}{\partial x_i} x_i = 0. \tag{4.27}$$

In other words, the sum of the two quasi-elasticities is equal to zero. Naturally, all this also holds for the binomial Probit model.

4.2 Estimation

In this section we discuss the Maximum Likelihood estimation method for the Logit and Probit models. The models are then written in terms of the joint density distribution $p(y|X; \beta)$ for the observed variables y given X, where β summarizes the model parameters β_0 to β_K. Remember that the variance of the error variable is fixed, and hence it does not have to be estimated. The likelihood function is defined as

$$L(\beta) = p(y|X; \beta). \tag{4.28}$$

Again it is convenient to consider the logarithmic likelihood function

$$l(\beta) = \log(L(\beta)). \tag{4.29}$$

Contrary to the Linear Regression model in section 3.2.2, it turns out that it is not possible to find an analytical solution for the value of β that maximizes the log-likelihood function. The maximization of the log-likelihood has to be done using a numerical optimization algorithm. Here, we opt for the Newton–Raphson method. For this method, we need the gradient $G(\beta)$ and the Hessian matrix $H(\beta)$, that is,

$$G(\beta) = \frac{\partial l(\beta)}{\partial \beta},$$
$$H(\beta) = \frac{\partial^2 l(\beta)}{\partial \beta \partial \beta'}. \tag{4.30}$$

It turns out that for the binomial Logit and Probit models, one can obtain elegant expressions for these two derivatives. The information matrix, which is useful for obtaining standard errors for the parameter estimates, is equal to $-E(H(\beta))$. Linearizing the optimization problem and solving it gives the sequence of estimates

$$\beta_{h+1} = \beta_h - H(\beta_h)^{-1}G(\beta_h), \tag{4.31}$$

where $G(\beta_h)$ and $H(\beta_h)$ are the gradient and Hessian matrix evaluated in β_h (see also section 3.2.2).

4.2.1 The Logit model

The likelihood function for the Logit model is the product of the choice probabilities over the i individuals, that is,

$$L(\beta) = \prod_{i=1}^{N}(\Lambda(X_i\beta))^{y_i}(1 - \Lambda(X_i\beta))^{1-y_i}, \tag{4.32}$$

and the log-likelihood is

$$l(\beta) = \sum_{i=1}^{N} y_i \log \Lambda(X_i\beta) + \sum_{i=1}^{N}(1 - y_i)\log(1 - \Lambda(X_i\beta)). \tag{4.33}$$

Owing to the fact that

$$\frac{\partial \Lambda(X_i\beta)}{\partial \beta} = \Lambda(X_i\beta)(1 - \Lambda(X_i\beta))X_i', \tag{4.34}$$

the gradient (or score) is given by

$$G(\beta) = \frac{\partial l(\beta)}{\partial \beta} = -\sum_{i=1}^{N}(\Lambda(X_i\beta))X_i' + \sum_{i=1}^{N} X_i'y_i, \tag{4.35}$$

and the Hessian matrix is given by

$$H(\beta) = \frac{\partial^2 l(\beta)}{\partial \beta \partial \beta'} = -\sum_{i=1}^{N} (\Lambda(X_i\beta))(1 - \Lambda(X_i\beta))X_i'X_i. \tag{4.36}$$

In Amemiya (1985) it is formally proved that the log-likelihood function is globally concave, which implies that the Newton–Raphson method converges to a unique maximum (the ML parameter estimates) for all possible starting values. The ML estimator is consistent, asymptotically normal and asymptotically efficient. The asymptotic covariance matrix of the parameters β can be estimated by $-H(\hat{\beta})^{-1}$, evaluated in the ML estimates. The diagonal elements of this $(K + 1) \times (K + 1)$ matrix are the estimated variances of the parameters in $\hat{\beta}$. With these, one can construct the z-scores for the estimated parameters in order to diagnose if the underlying parameters are significantly different from zero.

4.2.2   The Probit model

Along similar lines, one can consider ML estimation of the model parameters for the binary Probit model. The relevant likelihood function is now given by

$$L(\beta) = \prod_{i=1}^{N} (\Phi(X_i\beta))^{y_i} (1 - \Phi(X_i\beta))^{1-y_i}, \tag{4.37}$$

and the corresponding log-likelihood function is

$$l(\beta) = \sum_{i=1}^{N} y_i \log \Phi(X_i\beta) + \sum_{i=1}^{N} (1 - y_i) \log(1 - \Phi(X_i\beta)). \tag{4.38}$$

Differentiating $l(\beta)$ with respect to β gives

$$G(\beta) = \frac{\partial l(\beta)}{\partial \beta} = -\sum_{i=1}^{N} \frac{y_i - \Phi(X_i\beta)}{\Phi(X_i\beta)(1 - \Phi(X_i\beta))} \phi(X_i\beta)X_i', \tag{4.39}$$

and the Hessian matrix is given by

$$H(\beta) = \frac{\partial^2 l(\beta)}{\partial \beta \partial \beta'} = \sum_{i=1}^{N} \frac{\phi(X_i\beta)^2}{\Phi(X_i\beta)(1 - \Phi(X_i\beta))} X_i'X_i. \tag{4.40}$$

The asymptotic covariance matrix of the parameters β can again be estimated by $-H(\hat{\beta})^{-1}$, evaluated in the ML estimates. The diagonal elements of this $(K + 1) \times (K + 1)$ matrix are again the estimated variances of the parameters in $\hat{\beta}$.

4.2.3   Visualizing estimation results

Once the parameters have been estimated, there are various ways to examine the empirical results. Of course, one can display the parameter estimates and their associated z-scores in a table in order to see which of the parameters in β is perhaps equal to zero. If such parameters are found, one may decide to delete one or more variables. This would be useful in the case where one has a limited number of observations, because redundant variables in general reduce the z-scores of all variables. Hence, the inclusion of redundant variables may erroneously suggest that certain other variables are also not significant.

Because the above models for a binary dependent variable are nonlinear in the parameters β, it is not immediately clear how one should interpret their absolute values. One way to make more sense of the estimation output is to focus on the estimated cumulative distribution function. For the Logit model, this is equal to

$$\hat{\Pr}[Y_i = 1|X_i] = \Lambda(X_i\hat{\beta}). \tag{4.41}$$

One can now report the maximum value of $\hat{\Pr}[Y_i = 1|X_i]$, its minimum value and its mean, and also the values given maximum, mean and minimum values for the explanatory variables. A scatter diagram of the estimated quasi-elasticity

$$\hat{\Pr}[Y_i = 1|X_i](1 - \hat{\Pr}[Y_i = 1|X_i])\hat{\beta}_k x_{k,i}, \tag{4.42}$$

for a variable $x_{k,i}$ against this variable itself can also be insightful. In the empirical section below we will demonstrate a few potentially useful measures.

4.3   Diagnostics, model selection and forecasting

Once the parameters in binomial choice models have been estimated, it is again important to check the empirical adequacy of the model. Indeed, if a model is incorrectly specified, the interpretation of the parameters may be hazardous. Also, it is likely that the included parameters and their corresponding standard errors are calculated incorrectly. Hence, one should first check the adequacy of the model. If the model is found to be adequate, one may consider deleting possibly redundant variables or compare alternative models using selection criteria. Finally, when one or more suitable models have been found, one may evaluate them on within-sample or out-of-sample forecasting performance.

4.3.1   Diagnostics

As with the standard Linear Regression model, diagnostic tests are frequently based on the residuals. Ideally one would want to be able to estimate the values of ε_i in $y_i^* = X_i\beta + \varepsilon_i$, but unfortunately these values cannot be obtained because y_i^* is an unobserved (latent) variable. Hence, residuals can for example be obtained from comparing

$$\hat{\Pr}[Y_i = 1|X_i] = F(X_i\hat{\beta}) \\ = \hat{p}_i,$$

(4.43)

with the true observations on y_i. Because a Bernoulli distributed variable with mean p has variance $p(1 - p)$ (see also section A.2 in the Appendix), we have that the variance of the variable $(Y_i|X_i)$ is equal to $p_i(1 - p_i)$. This suggests that the standardized residuals

$$\hat{e}_i = \frac{y_i - \hat{p}_i}{\sqrt{\hat{p}_i(1 - \hat{p}_i)}}$$

(4.44)

can be used for diagnostic purposes.

An alternative definition of residuals can be obtained from considering the first-order conditions of the ML estimation method, that is

$$\frac{\partial l(\beta)}{\partial \beta} = \sum_{i=1}^{N} \frac{y_i - F(X_i\beta)}{F(X_i\beta)(1 - F(X_i\beta))} f(X_i\beta)X_i' = 0,$$

(4.45)

where $F(X_i\beta)$ can be $\Phi(X_i\beta)$ or $\Lambda(X_i\beta)$ and $f(X_i\beta)$ is then $\phi(X_i\beta)$ or $\lambda(X_i\beta)$, respectively. Similarly to the standard Linear Regression model, one can now define the residuals to correspond with

$$\frac{\partial l(\beta)}{\partial \beta} = \sum_{i=1}^{N} X_i'\hat{e}_i = 0,$$

(4.46)

which leads to

$$\hat{e}_i = \frac{y_i - F(X_i\hat{\beta})}{F(X_i\hat{\beta})(1 - F(X_i\hat{\beta}))} f(X_i\hat{\beta}).$$

(4.47)

Usually these residuals are called the generalized residuals. Large values of $\hat{e}_i$ may indicate the presence of outliers in y_i or in $\hat{p}_i$ (see Pregibon, 1981). Notice that the residuals are not normally distributed, and hence one can evaluate the residuals only against their average value and their standard deviation. Once outlying observations have been discovered, one might decide to leave out these observations while re-estimating the model parameters again.

A second check for model adequacy, which in this case concerns the error variable in the unobserved regression model ε_i, involves the presumed constancy of its variance. One may, for example, test the null hypothesis of a constant variance against

$$H_1 : V(\varepsilon_i) = \exp(2Z_i\gamma), \tag{4.48}$$

where V denotes "variance of", and where Z_i is a $(1 \times q)$ vector of variables and γ is a $(q \times 1)$ vector of unknown parameters. Davidson and MacKinnon (1993, section 15.4) show that a test for heteroskedasticity can be based on the artificial regression

$$\frac{y_i - \hat{p}_i}{\sqrt{\hat{p}_i(1 - \hat{p}_i)}} = \frac{f(-X_i\hat{\beta})}{\sqrt{\hat{p}_i(1 - \hat{p}_i)}} X_i\tau_1 + \frac{f(-X_i\hat{\beta})(-X_i\hat{\beta})}{\sqrt{\hat{p}_i(1 - \hat{p}_i)}} Z_i\tau_2 + \eta_i. \tag{4.49}$$

The relevant test statistic is calculated as the Likelihood Ratio test for the significance of the τ_2 parameters and it is asymptotically distributed as $\chi^2(q)$. Once heteroskedasticity has been discovered, one may consider a Probit model with

$$\varepsilon_i \sim N(0, \sigma_i^2), \text{ with } \sigma_i^2 = \exp(2Z_i\gamma); \tag{4.50}$$

see Greene (2000, p. 829) and Knapp and Seaks (1992) for an application.

The above diagnostic checks implicitly consider the adequacy of the functional form. There are, however, no clear guidelines as to how one should choose between a Logit and a Probit model. As noted earlier, the main differences between the two functions can be found in the tails of their distributions. In other words, when one considers a binary dependent variable that only seldom takes a value of 1, one may find different parameter estimates across the two models. A final decision between the two models can perhaps be made on the basis of out-of-sample forecasting.

4.3.2 *Model selection*

Once two or more models of the Logit or Probit type for a binomial dependent variable are found to pass relevant diagnostic checks, one may want to examine if certain (or all) variables can be deleted or if alternative models are to be preferred. These alternative models may include alternative regressors.

The relevance of individual variables can be based on the individual z-scores, which can be obtained from the parameter estimates combined with the diagonal elements of the estimated information matrix. The joint significance of g explanatory variables can be examined by using a Likelihood Ratio (LR) test. The test statistic can be calculated as

$$LR = -2\log\frac{L(\hat{\beta}_0)}{L(\hat{\beta}_A)} = -2(l(\hat{\beta}_0) - l(\hat{\beta})), \tag{4.51}$$

where $l(\hat{\beta}_0)$ denotes that the model contains only an intercept, and where $l(\hat{\beta})$ is the value of the maximum of the log-likelihood function for the model with the g variables included. Under the null hypothesis that the g variables are redundant, it holds that

$$LR \overset{a}{\sim} \chi^2(g). \tag{4.52}$$

The null hypothesis is rejected if the value of LR is sufficiently large when compared with the relevant critical values of the $\chi^2(g)$ distribution. If $g = K$, this LR test amounts to a measure of the overall fit.

An alternative measure of the overall fit is the R^2 measure. Windmeijer (1995) reviews several such measures for binomial dependent variable models, and based on simulations it appears that the measures proposed by McFadden (1974) and by McKelvey and Zavoina (1975) are the most reliable, in the sense that these are least dependent on the number of observations with $y_i = 1$. The McFadden R^2 is defined by

$$R^2 = 1 - \frac{l(\hat{\beta})}{l(\hat{\beta}_0)}. \tag{4.53}$$

Notice that the lower bound value of this R^2 is equal to 0, but that the upper bound is not equal to 1, because $l(\hat{\beta})$ cannot become equal to zero.

The R^2 proposed in McKelvey and Zavoina (1975) is slightly different, but it is found to be useful because it can be generalized to discrete dependent variable models with more than two ordered outcomes (see chapter 6). The intuition for this R^2 is that it measures the ratio of the variance of $\hat{y}_i^*$ and the variance of y_i^*, where $\hat{y}_i^*$ equals $X_i\hat{\beta}$. Some manipulation gives

$$R^2 = \frac{\sum_{i=1}^{N}(\hat{y}_i^* - \bar{y}_i^*)^2}{\sum_{i=1}^{N}(\hat{y}_i^* - \bar{y}_i^*)^2 + N\sigma^2}, \tag{4.54}$$

where $\bar{y}_i^*$ denotes the average value of $\hat{y}_i^*$, with $\sigma^2 = \frac{1}{3}\pi^2$ in the Logit model and $\sigma^2 = 1$ in the Probit model.

Finally, if one has more than one model within the Logit or Probit class of models, one may also consider familiar model selection criteria. In the notation of this chapter, the Akaike information criterion is defined as

$$AIC = \frac{1}{N}(-2l(\hat{\beta}) + 2n), \tag{4.55}$$

and the Schwarz information criterion is defined as

$$\text{BIC} = \frac{1}{N}(-2l(\hat{\beta}) + n \log N), \qquad (4.56)$$

where n denotes the number of parameters and N the number of observations.

4.3.3 Forecasting

A possible purpose of a model for a binomial dependent variable is to generate forecasts. One can consider forecasting within-sample or out-of-sample. For the latter forecasts, one needs to save a hold-out sample, containing observations that have not been used for constructing the model and estimating its parameters. Suppose that in that case there are N_1 observations for model building and estimation and that N_2 observations can be used for out-of-sample forecast evaluation.

The first issue of course concerns the construction of the forecasts. A common procedure is to predict that $Y_i = 1$, to be denoted as $\hat{y}_i = 1$, if $F(X_i\hat{\beta}) > c$, and to predict that $Y_i = 0$, denoted by $\hat{y}_i = 0$, if $F(X_i\hat{\beta}) \leq c$. The default option in many statistical packages is that c is 0.5. However, in practice one is free to choose the value of c. For example, one may also want to consider

$$c = \frac{\#(y_i = 1)}{N}, \qquad (4.57)$$

that is, the fraction of observations with $y_i = 1$.

Given the availability of forecasts, one can construct the prediction–realization table, that is,

	Predicted		
	$\hat{y}_i = 1$	$\hat{y}_i = 0$	
Observed			
$y_i = 1$	p_{11}	p_{10}	$p_{1\cdot}$
$y_i = 0$	p_{01}	p_{00}	$p_{0\cdot}$
	$p_{\cdot 1}$	$p_{\cdot 0}$	1

The fraction $p_{11} + p_{00}$ is usually called the hit rate. Based on simulation experiments, Veall and Zimmermann (1992) recommend the use of the measure suggested by McFadden et al. (1977), which is given by

$$F_1 = \frac{p_{11} + p_{00} - p_{\cdot 1}^2 - p_{\cdot 0}^2}{1 - p_{\cdot 1}^2 - p_{\cdot 0}^2}. \qquad (4.58)$$

The model with the maximum value for F_1 may be viewed as the model that has the best forecasting performance. Indeed, perfect forecasts would have been obtained if $F_1 = 1$. Strictly speaking, however, there is no lower bound to the value of F_1.

4.4 Modeling the choice between two brands

In this section we illustrate the Logit and Probit models for the choice between Heinz and Hunts tomato ketchup. The details of these data have already been given in section 2.2.2. We have 2,798 observations for 300 individuals. We leave out the last purchase made by each of these individuals, that is, we have $N_2 = 300$ data points for out-of-sample forecast evaluation. Of the N_2 observations there are 265 observations with $y_i = 1$, corresponding to the choice of Heinz. For within-sample analysis, we have $N_1 = 2,498$ observations, of which 2,226 amount to a choice for Heinz ($y_i = 1$). For each purchase occasion, we know whether or not Heinz and/ or Hunts were on display, and whether or not they were featured. We also have the price of both brands at each purchase occasion. The promotion variables are included in the models as the familiar 0/1 dummy variables, while we further decide to include the log of the ratio of the prices, that is,

$$\log\left(\frac{\text{price Heinz}}{\text{price Hunts}}\right),$$

which obviously equals $\log(\text{price Heinz}) - \log(\text{price Hunts})$.

The ML parameter estimates for the Logit and Probit models appear in table 4.1, as do the corresponding estimated standard errors. The intercept parameters are both positive and significant, and this matches with the larger number of purchases of Heinz ketchup. The promotion variables of Heinz do not have much explanatory value, as only display promotion is significant at the 5% level. In contrast, the promotion variables for Hunts are all significant and also take larger values (in an absolute sense). The joint effect of feature and display of Hunts (equal to -1.981) is largest. Finally, the price variable is significant and has the correct sign. When we compare the estimated values for the Logit and the Probit model, we observe that oftentimes $\hat{\beta}^{\text{Logit}} \approx 1.85\hat{\beta}^{\text{Probit}}$, where the factor 1.85 closely matches with

$$\sqrt{\frac{1}{3}\pi^2}.$$

As the results across the two models are very similar, we focus our attention only on the Logit model in the rest of this section.

Before we pay more attention to the interpretation of the estimated Logit model, we first consider its empirical adequacy. We start with the generalized

Table 4.1 *Estimation results for Logit and Probit models for the choice between Heinz and Hunts*

Variables	Logit model		Probit model	
	Parameter	Standard error	Parameter	Standard error
Intercept	3.290***	0.151	1.846***	0.076
Heinz, display only	0.526**	0.254	0.271**	0.129
Heinz, feature only	0.474	0.320	0.188	0.157
Heinz, feature and display	0.473	0.489	0.255	0.248
Hunts, display only	−0.651**	0.254	−0.376**	0.151
Hunts, feature only	−1.033***	0.361	−0.573***	0.197
Hunts, feature and display	−1.981***	0.479	−1.094***	0.275
log (price Heinz/Hunts)	−5.987***	0.401	−3.274***	0.217
max. log-likelihood value	−601.238		−598.828	

Notes:
*** Significant at the 0.01 level, ** at the 0.05 level, * at the 0.10 level.
The total number of observations is 2,498, of which 2,226 concern the choice for Heinz ($y_i = 1$).

residuals, as these are defined in (4.47). The mean value of these residuals is zero, and the standard deviation is 0.269. The maximum value of these residuals is 0.897 and the minimum value is −0.990. Hence, it seems that there may be a few observations which can be considered as outliers. It seems best, however, to decide about re-estimating the model parameters after having seen the results of other diagnostics and evaluation measures. Next, a test for the null hypothesis of homoskedasticity of the error variable ε_i against the alternative

$$H_1 : V(\varepsilon_i) = \exp\left(2\gamma_1 \log\left(\frac{\text{price Heinz}_i}{\text{price Hunts}_i}\right)\right) \tag{4.59}$$

results in a $\chi^2(1)$ test statistic value of 3.171, which is not significant at the 5% level (see section A.3 in the Appendix for the relevant critical value).

The McFadden R^2 (4.53) is 0.30, while the McKelvey and Zavoina R^2 measure (4.54) equals 0.61, which does not seem too bad for a large cross-section. The *LR* test for the joint significance of all seven variables takes a value of 517.06, which is significant at the 1% level. Finally, we consider within-sample and out-of-sample forecasting. In both cases, we set the cut-off point at 0.891, which corresponds with 2,226/2,498. For the 2,498 within-sample forecasts we obtain the following prediction–realization table, that is,

	Predicted		
	Heinz	Hunts	
Observed			
Heinz	0.692	0.199	0.891
Hunts	0.023	0.086	0.108
	0.715	0.285	1

The F_1 statistic takes a value of 0.455 and the hit rate p equals 0.778 (0.692 + 0.086).

For the 300 out-of-sample forecasts, where we again set the cut-off point c at 0.891, we obtain

	Predicted		
	Heinz	Hunts	
Observed			
Heinz	0.673	0.210	0.883
Hunts	0.020	0.097	0.117
	0.693	0.307	1

It can be seen that this is not very different from the within-sample results. Indeed, the F_1 statistic is 0.459 and the hit rate is 0.770. In sum, the Logit model seems very adequate, even though further improvement may perhaps be possible by deleting a few outlying data points.

We now continue with the interpretation of the estimation results in table 4.1. The estimated parameters for the promotion variables in this table suggest that the effects of the Heinz promotion variables on the probability of choosing Heinz are about equal, even though two of the three are not significant. In contrast, the effects of the Hunts promotion variables are 1.3 to about 5 times as large (in an absolute sense). Also, the Hunts promotions are most effective if they are held at the same time.

These differing effects can also be visualized by making a graph of the estimated probability of choosing Heinz against the log price difference for various settings of promotions. In figure 4.4 we depict four such settings. The top left graph depicts two curves, one for the case where there is no promotion whatsoever (solid line) and one for the case where Heinz is on display. It can be seen that the differences between the two curves are not substantial, although perhaps in the price difference range of 0.2 to 0.8, the higher price of Heinz can be compensated for by putting Heinz on display. The largest difference between the curves can be found in the bottom right graph, which

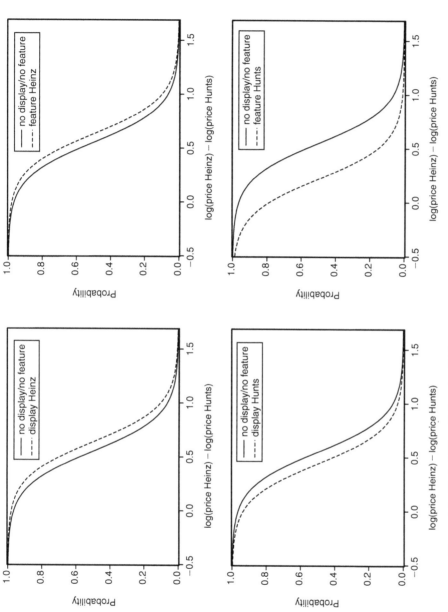

Figure 4.4   Probability of choosing Heinz

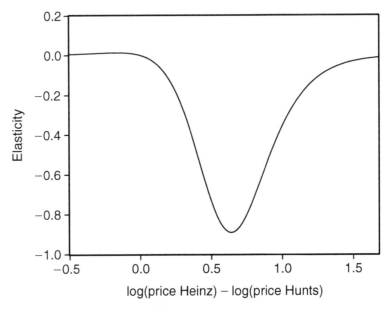

Figure 4.5   Quasi price elasticity

concerns the case where Hunts is featured. Clearly, when Heinz gets more expensive than Hunts, additional featuring of Hunts can substantially reduce the probability of buying Heinz.

Finally, in figure 4.5 we give a graph of a quasi price elasticity, that is,

$$-5.987 \, \hat{\Pr}[\text{Heinz}|X_i](1 - \hat{\Pr}[\text{Heinz}|X_i]) \log\left(\frac{\text{price Heinz}_i}{\text{price Hunts}_i}\right), \quad (4.60)$$

against

$$\log\left(\frac{\text{price Heinz}_i}{\text{price Hunts}_i}\right).$$

Moving from an equal price, where the log price ratio is equal to 0, towards the case where Heinz is twice as expensive (about 0.69) shows that the price elasticity increases rapidly in absolute sense. This means that going from a price ratio of, say, 1.4 to 1.5 has a larger negative effect on the probability of buying Heinz than going from, say, 1.3 to 1.4. Interestingly, when Heinz becomes much more expensive, for example it becomes more than three times as expensive, the price elasticity drops back to about 0. Hence, the structure of the Logit model implies that there is a price range that corresponds to highly sensitive effects of changes in a marketing instrument such as price.

4.5   Advanced topics

The models for a binomial dependent variable in this chapter have so far assumed the availability of a cross-section of observations, where N individuals could choose between two options. In the empirical example, these options concerned two brands, where we had information on a few (marketing) aspects of each purchase, such as price and promotion. Because sometimes one may know more about the individuals too, that is, one may know some household characteristics such as size and family income, one may aim to modify the Logit and Probit models by allowing for household heterogeneity. In other cases, these variables may not be sufficient to explain possible heterogeneity, and then one may opt to introduce unobserved heterogeneity in the models. In section 4.5.1, we give a brief account of including heterogeneity. In the next subsection we discuss a few models that can be useful if one has a panel of individuals, whose purchases over time are known. Finally, it can happen that the observations concerning one of the choice options outnumbers those of the other choice. For example, one brand may be seldom purchased. In that case, one can have a large number of observations with $y_i = 0$ and only very few with $y_i = 1$. To save time collecting explanatory variables for all $y_i = 0$ observations, one may decide to consider relatively few $y_i = 0$ observations. In section 4.5.3, we illustrate that in the case of a Logit model only a minor modification to the analysis is needed.

4.5.1   Modeling unobserved heterogeneity

It usually occurs that one has several observations of an individual over time. Suppose the availability of observations $y_{i,t}$ for $i = 1, 2, \ldots, N$ and $t = 1, 2, \ldots, T$. For example, one observes the choice between two brands made by household i in week t. Additionally, assume that one has explanatory variables $x_{i,t}$, which are measured over the same households and time period, where these variables are not all constant.

Consider again a binary choice model to model brand choice in week t for individual i, and for ease of notation assume that there is only a single explanatory variable, that is,

$$\Pr[Y_{i,t} = 1 | X_{i,t}] = F(\beta_0 + \beta_1 x_{i,t}), \tag{4.61}$$

and suppose that $x_{i,t}$ concerns a marketing-specific variable such as price in week t. If one has information on a household-specific variable h_i such as income, one can modify this model into

$$\Pr[Y_{i,t} = 1 | X_{i,t}, h_i] = F(\beta_{0,1} + \beta_{0,2} h_i + \beta_{1,1} x_{i,t} + \beta_{1,2} x_{i,t} h_i). \tag{4.62}$$

Through the cross-term $x_{i,t} h_i$ this model allows the effect of price on the probability of choosing, say, brand A, to depend also on household income.

It may, however, be that the effects of a variable such as price differ across households, but that a variable such as income is not good enough to describe this variation. It may also happen that one does not have information on such variables in the first place, while one does want to allow for heterogeneity. A common strategy is to extend (4.61) by allowing the parameters to vary across the households, that is, to apply

$$\Pr[Y_{i,t} = 1 | X_{i,t}] = F(\beta_{0,i} + \beta_{1,i} x_{i,t}). \tag{4.63}$$

Obviously, if some households do not buy one of the two brands, one cannot estimate these household-specific parameters. Additionally, one may not have enough observations over time to estimate each household-specific parameter (see Rossi and Allenby, 1993, for a discussion). It is in that case common practice to consider one of the following approaches to analyze a model such as (4.63).

The first amounts to assuming that the household-specific parameters are drawings from a population distribution. For example, one may assume that $\beta_{0,i} \sim N(\beta_0, \sigma_0^2)$ and $\beta_{1,i} \sim N(\beta_1, \sigma_1^2)$, where now the number of unknown parameters has been reduced to 4 population parameters instead of $2N$ parameters (2 per household); see, for example, Gönül and Srinivasan (1993) among many others for such an approach.

Another possible solution, which tends to be used quite frequently in marketing research (see Wedel and Kamakura, 1999), amounts to assuming the presence of latent classes. When there are S such classes in the population, the probability that a household belongs to these classes is modeled by the positive probabilities p_1 to p_{S-1} and $p_S = 1 - \sum_{s=1}^{S-1} p_s$. Because these probabilities are unknown, one has to estimate their values. In each class we have different β parameters, which are denoted $\beta_{0,s}$ and $\beta_{1,s}$. The likelihood function now reads

$$L(\theta) = \prod_{i=1}^{N} \sum_{s=1}^{S} p_s \left(\prod_{t=1}^{T} F(\beta_{0,s} + \beta_{1,s} x_{i,t})^{y_{i,t}} (1 - F(\beta_{0,s} + \beta_{1,s} x_{i,t}))^{1-y_{i,t}} \right), \tag{4.64}$$

where $\theta = (\beta_{0,1}, \ldots, \beta_{0,S}, \beta_{1,1}, \ldots, \beta_{1,S}, p_1, \ldots, p_{S-1})$. For a given value of the number of segments S, all parameters can be estimated by Maximum Likelihood. Wedel and Kamakura (1999) describe several useful estimation routines.

4.5.2 Modeling dynamics

When the binomial dependent variable concerns a variable that is measured over time, one may want to modify the basic model by including dynamics. Given that it is likely that households have some brand loyalty, one may want to include the choice made in the previous week. One possible extension of the binomial choice model is to allow for state dependence, where we again consider a single explanatory variable for convenience

$$y^*_{i,t} = \beta_0 + \beta_1 x_{i,t} + \phi y_{i,t-1} + \varepsilon_{i,t}$$

$$Y_{i,t} = 1 \text{ if } y^*_{i,t} > 0 \tag{4.65}$$

$$Y_{i,t} = 0 \text{ if } y^*_{i,t} \leq 0.$$

The parameter ϕ reflects some kind of loyalty. Notice that the observations on $y_{i,t-1}$ are known at time t, and hence, upon assuming that the distribution of $\varepsilon_{i,t}$ does not change with i or t, one can rely on the estimation routines discussed in section 4.2.

Two alternative models that also allow for some kind of brand loyalty assume

$$y^*_{i,t} = \beta_0 + \beta_1 x_{i,t} + \phi y^*_{i,t-1} + \varepsilon_{i,t} \tag{4.66}$$

and

$$y^*_{i,t} = \beta_0 + \beta_1 x_{i,t} + \beta_2 x_{i,t-1} + \phi y^*_{i,t-1} + \varepsilon_{i,t}. \tag{4.67}$$

These last two models include an unobserved explanatory variable on the right-hand side, and this makes parameter estimation more difficult.

4.5.3 Sample selection issues

In practice it may sometimes occur that the number of observations with $y_i = 0$ in the population outnumbers the observations with $y_i = 1$, or the other way around. A natural question now is whether one should analyze a sample that contains that many data with $y_i = 0$, or whether one should not start collecting all these data in the first place. Manski and Lerman (1977) show that in many cases this is not necessary, and that often only the likelihood function needs to be modified. In this section, we will illustrate that for the Logit model for a binomial dependent variable this adaptation is very easy to implement.

Suppose one is interested in $\Pr_p[Y_i = 1]$, where the subscript p denotes population, and where we delete the conditioning on X_i to save notation. Further, consider a sample is (to be) drawn from this population, and denote with $w_i = 1$ if an individual is observed and $w_i = 0$ if this is not the case. For this sample it holds that

$$Pr[Y_i = 1, W_i = 1] = Pr[W_i = 1 | Y_i = 1]Pr_p[Y_i = 1]$$
$$Pr[Y_i = 0, W_i = 1] = Pr[W_i = 1 | Y_i = 0]Pr_p[Y_i = 0]. \qquad (4.68)$$

Hence, for a sample from the population it holds that

$$Pr_s[Y_i = 1] = \frac{Pr[Y_i = 1, W_i = 1]}{Pr[Y_i = 1, W_i = 1] + Pr[Y_i = 0, W_i = 1]}, \qquad (4.69)$$

where the subscript s refers to the sample.

If the sample is random, that is,

$$Pr[W_i = 1 | Y_i = 1] = Pr[W_i = 1 | Y_i = 0] = \lambda, \qquad (4.70)$$

then

$$Pr_s[Y_i = 1] = \frac{\lambda Pr_p[Y_i = 1]}{\lambda Pr_p[Y_i = 1] + \lambda(1 - Pr_p[Y_i = 1])} \qquad (4.71)$$
$$= Pr_p[Y_i = 1].$$

If, however, the sample is not random, that is,

$$Pr[W_i = 1 | Y_i = 1] = \lambda$$
$$Pr[W_i = 1 | Y_i = 0] = \lambda - (1 - \kappa)\lambda = \kappa\lambda, \qquad (4.72)$$

implying that a fraction $1 - \kappa$ of the $y_i = 0$ observations is deleted, then one has that

$$Pr_s[Y_i = 1] = \frac{Pr_p[Y_i = 1]}{Pr_p[Y_i = 1] + \kappa(1 - Pr_p[Y_i = 1])}, \qquad (4.73)$$

which can be written as

$$Pr_s[Y_i = 1] = \frac{\kappa^{-1} Pr_p/(1 - Pr_p)}{1 + \kappa^{-1} Pr_p/(1 - Pr_p)}. \qquad (4.74)$$

For the Logit model, one can easily find the link between $Pr_s[Y_i = 1]$ and $Pr_p[Y_i = 1]$ because this model holds that the log odds ratio is

$$\frac{Pr_p[Y_i = 1]}{1 - Pr_p[Y_i = 1]} = \exp(X_i\beta), \qquad (4.75)$$

see (4.21). Substituting (4.75) into (4.74) gives

$$\Pr_s[Y_i = 1] = \frac{\kappa^{-1}\exp(X_i\beta)}{1+\kappa^{-1}\exp(X_i\beta)}$$

$$= \frac{\exp(-\log(\kappa)+X_i\beta)}{1+\exp(-\log(\kappa)+X_i\beta)}.$$

(4.76)

Hence, we only have to adjust the intercept parameter to correct for the fact that we have not included all $y_i = 0$. It follows from (4.76) that one needs only to add $\log(\kappa)$ to $\hat{\beta}_0$ to obtain the parameter estimates for the whole sample. Cramer et al. (1999) examine the loss of efficiency when observations from a sample are deleted, and they report that this loss is rather small.

5 An unordered multinomial dependent variable

In the previous chapter we considered the Logit and Probit models for a binomial dependent variable. These models are suitable for modeling binomial choice decisions, where the two categories often correspond to no/yes situations. For example, an individual can decide whether or not to donate to charity, to respond to a direct mailing, or to buy brand A and not B. In many choice cases, one can choose between more than two categories. For example, households usually can choose between many brands within a product category. Or firms can decide not to renew, to renew, or to renew and upgrade a maintenance contract. In this chapter we deal with quantitative models for such discrete choices, where the number of choice options is more than two. The models assume that there is no ordering in these options, based on, say, perceived quality. In the next chapter we relax this assumption.

The outline of this chapter is as follows. In section 5.1 we discuss the representation and interpretation of several choice models: the Multinomial and Conditional Logit models, the Multinomial Probit model and the Nested Logit model. Admittedly, the technical level of this section is reasonably high. We do believe, however, that considerable detail is relevant, in particular because these models are very often used in empirical marketing research. Section 5.2 deals with estimation of the parameters of these models using the Maximum Likelihood method. In section 5.3 we discuss model evaluation, although it is worth mentioning here that not many such diagnostic measures are currently available. We consider variable selection procedures and a method to determine some optimal number of choice categories. Indeed, it may sometimes be useful to join two or more choice categories into a new single category. To analyze the fit of the models, we consider within- and out-of-sample forecasting and the evaluation of forecast performance. The illustration in section 5.4 concerns the choice between four brands of saltine crackers. Finally, in section 5.5 we deal with modeling of unobserved heterogeneity among individuals, and modeling of dynamic choice behavior. In the appendix to this chapter we give the EViews code for three models, because these are not included in version 3.1 of this statistical package.

5.1 Representation and interpretation

In this chapter we extend the choice models of the previous chapter to the case with an unordered categorical dependent variable, that is, we now assume that an individual or household i can choose between J categories, where J is larger than 2. The observed choice of the individual is again denoted by the variable y_i, which now can take the discrete values $1, 2, \ldots, J$. Just as for the binomial choice models, it is usually the aim to correlate the choice between the categories with explanatory variables.

Before we turn to the models, we need to say something briefly about the available data, because we will see below that the data guide the selection of the model. In general, a marketing researcher has access to three types of explanatory variable. The first type corresponds to variables that are different across individuals but are the same across the categories. Examples are age, income and gender. We will denote these variables by X_i. The second type of explanatory variable concerns variables that are different for each individual and are also different across categories. We denote these variables by $W_{i,j}$. An example of such a variable in the context of brand choice is the price of brand j experienced by individual i on a particular purchase occasion. The third type of explanatory variable, summarized by Z_j, is the same for each individual but different across the categories. This variable might be the size of a package, which is the same for each individual. In what follows we will see that the models differ, depending on the available data.

5.1.1 The Multinomial and Conditional Logit models

The random variable Y_i, which underlies the actual observations y_i, can take only J discrete values. Assume that we want to explain the choice by the single explanatory variable x_i, which might be, say, age or gender. Again, it can easily be understood that a standard Linear Regression model such as

$$y_i = \beta_0 + \beta_1 x_i + \varepsilon_i, \tag{5.1}$$

which correlates the discrete choice y_i with the explanatory variable x_i, does not lead to a satisfactory model. This is because it relates a discrete variable with a continuous variable through a linear relation. For discrete outcomes, it therefore seems preferable to consider an extension of the Bernoulli distribution used in chapter 4, that is, the multivariate Bernoulli distribution denoted as

$$Y_i \sim \mathrm{MN}(1, \pi_1, \ldots, \pi_J) \tag{5.2}$$

(see section A.2 in the Appendix). This distribution implies that the probability that category j is chosen equals $\Pr[Y_i = j] = \pi_j$, $j = 1, \ldots, J$, with $\pi_1 + \pi_2 + \cdots + \pi_J = 1$. To relate the explanatory variables to the choice, one can make π_j a function of the explanatory variable, that is,

$$\pi_j = F_j(\beta_{0,j} + \beta_{1,j} x_i). \tag{5.3}$$

Notice that we allow the parameter $\beta_{1,j}$ to differ across the categories because the effect of variable x_i may be different for each category. If we have an explanatory variable $w_{i,j}$, we could restrict $\beta_{1,j}$ to β_1 (see below). For a binomial dependent variable, expression (5.3) becomes $\pi = F(\beta_0 + \beta_1 x_i)$. Because the probabilities π_j have to lie between 0 and 1, the function F_j has to be bounded between 0 and 1. Because it also must hold that $\sum_{j=1}^{J} \pi_j$ equals 1, a suitable choice for F_j is the logistic function. For this function, the probability that individual i will choose category j given an explanatory variable x_i is equal to

$$\Pr[Y_i = j | X_i] = \frac{\exp(\beta_{0,j} + \beta_{1,j} x_i)}{\sum_{l=1}^{J} \exp(\beta_{0,l} + \beta_{1,l} x_i)}, \quad \text{for } j = 1, \ldots, J, \tag{5.4}$$

where X_i collects the intercept and the explanatory variable x_i. Because the probabilities sum to 1, that is, $\sum_{j=1}^{J} \Pr[Y_i = j | X_i] = 1$, it can be understood that one has to assign a base category. This can be done by restricting the corresponding parameters to zero. Put another way, multiplying the numerator and denominator in (5.4) by a non-zero constant, for example $\exp(\alpha)$, changes the intercept parameters $\beta_{0,j}$ into $\beta_{0,j} + \alpha$ but the probability $\Pr[Y_i = j | X_i]$ remains the same. In other words, not all J intercept parameters are identified. Without loss of generality, one usually restricts $\beta_{0,J}$ to zero, thereby imposing category J as the base category. The same holds true for the $\beta_{1,j}$ parameters, which describe the effects of the individual-specific variables on choice. Indeed, if we multiply the nominator and denominator by $\exp(\alpha x_i)$, the probability $\Pr[Y_i = j | X_i]$ again does not change. To identify the $\beta_{1,j}$ parameters one therefore also imposes that $\beta_{1,J} = 0$. Note that the choice for a base category does not change the effect of the explanatory variables on choice.

So far, the focus has been on a single explanatory variable and an intercept for notational convenience, and this will continue in several of the subsequent discussions. Extensions to K_x explanatory variables are however straightforward, where we use the same notation as before. Hence, we write

$$\Pr[Y_i = j | X_i] = \frac{\exp(X_i \beta_j)}{\sum_{l=1}^{J} \exp(X_i \beta_l)} \quad \text{for } j = 1, \ldots, J, \tag{5.5}$$

where X_i is a $1 \times (K_x + 1)$ matrix of explanatory variables including the element 1 to model the intercept and β_j is a $(K_x + 1)$-dimensional parameter vector. For identification, one can set $\beta_J = 0$. Later on in this section we will also consider the explanatory variables W_i.

The Multinomial Logit model

The model in (5.4) is called the Multinomial Logit model. If we impose the identification restrictions for parameter identification, that is, we impose $\beta_J = 0$, we obtain for $K_x = 1$ that

$$\Pr[Y_i = j | X_i] = \frac{\exp(\beta_{0,j} + \beta_{1,j} x_i)}{1 + \sum_{l=1}^{J-1} \exp(\beta_{0,l} + \beta_{1,l} x_i)} \quad \text{for } j = 1, \ldots, J-1,$$

$$\Pr[Y_i = J | X_i] = \frac{1}{1 + \sum_{l=1}^{J-1} \exp(\beta_{0,l} + \beta_{1,l} x_i)}.$$

$$(5.6)$$

Note that for $J = 2$ (5.6) reduces to the binomial Logit model discussed in the previous chapter. The model in (5.6) assumes that the choices can be explained by intercepts and by individual-specific variables. For example, if x_i measures the age of an individual, the model may describe that older persons are more likely than younger persons to choose brand j.

A direct interpretation of the model parameters is not straightforward because the effect of x_i on the choice is clearly a nonlinear function in the model parameters β_j. Similarly to the binomial Logit model, to interpret the parameters one may consider the odds ratios. The odds ratio of category j versus category l is defined as

$$\Omega_{j|l}(X_i) = \frac{\Pr[Y_i = j | X_i]}{\Pr[Y_i = l | X_i]} = \frac{\exp(\beta_{0,j} + \beta_{1,j} x_i)}{\exp(\beta_{0,l} + \beta_{1,l} x_i)} \quad \text{for } l = 1, \ldots, J-1,$$

$$\Omega_{j|J}(x_i) = \frac{\Pr[Y_i = j | X_i]}{\Pr[Y_i = J | X_i]} = \exp(\beta_{0,j} + \beta_{1,j} x_i)$$

$$(5.7)$$

and the corresponding log odds ratios are

$$\log \Omega_{j|l}(X_i) = (\beta_{0,j} - \beta_{0,l}) + (\beta_{1,j} - \beta_{1,l}) x_i \quad \text{for } l = 1, \ldots, J-1,$$
$$\log \Omega_{j|J}(X_i) = \beta_{0,j} + \beta_{1,j} x_i.$$

$$(5.8)$$

Suppose that the $\beta_{1,j}$ parameters are equal to zero, we then see that positive values of $\beta_{0,j}$ imply that individuals are more likely to choose category j than the base category J. Likewise, individuals prefer category j over category l if $(\beta_{0,j} - \beta_{0,l}) > 0$. In this case the intercept parameters correspond with the average base preferences of the individuals. Individuals with a larger value for x_i tend to favor category j over category l if $(\beta_{1,j} - \beta_{1,l}) > 0$ and the other way around if $(\beta_{1,j} - \beta_{1,l}) < 0$. In other words, the difference $(\beta_{1,j} - \beta_{1,l})$ measures the change in the log odds ratio for a unit change in x_i. Finally, if we consider the odds ratio with respect to the base category J, the effects are determined solely by the parameter $\beta_{1,j}$.

The odds ratios show that a change in x_i may imply that individuals are more likely to choose category j compared with category l. It is important to recognize, however, that this does not necessarily mean that $\Pr[Y_i = j|X_i]$ moves in the same direction. Indeed, owing to the summation restriction, a change in x_i also changes the odds ratios of category j versus the other categories. The net effect of a change in x_i on the choice probability follows from the partial derivative of $\Pr[Y_i = j|X_i]$ with respect to x_i, which is given by

$$
\frac{\partial \Pr[Y_i = j|X_i]}{\partial x_i} = \frac{\left(1 + \sum_{l=1}^{J-1} \exp(\beta_{0,l} + \beta_{1,l}x_i)\right) \exp(\beta_{0,j} + \beta_{1,j}x_i)\beta_{1,j}x_i}{\left(1 + \sum_{l=1}^{J-1} \exp(\beta_{0,l} + \beta_{1,l}x_i)\right)^2}
$$

$$
- \frac{\exp(\beta_{0,j} + \beta_{1,j}x_i) \sum_{l=1}^{J-1} \exp(\beta_{0,l} + \beta_{1,l}x_i)\beta_{1,l}}{\left(1 + \sum_{l=1}^{J-1} \exp(\beta_{0,l} + \beta_{1,l}x_i)\right)^2}
$$

$$
= \Pr[Y_i = j|X_i]\left(\beta_{1,j} - \sum_{l=1}^{J-1} \beta_{1,l} \Pr[Y_i = l|X_i]\right).
$$

$$(5.9)$$

The sign of this derivative now depends on the sign of the term in parentheses. Because the probabilities depend on the value of x_i, the derivative may be positive for some values of x_i but negative for others. This phenomenon can also be observed from the odds ratios in (5.7), which show that an increase in x_i may imply an increase in the odds ratio of category j versus category l but a decrease in the odds ratio of category j versus some other category $s \neq l$. This aspect of the Multinomial Logit model is in marked contrast to the binomial Logit model, where the probabilities are monotonically increasing or decreasing in x_i. In fact, note that for only two categories $(J = 2)$ the partial derivative in (5.9) reduces to

$$
\Pr[Y_i = 1|X_i](1 - \Pr[Y_i = 1|X_i])\beta_{1,j}. \tag{5.10}
$$

Because obviously $\beta_{1,j} = \beta_1$, this is equal to the partial derivative in a binomial Logit model (see (4.19)).

The quasi-elasticity of x_i, which can also be useful for model interpretation, follows directly from the partial derivative (5.9), that is,

$$\frac{\partial \Pr[Y_i = j | X_i]}{\partial x_i} x_i = \Pr[Y_i = j | X_i] \left(\beta_{1,j} - \sum_{l=1}^{J-1} \beta_{1,l} \Pr[Y_i = l | X_i] \right) x_i.$$

$$(5.11)$$

This elasticity measures the percentage point change in the probability that category j is preferred owing to a percentage increase in x_i. The summation restriction concerning the J probabilities establishes that the sum of the elasticities over the alternatives is equal to zero, that is,

$$\sum_{j=1}^{J} \frac{\partial \Pr[Y_i = j | X_i]}{\partial x_i} x_i$$

$$= \sum_{j=1}^{J} \Pr[Y_i = j | X_i] \beta_{1,j} x_i - \sum_{j=1}^{J} (\Pr[Y_i = j | X_i] \sum_{l=1}^{J-1} \beta_{1,l} \Pr[Y_i = l | X_i] x_i)$$

$$= \sum_{j=1}^{J-1} \Pr[Y_i = j | X_i] \beta_{1,j} x_i - \sum_{l=1}^{J-1} (\Pr[Y_i = l | X_i] \beta_{1,l} x_i (\sum_{j=1}^{J} \Pr[Y_i = j | X_i])) = 0,$$

$$(5.12)$$

where we have used $\beta_{1,J} = 0$.

Sometimes it may be useful to interpret the Multinomial Logit model as a utility model, thereby building on the related discussion in section 4.1 for a binomial dependent variable. Suppose that an individual i perceives utility $u_{i,j}$ if he or she chooses category j, where

$$u_{i,j} = \beta_{0,j} + \beta_{1,j} x_i + \varepsilon_{i,j}, \quad \text{for } j = 1, \ldots, J \quad (5.13)$$

and $\varepsilon_{i,j}$ is an unobserved error variable. It seems natural to assume that individual i chooses category j if he or she perceives the highest utility from this choice, that is,

$$u_{i,j} = \max(u_{i,1}, \ldots, u_{i,J}). \quad (5.14)$$

The probability that the individual chooses category j therefore equals the probability that the perceived utility $u_{i,j}$ is larger than the other utilities $u_{i,l}$ for $l \neq j$, that is,

$$\Pr[Y_i = j | X_i] = \Pr[u_{i,j} > u_{i,1}, \ldots, u_{i,j} > u_{i,j-1}, u_{i,j} > u_{i,j+1}, \ldots,$$
$$u_{i,j} > u_{i,J} | X_i]. $$

$$(5.15)$$

The Conditional Logit model

In the Multinomial Logit model, the individual choices are correlated with individual-specific explanatory variables, which take the same value across the choice categories. In other cases, however, one may have explanatory variables that take different values across the choice options. One may, for example, explain brand choice by $w_{i,j}$, which denotes the price of brand j as experienced by household i on a particular purchase occasion. Another version of a logit model that is suitable for the inclusion of this type of variable is the Conditional Logit model, initially proposed by McFadden (1973). For this model, the probability that category j is chosen equals

$$\Pr[Y_i = j \,|\, W_i] = \frac{\exp(\beta_{0,j} + \gamma_1 w_{i,j})}{\sum_{l=1}^{J} \exp(\beta_{0,l} + \gamma_1 w_{i,l})} \quad \text{for } j = 1, \ldots, J. \quad (5.16)$$

For this model the choice probabilities depend on the explanatory variables denoted by $W_i = (W_{i,1}, \ldots, W_{i,J})$, which have a common impact γ_1 on the probabilities. Again, we have to set $\beta_{0,J} = 0$ for identification of the intercept parameters. However, the γ_1 parameter is equal for each category and hence it is always identified except for the case where $w_{i,1} = w_{i,2} = \ldots = w_{i,J}$.

The choice probabilities in the Conditional Logit model are nonlinear functions of the model parameter γ_1 and hence again model interpretation is not straightforward. To understand the effect of the explanatory variables, we again consider odds ratios. The odds ratio of category j versus category l is given by

$$\Omega_{j|l}(W_i) = \frac{\Pr[Y_i = j \,|\, W_i]}{\Pr[Y_i = l \,|\, W_i]} = \frac{\exp(\beta_{0,j} + \gamma_1 w_{i,j})}{\exp(\beta_{0,l} + \gamma_1 w_{i,l})} \quad \text{for } l = 1, \ldots, J$$

$$= \exp((\beta_{0,j} - \beta_{0,l}) + \gamma_1(w_{i,j} - w_{i,l}))$$

$$(5.17)$$

and the corresponding log odds ratio is

$$\log \Omega_{j|l}(W_i) = (\beta_{0,j} - \beta_{0,l}) + \gamma_1(w_{i,j} - w_{i,l}) \quad \text{for } l = 1, \ldots, J.$$

$$(5.18)$$

The interpretation of the intercept parameters is similar to that for the Multinomial Logit model. Furthermore, for positive values of γ_1, individuals favor category j more than category l for larger positive values of $(w_{i,j} - w_{i,l})$. For $\gamma_1 < 0$, we observe the opposite effect. If we consider a brand choice problem and $w_{i,j}$ represents the price of brand j, a negative value of γ_1 means that households are more likely to buy brand j instead of brand l as brand l gets increasingly more expensive. Due to symmetry, a unit change in $w_{i,j}$ leads to a change of γ_1 in the log odds ratio of category j versus l and a change of $-\gamma_1$ in the log odds ratio of l versus j.

The odds ratios for category j (5.17) show the effect of a change in the value of the explanatory variables on the probability that category j is chosen compared with another category $l \neq j$. To analyze the total effect of a change in $w_{i,j}$ on the probability that category j is chosen, we consider the partial derivative of $\Pr[Y_i = j | W_i]$ with respect to $w_{i,j}$, that is,

$$\frac{\partial \Pr[Y_i = j | W_i]}{\partial w_{i,j}} = \frac{\sum_{l=1}^{J} \exp(\beta_{0,l} + \gamma_1 w_{i,l}) \exp(\beta_{0,j} + \gamma_1 w_{i,j}) \gamma_1}{\left(\sum_{l=1}^{J} \exp(\beta_{0,l} + \gamma_1 w_{i,l}) \right)^2}$$

$$- \frac{\exp(\beta_{0,j} + \gamma_1 w_{i,j}) \exp(\beta_{0,j} + \gamma_1 w_{i,j}) \gamma_1}{\left(\sum_{l=1}^{J} \exp(\beta_{0,l} + \gamma_1 w_{i,l}) \right)^2}$$

$$= \gamma_1 \Pr[Y_i = j | W_i](1 - \Pr[Y_i = j | W_i]).$$

$$(5.19)$$

This partial derivative depends on the probability that category j is chosen and hence on the values of all explanatory variables in the model. The sign of this derivative, however, is completely determined by the sign of γ_1. Hence, in contrast to the Multinomial Logit specification, the probability varies monotonically with $w_{i,j}$.

Along similar lines, we can derive the partial derivative of the probability that an individual i chooses category j with respect to $w_{i,l}$ for $l \neq j$, that is,

$$\frac{\partial \Pr[Y_i = j | W_i]}{\partial w_{i,l}} = -\gamma_1 \Pr[Y_i = j | W_i] \Pr[Y_i = l | W_i]. \tag{5.20}$$

The sign of this cross-derivative is again completely determined by the sign of $-\gamma_1$. The value of the derivative itself also depends on the value of all explanatory variables through the choice probabilities. Note that the symmetry $\partial \Pr[Y_i = j | W_i]/\partial w_{i,l} = \partial \Pr[Y_i = l | W_i]/\partial w_{i,j}$ holds. If we consider brand choice again, where $w_{i,j}$ corresponds to the price of brand j as experienced by individual i, the derivatives (5.19) and (5.20) show that for $\gamma_1 < 0$ an increase in the price of brand j leads to a decrease in the probability that brand j is chosen and an increase in the probability that the other brands are chosen. Again, the sum of these changes in choice probabilities is zero because

$$\sum_{j=1}^{J} \frac{\partial \Pr[Y_i = j|W_i]}{\partial w_{i,l}} = \gamma_1 \Pr[Y_i = l|W_i](1 - \Pr[Y_i = l|W_i])$$

$$+ \sum_{j=1, j \neq l}^{J} -\gamma_1 \Pr[Y_i = j|W_i]\Pr[Y_i = l|W_i] = 0,$$

$$(5.21)$$

which simply confirms that the probabilities sum to one. The magnitude of each specific change in choice probability depends on γ_1 and on the probabilities themselves, and hence on the values of all $w_{i,l}$ variables. If all $w_{i,l}$ variables change similarly, $l = 1, \ldots, J$, the net effect of this change on the probability that, say, category j is chosen is also zero because it holds that

$$\sum_{l=1}^{J} \frac{\partial \Pr[Y_i = j|W_i]}{\partial w_{i,l}} = \gamma_1 \Pr[Y_i = l|W_i](1 - \Pr[Y_i = l|W_i])$$

$$+ \sum_{l=1, l \neq j}^{J} -\gamma_1 \Pr[Y_i = j|W_i]\Pr[Y_i = l|W_i] = 0,$$

$$(5.22)$$

where we have used $\sum_{l=1, l \neq j}^{J} \Pr[Y_i = l|W_i] = 1 - \Pr[Y_i = l|W_i]$. In marketing terms, for example for brand choice, this means that the model implies that an equal price change in all brands does not affect brand choice.

Quasi-elasticities and cross-elasticities follow immediately from the above two partial derivatives. The percentage point change in the probability that category j is chosen upon a percentage change in $w_{i,j}$ equals

$$\frac{\partial \Pr[Y_i = j|W_i]}{\partial w_{i,j}} w_{i,j} = \gamma_1 w_{i,j} \Pr[Y_i = j|W_i](1 - \Pr[Y_i = j|W_i]).$$

$$(5.23)$$

The percentage point change in the probability for j upon a percentage change in $w_{i,l}$ is simply

$$\frac{\partial \Pr[Y_i = j|W_i]}{\partial w_{i,l}} w_{i,l} = -\gamma_1 w_{i,l} \Pr[Y_i = j|W_i]\Pr[Y_i = l|W_i]. \quad (5.24)$$

Given (5.23) and (5.24), it is easy to see that

$$\sum_{j=1}^{J} \frac{\partial \Pr[Y_i = j|W_i]}{\partial w_{i,l}} w_{i,l} = 0 \quad \text{and} \quad \sum_{l=1}^{J} \frac{\partial \Pr[Y_i = j|w_i]}{\partial w_{i,l}} w_{i,l} = 0,$$

$$(5.25)$$

and hence the sum of all elasticities is equal to zero.

A general logit specification

So far, we have discussed the Multinomial and Conditional Logit models separately. In some applications one may want to combine both models in a general logit specification. This specification can be further extended by including explanatory variables Z_j that are different across categories but the same for each individual. Furthermore, it is also possible to allow for different γ_1 parameters for each category in the Conditional Logit model (5.16). Taking all this together results in a general logit specification, which for one explanatory variable of either type reads as

$$\Pr[Y_i = j | X_i, W_i, Z] = \frac{\exp(\beta_{0,j} + \beta_{1,j} x_i + \gamma_{1,j} w_{i,j} + \alpha z_j)}{\sum_{l=1}^{J} \exp(\beta_{0,l} + \beta_{1,l} x_i + \gamma_{1,l} w_{i,l} + \alpha z_l)},$$
$$\text{for } j = 1, \ldots, J,$$

(5.26)

where $\beta_{0,J} = \beta_{1,J} = 0$ for identification purposes and $Z = (z_1, \ldots, z_J)$. Note that it is not possible to modify α into α_j because the z_j variables are in fact already proportional to the choice-specific intercept terms.

The interpretation of the logit model (5.26) follows again from the odds ratio

$$\frac{\Pr[Y_i = j | x_i, w_i, z]}{\Pr[Y_i = l | x_i, w_i, z]} = \exp((\beta_{0,j} - \beta_{0,l}) + (\beta_{1,j} - \beta_{1,l}) x_i$$
$$+ \gamma_{1,j} w_{i,j} - \gamma_{1,l} w_{i,l} + \alpha(z_j - z_l)).$$

(5.27)

For most of the explanatory variables, the effects on the odds ratios are the same as in the Conditional and Multinomial Logit model specification. The exception is that it is not the difference between $w_{i,j}$ and $w_{i,l}$ that affects the odds ratio but the linear combination $\gamma_{1,j} w_{i,j} - \gamma_{1,l} w_{i,l}$. Finally, partial derivatives and elasticities for the net effects of changes in the explanatory variables on the probabilities can be derived in a manner similar to that for the Conditional and Multinomial Logit models. Note, however, that the symmetry $\partial \Pr[Y_i = j | X_i, W_i, Z]/\partial w_{i,l} = \partial \Pr[Y_i = l | X_i, W_i, Z]/\partial w_{i,j}$ does not hold any more.

The independence of irrelevant alternatives

The odds ratio in (5.27) shows that the choice between two categories depends only on the characteristics of the categories under consideration. Hence, it does not relate to the characteristics of other categories or to the number of categories that might be available for consideration. Naturally, this is also true for the Multinomial and Conditional Logit models, as can be seen from (5.7) and (5.17), respectively. This property of these models is known as the independence of irrelevant alternatives (IIA).

Although the IIA assumption may seem to be a purely mathematical issue, it can have important practical implications, in particular because it may not be a realistic assumption in some cases. To illustrate this, consider an individual who can choose between two mobile telephone service providers. Provider A offers a low fixed cost per month but charges a high price per minute, whereas provider B charges a higher fixed cost per month, but has a lower price per minute. Assume that the odds ratio of an individual is 2 in favor of provider A, then the probability that he or she will choose provider A is 2/3 and the probability that he or she will opt for provider B is 1/3. Suppose now that a third provider called C enters the market, offering exactly the same service as provider B. Because the service is the same, the individual should be indifferent between providers B and C. If, for example, the Conditional Logit model in (5.16) holds, the odds ratio of provider A versus provider B would still have to be 2 because the odds ratio does not depend on the characteristics of the alternatives. However, provider C offers the same service as provider B and therefore the odds ratio of A versus C should be equal to 2 as well. Hence, the probability that the individual will choose provider A drops from 2/3 to 1/2 and the remaining probability is equally divided between providers B and C (1/4 each). This implies that the odds ratio of provider A versus an alternative with high fixed cost and low variable cost is now equal to 1. In sum, one would expect provider B to suffer most from the entry of provider C (from 1/3 to 1/4), but it turns out that provider A becomes less attractive at a faster rate (from 2/3 to 1/2).

This hypothetical example shows that the IIA property of a model may not always make sense. The origin of the IIA property is the assumption that the error variables in (5.13) are uncorrelated and that they have the same variance across categories. In the next two subsections, we discuss two choice models that relax this assumption and do not incorporate this IIA property. It should be stressed here that these two models are a bit more complicated than the ones discussed so far. In section 5.3 we discuss a formal test for the validity of IIA.

5.1.2   *The Multinomial Probit model*

One way to derive the logit models in the previous section starts off with a random utility specification, (see (5.13)). The perceived utility for category j for individual i denoted by $u_{i,j}$ is then written as

$$u_{i,j} = \beta_{0,j} + \beta_{1,j} x_i + \varepsilon_{i,j}, \quad \text{for } j = 1, \ldots, J, \tag{5.28}$$

where $\varepsilon_{i,j}$ are unobserved random error variables for $i = 1, \ldots, N$ and where x_i is an individual-specific explanatory variable as before. Individual i

chooses alternative j if he or she perceives the highest utility from this alternative. The corresponding choice probability is defined in (5.15). The probability in (5.15) can be written as a J-dimensional integral

$$\int_{-\infty}^{\infty} \int_{-\infty}^{u_{i,j}} \cdots \int_{-\infty}^{u_{i,j}} f(u_{i,1}, \ldots, u_{i,J}) \, du_{i,j} \, du_{i,1} \ldots du_{i,j-1} \, du_{i,j+1} \ldots, du_{i,J},$$

$$(5.29)$$

where f denotes the joint probability density function of the unobserved utilities. If one now assumes that the error variables are independently distributed with a type-I extreme value distribution, that is, that the density function of $\varepsilon_{i,j}$ is

$$f(\varepsilon_{i,j}) = \exp(-\exp(-\varepsilon_{i,j})), \quad \text{for } j = 1, \ldots, J,$$ $$(5.30)$$

it can be shown that the choice probabilities (5.29) simplify to (5.6); see McFadden (1973) or Amemiya (1985, p. 297) for a detailed derivation. For this logit model the IIA property holds. This is caused by the fact that the error terms $\varepsilon_{i,j}$ are independently and identically distributed.

In some cases the IIA property may not be plausible or useful and an alternative model would then be more appropriate. The IIA property disappears if one allows for correlations between the error variables and/or if one does not assume equal variances for the categories. To establish this, a straightforward alternative to the Multinomial Logit specification is the Multinomial Probit model. This model assumes that the J-dimensional vector of error terms $\varepsilon_i = (\varepsilon_{i,1}, \ldots, \varepsilon_{i,J})$ is normally distributed with mean zero and a $J \times J$ covariance matrix Σ, that is,

$$\varepsilon_i \sim \mathrm{N}(0, \Sigma)$$ $$(5.31)$$

(see, for example, Hausman and Wise, 1978, and Daganzo, 1979). Note that, when the covariance matrix is an identity matrix, the IIA property will again hold. However, when Σ is a diagonal matrix with different elements on the main diagonal and/or has non-zero off-diagonal elements, the IIA property does not hold.

Similarly to logit models, several parameter restrictions have to be imposed to identify the remaining parameters. First of all, one again needs to impose that $\beta_{0,J} = \beta_{1,J} = 0$. This is, however, not sufficient, and hence the second set of restrictions concerns the elements of the covariance matrix. Condition (5.14) shows that the choice is determined not by the levels of the utilities $u_{i,j}$ but by the differences in utilities $(u_{i,j} - u_{i,l})$. This implies that a $(J-1) \times (J-1)$ covariance matrix completely determines all identified variances and covariances of the utilities and hence only $J(J-1)/2$ elements of Σ are identified. Additionally, it follows from (5.14) that multiplying each utility $u_{i,j}$ by the same constant α does not change the choice and hence we have to scale the utilities by restricting one of the diagonal elements of Σ to be 1. A detailed discussion on parameter identification in the Multinomial Probit model can be found in, for example, Bunch (1991) and Keane (1992).

The random utility specification (5.28) can be adjusted to obtain a general probit specification in the same manner as for the logit model. For example, if we specify

$$u_{i,j} = \beta_{0,j} + \gamma_j w_{i,j} + \varepsilon_{i,j} \quad \text{for } j = 1, \ldots, J, \tag{5.32}$$

we end up with a Conditional Probit model.

The disadvantage of the Multinomial Probit model with respect to the Multinomial Logit model is that there is no easy expression for the choice probabilities (5.15) that would facilitate model interpretation using odds ratios. In fact, to obtain the choice probabilities, one has to evaluate (5.29) using numerical integration (see, for example, Greene, 2000, section 5.4.2). However, if the number of alternatives J is larger than 3 or 4, numerical integration is no longer feasible because the number of function evaluations becomes too large. For example, if one takes n grid points per dimension, the number of function evaluations becomes n^J. To compute the choice probabilities for large J, one therefore resorts to simulation techniques. The techniques also have to be used to compute odds ratios, partial derivatives and elasticities. We consider this beyond the scope of this book and refer the reader to, for example, Börsch-Supan and Hajivassiliou (1993) and Greene (2000, pp. 183–185) for more details.

5.1.3   The Nested Logit model

It is also possible to extend the logit model class in order to cope with the IIA property (see, for example, Maddala, 1983, pp. 67–73, Amemiya, 1985, pp. 300–307, and Ben-Akiva and Lerman, 1985, ch. 10). A popular extension is the Nested Logit model. For this model it is assumed that the categories can be divided into clusters such that the variances of the error terms of the random utilities in (5.13) are the same within each cluster but different across clusters. This implies that the IIA assumption holds within each cluster but not across clusters. For brand choice, one may, for example, assign brands to a cluster with private labels or to a cluster with national brands:

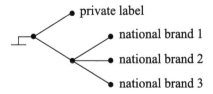

Another example is the contract renewal decision problem discussed in the introduction to this chapter, which can be represented by:

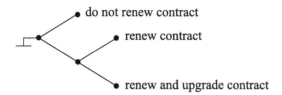

do not renew contract

renew contract

renew and upgrade contract

The first cluster corresponds to no renewal, while the second cluster contains the categories corresponding to renewal. Although the trees suggest that there is some sequence in decision-making (renew no/yes followed by upgrade no/yes), this does not have to be the case.

In general, we may divide the J categories into M clusters, each containing J_m categories $m = 1, \ldots, M$ such that $\sum_{m=1}^{M} J_m = J$. The random variable Y_i, which models choice, is now split up into two random variables (C_i, S_i) with realizations c_i and s_i, where c_i corresponds to the choice of the cluster and s_i to the choice among the categories within this cluster. The probability that individual i chooses category j in cluster m is equal to the joint probability that the individual chooses cluster m and that category j is preferred within this cluster, that is,

$$\Pr[Y_i = (j, m)] = \Pr[C_i = m \wedge S_i = j]. \tag{5.33}$$

One can write this probability as the product of a conditional probability of choice given the cluster and a marginal probability for the cluster

$$\Pr[C_i = m \wedge S_i = j] = \Pr[S_i = j | C_i = m] \Pr[C_i = m] \tag{5.34}$$

To model the choice within each cluster, one specifies a Conditional Logit model,

$$\Pr[S_i = j | C_i = m, Z] = \frac{\exp(Z_{j|m}\gamma)}{\sum_{j=1}^{J_m} \exp(Z_{j|m}\gamma)}, \tag{5.35}$$

where $Z_{j|m}$ denote the variables that have explanatory value for the choice within cluster m, for $j = 1, \ldots, J_m$.

To model the choice between the clusters we consider the following logit specification

$$\Pr[C_i = m | Z] = \frac{\exp(Z_m\alpha + \tau_m I_m)}{\sum_{l=1}^{M} \exp(Z_l\alpha + \tau_l I_l)}, \tag{5.36}$$

where Z_m denote the variables that explain the choice of the cluster m and I_m denote the inclusive value of cluster m defined as

$$I_m = \log \sum_{j=1}^{J_m} \exp(Z_{j|m}\gamma), \quad \text{for } m = 1, \ldots, M. \tag{5.37}$$

The inclusive value captures the differences in the variance of the error terms of the random utilities between each cluster (see also Amemiya, 1985, p. 300, and Maddala, 1983, p. 37). To ensure that choices by individuals correspond to utility-maximizing behavior, the restriction $\tau_m \geq 1$ has to hold for $m = 1, \ldots, M$. These restrictions also guarantee the existence of nest/cluster correlations (see Ben-Akiva and Lerman, 1985, section 10.3, for details).

The model in (5.34)–(5.37) is called the Nested Logit model. As we will show below, the IIA assumption is not implied by the model as long as the τ_m parameters are unequal to 1. Indeed, if we set the τ_m parameters equal to 1 we obtain

$$\Pr[C_i = m \wedge S_i = j|Z] = \frac{\exp(Z_m\alpha + Z_{j|m}\gamma)}{\sum_{l=1}^{M} \sum_{j=1}^{J_m} \exp(Z_l\alpha + Z_{j|l}\gamma)}, \tag{5.38}$$

which is in fact a rewritten version of the Conditional Logit model (5.16) if Z_m and $Z_{j|m}$ are the same variables.

The parameters of the Nested Logit model cannot be interpreted directly. Just as for the Multinomial and Conditional Logit models, one may consider odds ratios to interpret the effects of explanatory variables on choice. The interpretation of these odds ratios is the same as in the above logit models. Here, we discuss the odds ratios only with respect to the IIA property of the model. The choice probabilities within a cluster (5.35) are modeled by a Conditional Logit model, and hence the IIA property holds within each cluster. This is also the case for the choices between the clusters because the ratio of $\Pr[C_i = m_1|Z]$ and $\Pr[C_i = m_2|Z]$ does not depend on the explanatory variables and inclusive values of the other clusters. The odds ratio of the choice of category j in cluster m_1 versus the choice of category l in cluster m_2, given by

$$\frac{\Pr[Y_i = (j, m_1)|Z]}{\Pr[Y_i = (l, m_2)|Z]} = \frac{\exp(Z_{m_1}\alpha + \tau_{m_1}I_{m_1})\exp(Z_{j|m_1}\gamma)\sum_{j=1}^{J_{m_2}} \exp(Z_{j|m_2}\gamma)}{\exp(Z_{m_2}\alpha + \tau_{m_2}I_{m_2})\exp(Z_{l|m_2}\gamma)\sum_{j=1}^{J_{m_1}} \exp(Z_{j|m_1}\gamma)}, \tag{5.39}$$

is seen to depend on all categories in both clusters unless $\tau_{m_1} = \tau_{m_2} = 1$. In other words, the IIA property does not hold if one compares choices across clusters.

Partial derivatives and quasi-elasticities can be derived in a manner similar to that for the logit models discussed earlier. For example, the partial derivative of the probability that category j belonging to cluster m is chosen to the cluster-specific variables $Z_{j|m}$ equals

$$\frac{\partial \Pr[C_i = m \wedge S_i = j]}{\partial Z_{j|m}} = \Pr[C_i = m|Z]\frac{\partial \Pr[S_i = j|C_i = m]}{\partial Z_{j|m}}$$

$$+ \Pr[S_j = j|C_i = m]\frac{\partial \Pr[C_i = m]}{\partial Z_{j|m}}$$

$$= \gamma \Pr[C_i = m]\Pr[S_i = j|C_i = m]$$
$$(1 - \Pr[S_i = j|C_i = m])$$
$$+ \tau_m \gamma \Pr[S_i = j|C_i = m]\Pr[C_i = m]$$
$$(1 - \Pr[S_i = m])\exp(Z_{j|m}\gamma - I_m),$$

$$(5.40)$$

where the conditioning on Z is omitted for notational convenience. This expression shows that the effects of explanatory variables on the eventual choice are far from trivial.

Several extensions to the Nested Logit model in (5.34)–(5.37) are also possible. We may include individual-specific explanatory variables and explanatory variables that are different across categories and individuals in a straightforward way. Additionally, the Nested Logit model can even be further extended to allow for new clusters within each cluster. The complexity of the model increases with the number of cluster divisions (see also Amemiya, 1985, pp. 300–306, and especially Ben-Akiva and Lerman, 1985, ch. 10, for a more general introduction to Nested Logit models). Unfortunately, there is no general rule or testing procedure to determine an appropriate division into clusters, which makes the clustering decision mainly a practical one.

5.2 Estimation

Estimates of the model parameters discussed in the previous sections can be obtained via the Maximum Likelihood method. The likelihood functions of the models presented above are all the same, except for the fact that they differ with respect to the functional form of the choice probabilities. In all cases the likelihood function is the product of the probabilities of the chosen categories over all individuals, that is,

$$L(\theta) = \prod_{i=1}^{N}\prod_{j=1}^{J}\Pr[Y_i = j]^{I[y_i=j]}, \qquad (5.41)$$

where $I[\cdot]$ denotes a 0/1 indicator function that is 1 if the argument is true and 0 otherwise, and where θ summarizes the model parameters. To save on notation we abbreviate $\Pr[Y_i = j|\cdot]$ as $\Pr[Y_i = j]$. The logarithm of the likelihood function is

$$l(\theta) = \sum_{i=1}^{N} \sum_{j=1}^{J} I[y_i = j] \log \Pr[Y_i = j]. \tag{5.42}$$

The ML estimator is the parameter value $\hat{\theta}$ that corresponds to the largest value of the (log-)likelihood function over the parameters. This maximum can be found by solving the first-order condition

$$\frac{\partial l(\theta)}{\partial \theta} = \sum_{i=1}^{N} \sum_{j=1}^{J} I[y_i = j] \frac{\partial \log \Pr[Y_i = j]}{\partial \theta}$$

$$= \sum_{i=1}^{N} \sum_{j=1}^{J} \frac{I[y_i = j]}{\Pr[Y_i = j]} \frac{\partial \Pr[Y_i = j]}{\partial \theta} = 0. \tag{5.43}$$

Because the log-likelihood function is nonlinear in the parameters, it is not possible to solve the first-order conditions analytically. Therefore, numerical optimization algorithms, such as Newton–Raphson, have to be used to maximize the log-likelihood function. As described in chapter 3, the ML estimates can be found by iterating over

$$\theta_h = \theta_{h-1} - H(\theta_{h-1})^{-1} G(\theta_{h-1}), \tag{5.44}$$

until convergence, where $G(\theta)$ and $H(\theta)$ are the first- and second-order derivatives of the log-likelihood function (see also section 3.2.2).

In the remainder of this section we discuss parameter estimation of the models for a multinomial dependent variable discussed above in detail and we provide mathematical expressions for $G(\theta)$ and $H(\theta)$.

5.2.1   The Multinomial and Conditional Logit models

Maximum Likelihood estimation of the parameters of the Multinomial and Conditional Logit models is often discussed separately. However, in practice one often has a combination of the two specifications, and therefore we discuss the estimation of the combined model given by

$$\Pr[Y_i = j] = \frac{\exp(X_i \beta_j + W_{i,j} \gamma)}{\sum_{l=1}^{J} \exp(X_i \beta_l + W_{i,j} \gamma)} \quad \text{for } j = 1, \ldots, J, \tag{5.45}$$

where $W_{i,j}$ is a $1 \times K_w$ matrix containing the explanatory variables for category j for individual i and where γ is a K_w-dimensional vector. The estimation of the parameters of the separate models can be done in a straightforward way using the results below.

The model parameters contained in θ are $(\beta_1, \ldots, \beta_J, \gamma)$. The first-order derivative of the likelihood function called the gradient $G(\theta)$ is given by

$$G(\theta) = \left(\frac{\partial l(\theta)}{\partial \beta_1'}, \ldots, \frac{\partial l(\theta)}{\partial \beta_J'}, \frac{\partial l(\theta)}{\partial \gamma} \right)'. \tag{5.46}$$

To derive the specific first-order derivatives, we first consider the partial derivatives of the choice probabilities with respect to the model parameters. The partial derivatives with respect to the β_j parameters are given by

$$\frac{\partial \Pr[Y_i = j]}{\partial \beta_j} = \Pr[Y_i = j](1 - \Pr[Y_i = j])X_i' \quad \text{for } j = 1, \ldots, J-1$$

$$\frac{\partial \Pr[Y_i = l]}{\partial \beta_j} = -\Pr[Y_i = l]\Pr[Y_i = j]X_i' \quad \text{for } j = 1, \ldots, J-1 \neq l. \tag{5.47}$$

The partial derivative with respect to γ equals

$$\frac{\partial \Pr[Y_j = j]}{\partial \gamma} = \Pr[Y_i = j]\left(W_{i,j}' - \sum_{l=1}^{J} \Pr[Y_i = l]W_{i,l}' \right). \tag{5.48}$$

If we substitute (5.47) and (5.48) in the first-order derivative of the log-likelihood function (5.46), we obtain the partial derivatives with respect to the model parameters. For the β_j parameters these become

$$\frac{\partial l(\theta)}{\partial \beta_j} = \sum_{i=1}^{N} (I[y_i = j] - \Pr[Y_i = j])X_i' \quad \text{for } j = 1, \ldots, J-1. \tag{5.49}$$

Substituting (5.48) in (5.43) gives

$$\frac{\partial l(\theta)}{\partial \gamma} = \sum_{i=1}^{N}\sum_{j=1}^{J} \frac{I[y_i = j]}{\Pr[Y_i = j]} \Pr[Y_i = j]\left(W_{i,j}' - \sum_{l=1}^{J} \Pr[Y_i = l]W_{i,l}' \right)$$

$$= \sum_{i=1}^{N}\sum_{j=1}^{J} I[y_i = j]\left(W_{i,j}' - \sum_{l=1}^{J} \Pr[Y_i = l]W_{i,l}' \right). \tag{5.50}$$

It is immediately clear that it is not possible to solve equation (5.43) for β_j and γ analytically. Therefore we use the Newton–Raphson algorithm in (5.44) to find the maximum.

The optimization algorithm requires the second-order derivative of the log-likelihood function, that is, the Hessian matrix, given by

$$
H(\theta) = \begin{pmatrix}
\dfrac{\partial^2 l(\theta)}{\partial \beta_1 \partial \beta_1'} & \cdots & \dfrac{\partial^2 l(\theta)}{\partial \beta_1 \partial \beta_{J-1}'} & \dfrac{\partial^2 l(\theta)}{\partial \beta_1 \partial \gamma'} \\[2ex]
\vdots & \ddots & \vdots & \vdots \\[2ex]
\dfrac{\partial^2 l(\theta)}{\partial \beta_{J-1} \partial \beta_1'} & \cdots & \dfrac{\partial^2 l(\theta)}{\partial \beta_{J-1} \partial \beta_{J-1}'} & \dfrac{\partial^2 l(\theta)}{\partial \beta_{J-1} \partial \gamma'} \\[2ex]
\dfrac{\partial^2 l(\theta)}{\partial \gamma \partial \beta_1'} & \cdots & \dfrac{\partial^2 l(\theta)}{\partial \gamma \partial \beta_{J-1}'} & \dfrac{\partial^2 l(\theta)}{\partial \gamma \partial \gamma'}
\end{pmatrix}. \tag{5.51}
$$

To obtain this matrix, we need the second-order partial derivatives of the log-likelihood with respect to β_j and γ and cross-derivatives. These derivatives follow from the first-order derivatives of the log-likelihood function (5.49) and (5.50) and the probabilities (5.47) and (5.48). Straightforward substitution gives

$$
\frac{\partial^2 l(\theta)}{\partial \beta_j \partial \beta_j'} = -\sum_{i=1}^{N} \Pr[Y_i = j](1 - \Pr[Y_i = j]) X_j' X_j \quad \text{for } j = 1, \ldots, J-1
$$

$$
\frac{\partial^2 l(\theta)}{\partial \gamma \partial \gamma'} = -\sum_{i=1}^{N} \sum_{j=1}^{J} I[y_i = j] \sum_{l=1}^{J} \Pr[Y_i = l]
$$

$$
\left(W_{i,l}' W_{i,l} - \sum_{j=1}^{J} \Pr[Y_i = j] W_{i,j}' W_{i,l} \right) \tag{5.52}
$$

and the cross-derivatives equal

$$
\frac{\partial^2 l(\theta)}{\partial \beta_j \partial \beta_l'} = \sum_{i=1}^{N} \Pr[Y_i = j] \Pr[Y_i = l] X_i' X_i \quad \text{for } j = 1, \ldots, J-1 \neq l
$$

$$
\frac{\partial^2 l(\theta)}{\partial \beta_j \partial \gamma'} = \sum_{i=1}^{N} \Pr[Y_i = j] \left(W_{i,j}' X_i - \sum_{l=1}^{J} \Pr[Y_i = l] W_{i,l}' X_i \right)
$$

$$
\text{for } j = 1, \ldots, J-1. \tag{5.53}
$$

The ML estimator is found by iterating over (5.44), where the expressions for $G(\theta)$ and $H(\theta)$ are given in (5.46) and (5.51). It can be shown that the log-likelihood is globally concave (see Amemiya, 1985). This implies that the Newton–Raphson algorithm (5.44) will converge to a unique optimum for all possible starting values. The resultant ML estimator $\hat{\theta} = (\hat{\beta}_1, \ldots, \hat{\beta}_{J-1}, \hat{\gamma})$ is asymptotically normally distributed with the true parameter value θ as its mean and the inverse of the information matrix as its covariance matrix. This information matrix can be estimated by $-H(\hat{\theta})$, where $H(\theta)$ is defined in (5.51) such that

$$\hat{\theta} \overset{a}{\sim} N(\theta, (-H(\hat{\theta}))^{-1}). \tag{5.54}$$

This result can be used to make inferences about the significance of the parameters. In sections 5.A.1 and 5.A.2 of the appendix to this chapter we give the EViews code for estimating Multinomial and Conditional Logit models.

5.2.2 The Multinomial Probit model

The parameters of the Multinomial and Conditional Probit models can be estimated in the same way as the logistic alternatives. The log-likelihood function is given by (5.42) with $\Pr[Y_i = j]$ defined in (5.29) under the assumption that the error terms are multivariate normally distributed. For the Multinomial Probit model, the parameters are summarized by $\theta = (\beta_1, \dots, \beta_{J-1}, \Sigma)$. One can derive the first-order and second-order derivatives of the choice probabilities to the parameters in θ, which determine the gradient and Hessian matrix. We consider this rather complicated derivation beyond the scope of this book. The interested reader who wants to estimate Multinomial Probit models is referred to McFadden (1989), Geweke et al. (1994) and Bolduc (1999), among others.

5.2.3 The Nested Logit model

There are two popular ways to estimate the parameters $\theta = (\alpha, \gamma, \tau_1, \dots, \tau_m)$ of the Nested Logit model (see also Ben-Akiva and Lerman, 1985, section 10.4). The first method amounts to a two-step ML procedure. In the first step, one estimates the γ parameters by treating the choice within a cluster as a standard Conditional Logit model. In the second step one considers the choice between the clusters as a Conditional Logit model and estimates the α and τ_m parameters, where $\hat{\gamma}$ is used to compute the inclusive values I_m for all clusters. Because this is a two-step estimator, the estimate of the covariance matrix obtained in the second step has to be adjusted (see McFadden, 1984).

The second estimation method is a full ML approach. The log-likelihood function is given by

$$l(\theta) = \sum_{i=1}^{N} \sum_{m=1}^{M} \sum_{j=1}^{J_m} I[y_i = (j, m)] \log \Pr[S_i = j | C_i = m] \Pr[C_i = m].$$

$$\tag{5.55}$$

The log-likelihood function is maximized over the parameter space θ. Expressions for the gradient and Hessian matrix can be derived in a straightforward way. In practice, one may opt for numerical first- and second-order derivatives. In section 5.A.3 we give the EViews code for estimating a Nested Logit model.

5.3   Diagnostics, model selection and forecasting

Once the parameters of a model for a multinomial dependent variable have been estimated, one should check the empirical validity of the model. Again, the interpretation of the estimated parameters and their standard errors may be invalid if the model is not well specified. Unfortunately, at present there are not many diagnostic checks for multinomial choice models. If the model is found to be adequate, one may consider deleting redundant variables or combining several choice categories using statistical tests or model selection criteria. Finally, one may evaluate the models on their within-sample and/or out-of-sample forecasting performance.

5.3.1   Diagnostics

At present, there are not many diagnostic tests for multinomial choice models. Many diagnostic tests are based on the properties of the residuals. However, the key problem of an unordered multinomial choice model lies in the fact that there is no natural way to construct a residual. A possible way to analyze the fit of the model is to compare the value of the realization y_i with the estimated probability. For example, in a Multinomial Logit model the estimated probability that category j is chosen by individual i is simply

$$\hat{p}_{i,j} = \hat{\Pr}[Y_i = j | X_i] = \frac{\exp(X_i \hat{\beta}_j)}{\sum_{l=1}^{J} \exp(X_i \hat{\beta}_l)}. \tag{5.56}$$

This probability has to be 1 if j is the true value of Y_i and zero for the other categories. As the maximum of the log-likelihood function (5.42) is just the sum of the estimated probabilities of the observed choices, one may define as residual

$$\hat{e}_i = 1 - \hat{p}_i, \tag{5.57}$$

where $\hat{p}_i$ is the estimated probability of the chosen alternative, that is $\hat{p}_i = \hat{\Pr}[Y_i = y_i | X_i]$. This residual has some odd properties. It is always positive and smaller or equal to 1. The interpretation of these residuals is therefore difficult (see also Cramer, 1991, section 5.4). They may, however, be useful for detecting outlying observations.

A well-known specification test in Multinomial and Conditional Logit models is due to Hausman and McFadden (1984) and it concerns the IIA property. The idea behind the test is that deleting one of the categories should not affect the estimates of the remaining parameters if the IIA assumption is valid. If it is valid, the estimation of the odds of two outcomes should not depend on alternative categories. The test amounts to checking whether the difference between the parameter estimates based on all categories and the parameter estimates when one or more categories are neglected is significant.

Let $\hat{\theta}_r$ denote the ML estimator of the logit model, where we have deleted one or more categories, and $\hat{V}(\hat{\theta}_r)$ the estimated covariance matrix of these estimates. Because the number of parameters for the unrestricted model is larger than the number of parameters for the restricted model, one removes the superfluous parameters from the ML estimates of the parameters of the unrestricted model $\hat{\theta}$, resulting in $\hat{\theta}_f$. The corresponding estimated covariance matrix is denoted by $\hat{V}(\hat{\theta}_f)$. The Hausman-type test of the validity of the IIA property is now defined as:

$$H_{\text{IIA}} = (\hat{\theta}_r - \hat{\theta}_f)'(\hat{V}(\hat{\theta}_r) - \hat{V}(\hat{\theta}_f))^{-1}(\hat{\theta}_r - \hat{\theta}_f). \tag{5.58}$$

The test statistic is asymptotically χ^2 distributed with degrees of freedom equal to the number of parameters in θ_r. The IIA assumption is rejected for large values of H_{IIA}. It may happen that the test statistic is negative. This is evidence that the IIA holds (see Hausman and McFadden, 1984, p. 1226). Obviously, if the test for the validity of IIA is rejected, one may opt for a Multinomial Probit model or a Nested Logit model.

5.3.2 Model selection

If one has obtained one or more empirically adequate models for a multinomial dependent variable, one may want to compare the different models. One may also want to examine whether or not certain redundant explanatory variables may be deleted.

The significance of individual explanatory variables can be based on the z-scores of the estimated parameters. These follow from the estimated parameters divided by their standard errors, which result from the square root of the diagonal elements of the estimated covariance matrix. If one wants to test for the redundancy of, say, g explanatory variables, one can use a likelihood ratio test. The relevant test statistic equals

$$\text{LR} = -2(l(\hat{\theta}_N) - l(\hat{\theta}_A)), \tag{5.59}$$

where $l(\hat{\theta}_N)$ and $l(\hat{\theta}_A)$ are the values of the log-likelihood function under the null and alternative hypotheses, respectively. Under the null hypothesis, this likelihood ratio test is asymptotically χ^2 distributed with g degrees of free-dom.

It may sometimes also be of interest to see whether the number of cate-gories may be reduced, in particular where there are, for example, many brands, of which a few are seldom purchased. Cramer and Ridder (1991) propose a test for the reduction of the number of categories in the Multinomial Logit model. Consider again the log odds ratio of j versus l defined in (5.8), and take for simplicity a single explanatory variable

$$\log \Omega_{j|l}(X_i) = \beta_{0,j} - \beta_{0,l} + (\beta_{1,j} - \beta_{1,l})x_i. \tag{5.60}$$

If $\beta_{1,j} = \beta_{1,l}$, the variable x_i cannot explain the difference between categories j and l. In that case the choice between j and l is fully explained by the intercept parameters $(\beta_{0,j} - \beta_{0,l})$. Hence,

$$\pi = \frac{\exp(\beta_{0,j})}{\exp(\beta_{0,j}) + \exp(\beta_{0,l})} \tag{5.61}$$

determines the fraction of $y_i = j$ observations in a new combined category $(j + l)$. A test for such a combination can thus be based on checking the equality of $\beta_{1,j}$ and $\beta_{1,l}$.

In general, a test for combining two categories j and l amounts to testing for the equality of β_j and β_l apart from the intercepts parameters. This equality restriction can be tested with a standard Likelihood Ratio test. The value of the log-likelihood function under the alternative hypothesis can be obtained from (5.42). Under the null hypothesis one has to estimate the model under the restriction that the β parameters (apart from the inter-cepts) of two categories are the same. This can easily be done as the log-likelihood function under the null hypothesis that categories j and l can be combined can be written as

$$
\begin{aligned}
l(\theta_N) = {}& \sum_{i=1}^{N} \sum_{s=1, s\neq l}^{J} I[y_i = s] \log \Pr[Y_i = s] \\
& + I[y_i = j \vee y_i = l] \Pr[Y_i = j] \\
& + \sum_{i=1}^{N} (I[y_i = j] \log \pi + I[y_i = 1] \log(1 - \pi)).
\end{aligned}
\tag{5.62}
$$

This log-likelihood function consists of two parts. The first part is the log-likelihood function of a Multinomial Logit model under the restriction $\beta_j = \beta_l$ including the intercept parameters. This is just a standard Multinomial Logit model. The last part of the log-likelihood function is a simple binomial model. The ML estimator of π is the ratio of the number of observations for which $y_i = j$ divided by the number of observations that y_i $= j$ or l, that is,

$$\hat{\pi} = \frac{\#(y_i = j)}{\#(y_i = j) + \#(y_i = l)}. \tag{5.63}$$

Under the null hypothesis that the categories may be combined, the LR statistic is asymptotically χ^2 distributed with degrees of freedom equal to K_x (the number of parameters in β_j minus the intercept). Tests for the combination of more than two categories follow in the same way (see Cramer and Ridder, 1991, for more details).

As we have already discussed in the previous subsection, it is difficult to define residuals for multinomial choice models. To construct an overall measure of fit, one therefore usually opts for a pseudo-R^2 measure. One such measure is the McFadden R^2 given by

$$R^2 = 1 - \frac{l(\hat{\theta})}{l(\hat{\theta}_0)}, \tag{5.64}$$

where $l(\hat{\theta}_0)$ is the value of the log likelihood function if the model contains only intercept parameters. The lower bound of the R^2 in (5.64) is 0, but the upper bound is not equal to 1, because $l(\hat{\theta})$ will never be 0. An alternative R^2 measure is derived in Maddala (1983, p. 39), that is,

$$\bar{R}^2 = \frac{1 - \left(\frac{L(\hat{\theta}_0)}{L(\hat{\theta})}\right)^{2/N}}{1 - (L(\hat{\theta}_0))^{2/N}}, \tag{5.65}$$

where $L(\hat{\theta}_0)$ is the value of the likelihood function when the model contains only intercept parameters and N is the number of individuals. This R^2 measure has a lower bound of 0 if $L(\hat{\theta}_0) = L(\hat{\theta})$ and an upper bound of 1 if $L(\hat{\theta}) = 1$. This upper bound corresponds with a perfect fit because it implies that all residuals in (5.57) are zero.

Finally, if one wants to compare models with different sets of explanatory variables, one may use the familiar AIC and BIC model selection criteria as discussed in chapters 3 and 4.

5.3.3 Forecasting

A final stage in a model selection procedure may be the evaluation of the forecasting performance of one or more selected models. We may consider within-sample and out-of-sample forecasts. In the latter case one needs a hold-out sample, which is not used for the estimation of the model parameters.

To generate forecasts, one computes the estimated choice probabilities. For a Multinomial Logit model this amounts to computing

$$\hat{p}_{i,j} = \hat{\Pr}[Y_i = j | X_i] = \frac{\exp(X_i \hat{\beta}_j)}{\sum_{l=1}^{J} \exp(X_i \hat{\beta}_l)} \quad \text{for } j = 1, \dots, J. \tag{5.66}$$

The next step consists of translating these probabilities into a discrete choice. One may think that a good forecast of the choice equals the expectation of Y_i given X_i, that is,

$$E[Y_i | X_i] = \sum_{j=1}^{J} \hat{p}_{i,j} j, \tag{5.67}$$

but this is not the case because the value of this expectation depends on the ordering of the choices from 1 to J, and this ordering was assumed to be irrelevant. In practice, one usually opts for the rule that the forecast for Y_i is the value of j that corresponds to the highest choice probability, that is

$$\hat{y}_i = j \text{ if } \hat{p}_{i,j} = \max(\hat{p}_{i,1}, \dots, \hat{p}_{i,J}). \tag{5.68}$$

To evaluate the forecasts, one may consider the percentage of correct hits for each model. These follow directly from a prediction–realization table:

		Predicted					
		$\hat{y}_i = 1$	...	$\hat{y}_i = j$	...	$\hat{y}_i = J$	
Observed							
	$y_i = 1$	p_{11}	...	p_{1j}	...	p_{1J}	$p_{1\cdot}$
	$\vdots$	$\vdots$	...	$\vdots$	...	$\vdots$	$\vdots$
	$y_i = j$	p_{j1}	...	p_{jj}	...	p_{jJ}	$p_{j\cdot}$
	$\vdots$	$\vdots$	...	$\vdots$	...	$\vdots$	$\vdots$
	$y_i = J$	p_{J1}	...	p_{Jj}	...	p_{JJ}	$p_{J\cdot}$
		$p_{\cdot 1}$	...	$p_{\cdot j}$	...	$p_{\cdot J}$	1

The value $p_{11} + \dots + p_{jj} + \dots + p_{JJ}$ can be interpreted as the hit rate. A useful forecasting criterion can generalize the F_1 measure in chapter 4, that is,

$$F_1 = \frac{\sum_{j=1}^{J} p_{jj} - p_{\cdot j}^2}{1 - \sum_{j=1}^{J} p_{\cdot j}^2} \tag{5.69}$$

The model with the maximum value for F_1 may be viewed as the model that has the best forecasting performance.

Table 5.1 *Parameter estimates of a Conditional Logit model for the choice between four brands of saltine crackers*

Variables	Parameter	Standard error
Intercepts		
Private label	−1.814***	0.091
Sunshine	−2.464***	0.084
Keebler	−1.968***	0.074
Marketing variables		
Display	0.048	0.067
Feature	0.412***	0.154
Display and feature	0.580***	0.118
Price	−3.172***	0.194
max. log-likelihood value	−3215.83	

Notes:
***Significant at the 0.01 level, ** at the 0.05 level, * at the 0.10 level
The total number of observations is 3,156.

5.4 Modeling the choice between four brands

As an illustration of the modeling of an unordered multinomial dependent variable, we consider the choice between four brands of saltine crackers. The brands are called Private label, Sunshine, Keebler and Nabisco. The data were described in section 2.2.3. We have a scanner data set of $N = 3,292$ purchases made by 136 households. For each purchase, we have the actual price of the purchased brand, the shelf price of the other brands and four times two dummy variables which indicate whether the brands were on display or featured.

To describe brand choice we consider the Conditional Logit model in (5.16), where we include as explanatory variables per category the price of the brand and three 0/1 dummy variables indicating whether a brand was on display only or featured only or jointly on display and featured. To allow for out-of-sample evaluation of the model, we exclude the last purchases of each household from the estimation sample. Hence, we have 3,156 observations for parameter estimation.

Table 5.1 shows the ML parameter estimates of the Conditional Logit model with corresponding estimated standard errors. The model parameters are estimated using EViews 3.1 (see section 5.A.2 for the EViews code). The model contains three intercepts because the intercept for Nabisco is set equal to zero for identification. The three intercept parameters are all negative and significant, thereby confirming that Nabisco is the market leader (see section 2.2.3). Feature and joint display and feature have a significant positive effect on brand choice, but their effects do not seem to be significantly different. This suggests that the effect of a single display is not significant, which is confirmed by its individual insignificant parameter. The negative significant price coefficient indicates that an increase in the price of a brand leads to a smaller probability that the brand is chosen. The likelihood ratio test for the significance of the four explanatory variables (apart from the three intercepts) equals 324.33, and the effect of the four explanatory variables on brand choice is significant at the 1% level.

To evaluate the model, we first consider the test for the validity of IIA. We remove the Private label category from the data set and we estimate the parameters in a Conditional Logit model for the three national brands. The Hausman-type statistic H_{IIA} (see (5.58)), which compares the parameter estimates of the model with four brands with the parameter estimates of the model with three brands, equals 32.98. This statistic is asymptotically $\chi^2(6)$ distributed under the null hypothesis, and hence the IIA property is rejected at the 5% level.

To account for the absence of IIA, we opt for a Nested Logit model for the same data. We split the brands into two clusters. The first cluster contains Private label and the second cluster the three national brands, that is,

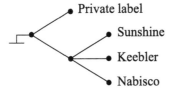

To model the brand choices within the national brands cluster, we take a Conditional Logit model (see (5.35)) with $J_m = 3$. As explanatory variables, we take price, display only, feature only and display and feature, and two intercept parameters (Nabisco is the base brand within the cluster). Because the Private label cluster contains only one brand, we do not have to specify a logit model for this cluster. The choice probabilities between the two clusters are modeled by (5.36) with $M = 2$. As explanatory variables we take the price, display only, feature only and display and feature of Private label. Additionally, we include a Private label intercept and the inclusive value of the national brand cluster with parameter τ. We impose that the price, display and feature effects in the probabilities that model the cluster choices denoted by α in (5.36) are the same as the price, display and feature effects of

Table 5.2 *Parameter estimates of a Nested Logit model for the choice between four brands of saltine crackers*

Variables	Parameter	Standard error
Intercepts		
Private label	−2.812***	0.339
Sunshine	−2.372***	0.056
Keebler	−1.947***	0.074
Marketing variables		
Display	0.075	0.057
Feature	0.442***	0.132
Display and feature	0.631***	0.107
Price	−2.747***	0.205
$\hat{\tau}$	1.441***	0.147
max. log-likelihood value	−3210.43	

Notes:
***Significant at the 0.01 level, ** at the 0.05 level, * at the 0.10 level
The total number of observations is 3,156.

the choice probabilities in the national brand cluster, denoted by γ in (5.35). This restriction implies that, for $\tau = 1$, the model simplifies to the same Conditional Logit model as considered above. Hence, we can simply test the Nested Logit model against the Conditional Logit model using a Likelihood Ratio test.

Table 5.2 shows the ML parameter estimates of the above Nested Logit model. The model parameters are estimated using EViews 3.1 (see section 5.A.3 for the EViews code). The parameter estimates are rather similar to the estimates in table 5.1. The display and feature parameters are slightly higher, while the price parameter is lower. Fortunately, the $\hat{\tau}$ parameter is larger than 1, which ensures utility-maximizing behavior. The standard error of $\hat{\tau}$ shows that $\hat{\tau}$ is more than two standard errors away from 1, which suggests that we cannot restrict τ to be 1. The formal LR test for $\tau = 1$ equals 10.80 and hence we can reject the null hypothesis of the Conditional Logit model against the Nested Logit specification. This means that the Nested Logit model is preferred.

The McFadden R^2 in (5.64) of the Conditional Logit model equals 0.05, while the alternative $\bar{R}^2$ (5.65) equals 0.11. The R^2 measures for the Nested

Logit model are almost the same. Hence, although the model is significantly different, there is not much difference in fit.

To compare the forecast performance of both models we construct the prediction–realization tables. For the 3,156 within-sample forecasts of the Conditional Logit model and Nested Logit model the prediction–realization table is:

	Predicted				
	Private label	Sunshine	Keebler	Nabisco	
Observed					
Private label	0.09 (0.09)	0.00 (0.00)	0.00 (0.00)	0.23 (0.23)	0.32 (0.32)
Sunshine	0.01 (0.01)	0.00 (0.00)	0.00 (0.00)	0.06 (0.06)	0.07 (0.07)
Keebler	0.01 (0.02)	0.00 (0.00)	0.00 (0.00)	0.06 (0.05)	0.07 (0.07)
Nabisco	0.06 (0.08)	0.00 (0.00)	0.00 (0.00)	0.48 (0.46)	0.54 (0.54)
	0.18 (0.20)	0.00 (0.00)	0.00 (0.00)	0.82 (0.80)	1

where the Nested Logit model results appear in parentheses. The small inconsistencies in the table are due to rounding errors. We see that there is not much difference in the forecast performance of both models. The hit rate is 0.57 (= 0.09 + 0.48) for the Conditional Logit model and 0.55 for the Nested Logit model. The F_1 measures are 0.025 and 0.050 for the Conditional and Nested Logit models, respectively. Both models perform reasonably well in forecasting Private label and Nabisco purchases, but certainly not purchases of Sunshine and Keebler.

For the 136 out-of-sample forecasts, the prediction–realization table becomes:

	Predicted				
	Private label	Sunshine	Keebler	Nabisco	
Observed					
Private label	0.14 (0.15)	0.00 (0.00)	0.00 (0.00)	0.15 (0.15)	0.29 (0.29)
Sunshine	0.03 (0.03)	0.00 (0.00)	0.00 (0.00)	0.01 (0.01)	0.04 (0.04)
Keebler	0.01 (0.02)	0.00 (0.00)	0.00 (0.00)	0.07 (0.07)	0.09 (0.09)
Nabisco	0.14 (0.15)	0.00 (0.00)	0.00 (0.00)	0.43 (0.42)	0.57 (0.57)
	0.32 (0.35)	0.00 (0.00)	0.00 (0.00)	0.68 (0.65)	1

where the results for the Nested Logit model again appear in parentheses. Again, small inconsistencies in the table are due to rounding errors. The out-of-sample hit rate for both models is 0.57, which is (about) as good as the in-sample hit rates. The F_1 measures are however worse, -0.46 and -0.40 for the Conditional and Nested Logit models, respectively. We notice the same pattern as for the within-sample forecasts. Both models predict the purchases of Private label and Nabisco reasonably well, but fail to forecast purchases of Sunshine and Keebler. This indicates that it must be possible to improve the model.

A promising way of improving the model is perhaps to allow households to have different base preferences and to allow that some households are more price sensitive than others by introducing unobserved household heterogeneity, as is done in Jain et al. (1994). This topic is beyond the scope of this application and some discussion on this matter is postponed to the advanced topics section. In this section, we will continue with model interpretation, where we focus on the Conditional Logit model.

Figure 5.1 displays the choice probabilities as a function of the prices of the four brands for the estimated Conditional Logit model. For example, the upper left cell displays the choice probabilities for the four brands as a function of the price of Private label. The prices of the other brands are set at their sample mean. We assume no display or feature. An increase in the price of Private label leads to a decrease in the choice probability of Private label and an increase in the choice probabilities of the national brands. For high prices of Private label, Nabisco is by far the most popular brand. This is also the case for high prices of Sunshine and Keebler. For high prices of Nabisco, Private label is the most popular brand. In marketing terms, this suggests that Nabisco is the most preferred brand when it comes to competitive actions. Also, the direct competitor to Nabisco seems to be Private Label.

The choice probabilities for Sunshine and Keebler seem to behave in a roughly similar way. The second and third graphs are very similar and in the two other graphs the choice probabilities are almost the same for all prices. This suggests that we could test whether or not it is possible to combine both categories; it is, however, not possible because the values of the explanatory variables for Sunshine and Keebler are different. Hence, one could now calculate some kind of an average price and average promotion activity, and combine the two as one brand. An LR test to check whether this is allowed is, however, not possible.

Figure 5.2 shows the quasi price elasticities of the four brands. Because price elasticities depend on the value of the prices of the other brands, we set these prices at their sample mean value. We assume again that there is no display or feature. The price elasticities of Private label, Sunshine and Keebler have the same pattern. For small values of the price, we see a decrease in price elasticity, but for prices larger than US$0.75 we see an increase. Nabisco is less price sensitive than the other brands for small values of the price but much more price sensitive if the price is larger than US$0.80. Finally, for Nabisco the turning point from a decrease to an increase in price elasticity is around a hypothetical price of US$1.30. The main message to take from figure 5.2 is that a Conditional Logit model implies nonlinear patterns in elasticities.

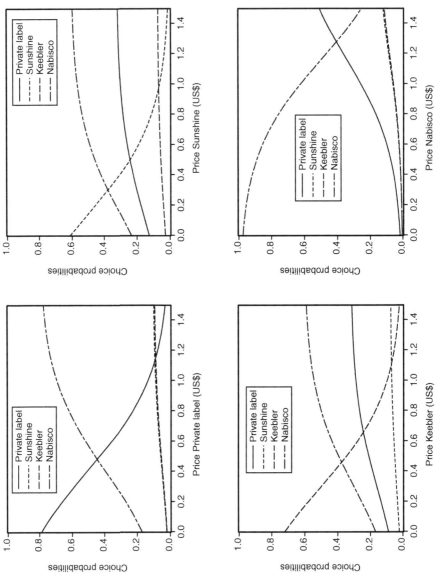

Figure 5.1   Choice probabilities versus price

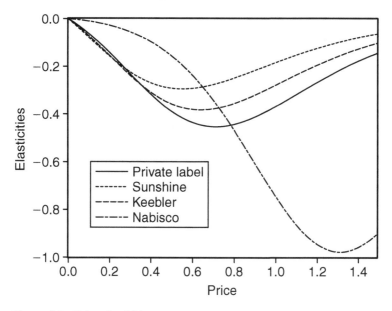

Figure 5.2   Price elasticities

5.5   Advanced topics

So far, the discussion on models for a multinomial unordered dependent variable has been based on the availability of a cross-section of observations, where N individuals could choose from J categories. In many marketing applications one can have several observations of individuals over time. In the advanced topics section of chapter 4 we have already seen that we may use this extra information to estimate unobserved heterogeneity and analyze choice dynamics, and here we extend it to the above discussed models. In section 5.5.1 we discuss modeling of unobserved heterogeneity for the multinomial choice models and in section 5.5.2 we discuss ways to introduce dynamics in choice models.

5.5.1   Modeling unobserved heterogeneity

Let $y_{i,t}$ denote the choice of individual i from J categories at time t, $t = 1, \ldots, T$. To model the choice behavior of this individual, consider again the Conditional Logit model with one explanatory variable

$$\Pr[Y_{i,t} = j | w_{i,t}] = \frac{\exp(\beta_{0,j} + \gamma_1 w_{i,j,t})}{\sum_{l=1}^{J} \exp(\beta_{0,l} + \gamma_1 w_{i,l,t})} \quad \text{for } j = 1, \ldots, J,$$

$$(5.70)$$

where $w_{i,j,t}$ denotes the explanatory variable belonging to category j experienced by individual i at time t. It is likely that individuals will have different base preferences. To capture these differences, one usually includes individual-specific explanatory variables such as age or gender to the model. In many cases these variables are not available. To capture differences in base preferences in these cases one may replace the intercepts $\beta_{0,j}$ in (5.70) by individual-specific intercepts $\beta_{0,j,i}$.

It is not always possible to estimate individual-specific intercepts. If an individual does not consider one or more categories, it is not possible to estimate all individual-specific intercepts. To solve this problem, one usually assumes that the $\beta_{0,j,i}$ parameters are draws from a distribution, which describes the distribution of the base preferences in the population of individuals. There are several possibilities for the functional form of the distribution. One may, for example, assume that the vector of individual-specific intercepts $\beta_{0,i} = (\beta_{0,1,i}, \ldots, \beta_{0,J-1,i})$ is normally distributed with mean β_0 and covariance matrix Σ_{β_0}, that is,

$$\beta_{0,i} \sim N(\beta_0, \Sigma_{\beta_0}) \tag{5.71}$$

(see, for example, Gönül and Srinivasan, 1993, and Rossi and Allenby, 1993).

Another frequently used approach in marketing research is to assume that there are S latent classes in the population (see also section 4.5). The intercept parameters for class s are $\beta_{0,s}$ and the probability that an individual belongs to this class equals p_s with $\sum_{s=1}^{S} p_s = 1$ (see, for example, Kamakura and Russell, 1989, and Jain et al., 1994). The likelihood function now becomes

$$L(\theta) = \prod_{i=1}^{N} \left(\sum_{s=1}^{S} p_s \left(\prod_{t=1}^{T} \prod_{j=1}^{J} \Pr[Y_{i,t} = j; \beta_{0,s}, \gamma_1]^{I[y_{i,t}=j]} \right) \right). \tag{5.72}$$

To estimate the parameters of the model, one maximizes the likelihood function with respect to the parameters $\theta = (\beta_{0,1}, \ldots, \beta_{0,S}, p_1, \ldots, p_{S-1}, \gamma_1)$ (see, for example, Wedel and Kamakura, 1999).

Apart from different base preferences, the effects of explanatory variables on choice may be different for individuals. This can be modeled in the same way as for the intercept parameters, that is, one replaces γ_1 in (5.70) by the individual-specific parameter $\gamma_{1,i}$.

5.5.2   Modeling dynamics

Dynamic structures can be incorporated in the model in several ways. The easiest way is to allow for state dependence and to include a lagged choice variable to the model that denotes whether the category is chosen at time $t - 1$, that is,

$$\Pr[Y_{i,t} = j | w_{i,t}] = \frac{\exp(\beta_{0,j} + \gamma_1 w_{i,j,t} + \delta I[y_{i,t-1} = j])}{\sum_{l=1}^{J} \exp(\beta_{0,l} + \gamma_1 w_{i,l,t} + \delta I[y_{i,t-1} = l])} \qquad (5.73)$$
$$\text{for } j = 1, \ldots, J,$$

where $I[y_{i,t-1} = j]$ is a 0/1 dummy variable that is 1 if the individual chooses category j at time $t - 1$ and zero otherwise, and δ is a parameter (see, for example, Roy et al., 1996). Other possibilities concern introducing an auto-regressive structure on the error variables $\varepsilon_{i,j}$ in (5.28) (see, for example, McCulloch and Rossi, 1994, Geweke et al., 1997, and Paap and Franses, 2000).

Finally, another way to include past choice behavior in a model is used in Guadagni and Little (1983). They introduce a brand loyalty variable in their logit brand choice model. This variable is an exponentially weighted average of past purchase decisions. The brand loyalty variable for brand j for individual i, $b_{i,j,t}$, is defined as

$$b_{i,j,t} = \delta b_{i,j,t-1} + (1 - \delta) I[y_{i,t-1} = j], \qquad (5.74)$$

with $0 < \delta < 1$. To start up brand loyalty, we set $b_{i,j,1}$ equal to δ if j was the first choice of individual i and $(1 - \delta)/(J - 1)$ otherwise. The value of δ has to be estimated from the data.

5.A.   EViews Code

This appendix provides the EViews code we used to estimate the models in section 5.4. In the code the following abbreviations are used for the variables:

- pri, sun, kee and nab are 0/1 dummy variables indicating whether the brand has been chosen;
- dispri, dissun, diskee and disnab are 0/1 dummy variables indicating whether the corresponding brand was on display only;
- feapri, feasun, feakee and feanab are 0/1 dummy variables indicating whether the corresponding brand was featured only;
- fedipri, fedisun, fedikee and fedinab are 0/1 dummy variables indicating whether the corresponding brand was displayed and featured at the same time;
- pripri, prisun, prikee and prinab are the prices of the four brands;
- hhsize and inc denote household size and family income. These variables are not in our genuine data set, and serve for illustrative purposes only.

5.A.1   The Multinomial Logit model

```
load c:\data\cracker.wf1

' Declare coefficient vectors to use in Maximum Likelihood estimation
coef(3) a1
coef(3) b1
coef(3) b2

' Specify log-likelihood for Multinomial Logit
model logl mnl
mnl.append @logl loglmnl

' Define the exponent for each choice
mnl.append xb1=a1(1)+b1(1)*hhsize+b2(1)*inc
mnl.append xb2=a1(2)+b1(2)*hhsize+b2(2)*inc
mnl.append xb3=a1(3)+b1(3)*hhsize+b2(3)*inc
mnl.append denom=1+exp(xb2)+exp(xb3)+exp(xb4)

mnl.append loglmnl=pri*xb1+sun*xb2+kee*xb3-log(denom)

' Estimate by Maximum Likelihood
smpl 1 3292
mnl.ml(d)
show mnl.output
```

5.A.2   The Conditional Logit model

```
load c:\data\cracker.wf1

' Declare coefficient vectors to use in Maximum Likelihood estimation
coef(3) a1
coef(4) b1

' Specify log-likelihood for Conditional Logit model
logl cl
cl.append @logl loglcl

' Define the exponent for each choice
cl.append xb1=a1(1)+b1(1)*dispri+b1(2)*feapri+b1(3)*fedipri+b1(4)*pripri
cl.append xb2=a1(2)+b1(1)*dissun+b1(2)*feasun+b1(3)*fedisun+b1(4)*prisun
cl.append xb3=a1(3)+b1(1)*diskee+b1(2)*feakee+b1(3)*fedikee+b1(4)*prikee
cl.append xb4=b1(1)*disnab+b1(2)*feanab+b1(3)*fedinab+b1(4)*prinab
cl.append denom=exp(xb1)+exp(xb2)+exp(xb3)+exp(xb4)

cl.append loglcl=pri*xb1+sun*xb2+kee*xb3+nab*xb4-log(denom)
```

```
' Estimate by Maximum Likelihood
smpl 1 3292
cl.ml(d)
show cl.output
```

5.A.3   The Nested Logit model

```
load c:\data\cracker.wf1
```

```
' Declare coefficient vectors to use in Maximum Likelihood estimation
coef(3) a1
coef(4) b1
coef(1) c1
```

```
' Specify log-likelihood for Nested Logit model
logl nl
nl.append @logl loglnl
```

```
' National brands cluster
nl.append xb21=a1(1)+b1(1)*dissun+b1(2)*feasun+b1(3)*fedisun+b1(4)*prisun
nl.append xb22=a1(2)+b1(1)*diskee+b1(2)*feakee+b1(3)*fedikee+b1(4)*prikee
nl.append xb23=b1(1)*disnab+b1(2)*feanab+b1(3)*fedinab+b1(4)*prinab
```

```
' Private label + inclusive value
nl.append xb11=a1(3)+b1(1)*dispri+b1(2)*feapri+b1(3)*fedipri+b1(4)*pripri
nl.append ival=log(exp(xb21)+exp(xb22)+exp(xb23))
```

```
' Cluster probabilities
nl.append prob1=exp(xb11)/(exp(xb11)+exp(c1(1)*ival))
nl.append prob2=exp(c1(1)*ival)/(exp(xb11)+exp(c1(1)*ival))
```

```
' Conditional probabilities within national brands cluster
nl.append prob22=exp(xb21)/(exp(xb21)+exp(xb22)+exp(xb23))
nl.append prob23=exp(xb22)/(exp(xb21)+exp(xb22)+exp(xb23))
nl.append prob24=exp(xb23)/(exp(xb21)+exp(xb22)+exp(xb23))
```

```
nl.append loglnl=pri*log(prob1)+sun*log(prob2*prob22)
                +kee*log(prob2*prob23)+nab*log(prob2*prob24)
```

```
' Estimate by Maximum Likelihood
smpl 1 3292
nl.ml(d)
show nl.output
```

6   An ordered multinomial dependent variable

In this chapter we focus on the Logit model and the Probit model for an ordered dependent variable, where this variable is not continuous but takes discrete values. Such an ordered multinomial variable differs from an unordered variable by the fact that individuals now face a ranked variable. Examples of ordered multinomial data typically appear in questionnaires, where individuals are, for example, asked to indicate whether they strongly disagree, disagree, are indifferent, agree or strongly agree with a certain statement, or where individuals have to evaluate characteristics of a (possibly hypothetical) brand or product on a five-point Likert scale. It may also be that individuals themselves are assigned to categories, which sequentially concern a more or less favorable attitude towards some phenomenon, and that it is then of interest to the market researcher to examine which explanatory variables have predictive value for the classification of individuals into these categories. In fact, the example in this chapter concerns this last type of data, where we analyze individuals who are all customers of a financial investment firm and who have been assigned to three categories according to their risk profiles. Having only bonds corresponds with low risk and trading in financial derivatives may be viewed as more risky. It is the aim of this empirical analysis to investigate which behavioral characteristics of the individuals can explain this classification.

The econometric models which are useful for such an ordered dependent variable are called ordered regression models. Examples of applications in marketing research usually concern customer satisfaction, perceived customer value and perceptual mapping (see, for example, Katahira, 1990, and Zemanek, 1995, among others). Kekre et al. (1995) use an Ordered Probit model to investigate the drivers of customer satisfaction for software products. Sinha and DeSarbo (1998) propose an Ordered Probit-based model to examine the perceived value of compact cars. Finally, an application in financial economics can be found in Hausman et al. (1992).

The outline of this chapter is as follows. In section 6.1 we discuss the model representations of the Ordered Logit and Probit models, and we address parameter interpretation in some detail. In section 6.2 we discuss Maximum Likelihood estimation. Not many textbooks elaborate on this topic, and therefore we supply ample details. In section 6.3 diagnostic measures, model selection and forecasting are considered. Model selection is confined to the selection of regressors. Forecasting deals with within-sample or out-of-sample classification of individuals to one of the ordered categories. In section 6.4 we illustrate the two models for the data set on the classification of individuals according to risk profiles. Elements of this data set were discussed in chapter 2. Finally, in section 6.5 we discuss a few other models for ordered categorical data, and we will illustrate the effects of sample selection if one wants to handle the case where the observations for one of the categories outnumber those in other categories.

6.1 Representation and interpretation

This section starts with a general introduction to the model framework for an ordered dependent variable. Next, we discuss the representation of an Ordered Logit model and an Ordered Probit model. Finally, we provide some details on how one can interpret the parameters of these models.

6.1.1 Modeling an ordered dependent variable

As already indicated in chapter 4, the most intuitively appealing way to introduce an ordered regression model starts off with an unobserved (latent) variable y_i^*. For convenience, we first assume that this latent variable correlates with a single explanatory variable x_i, that is,

$$y_i^* = \beta_0 + \beta_1 x_i + \varepsilon_i, \tag{6.1}$$

where for the moment we leave the distribution of ε_i unspecified. This latent variable might measure, for example, the unobserved willingness of an individual to take a risk in a financial market. Another example concerns the unobserved attitude towards a certain phenomenon, where this attitude can range from very much against to very much in favor. In chapter 4 we dealt with the case that this latent variable gets mapped onto a binomial variable Y_i by the rule

$$
\begin{aligned}
Y_i &= 1 \quad \text{if } y_i^* > 0 \\
Y_i &= 0 \quad \text{if } y_i^* \leq 0.
\end{aligned}
\tag{6.2}
$$

In this chapter we extend this mapping mechanism by allowing the latent variable to get mapped onto more than two categories, with the implicit assumption that these categories are ordered.

Mapping y_i^* onto a multinomial variable, while preserving the fact that y_i^* is a continuous variable that depends linearly on an explanatory variable, and thus making sure that this latent variable gets mapped onto an ordered categorical variable, can simply be done by extending (6.2) to have more than two categories. More formally, (6.2) can be modified as

$$
\begin{aligned}
Y_i &= 1 \quad \text{if} \quad \alpha_0 < y_i^* \le \alpha_1 \\
Y_i &= j \quad \text{if} \quad \alpha_{j-1} < y_i^* \le \alpha_j \quad \text{for } j = 2, \ldots, J-1 \\
Y_i &= J \quad \text{if} \quad \alpha_{J-1} < y_i^* \le \alpha_J,
\end{aligned}
\tag{6.3}
$$

where α_0 to α_J are unobserved thresholds. This amounts to the indicator variable $I[y_i = j]$, which is 1 if observation y_i belongs to category j and 0 otherwise, for $i = 1, \ldots, N$, and $j = 1, \ldots, J$. To preserve the ordering, the thresholds α_i in (6.3) must satisfy $\alpha_0 < \alpha_1 < \alpha_2 < \ldots < \alpha_{J-1} < \alpha_J$. Because the boundary values of the latent variable are unknown, one can simply set $\alpha_0 = -\infty$ and $\alpha_J = +\infty$, and hence there is no need to try to estimate their values. The above equations can be summarized as that an individual i gets assigned to category j if

$$
\alpha_{j-1} < y_i^* \le \alpha_j, \quad j = 1, \ldots, J.
\tag{6.4}
$$

In figure 6.1, we provide a scatter diagram of y_i^* against x_i, when the data are again generated according to the DGP that was used in previous chapters, that is,

$$
\begin{aligned}
x_i &= 0.0001i + \varepsilon_{1,i} \quad \text{with } \varepsilon_{1,i} \sim N(0, 1) \\
y_i^* &= -2 + x_i + \varepsilon_{2,i} \quad \text{with } \varepsilon_{2,i} \sim N(0, 1),
\end{aligned}
\tag{6.5}
$$

where i is $1, 2, \ldots, N = 1,000$. For illustration, we depict the distribution of y_i^* for three observations x_i. We assume that α_1 equals -3 and α_2 equals -1. For an observation with $x_i = -2$, we observe that it is most likely (as indicated by the size of the shaded area) that the individual gets classified into the bottom category, that is, where $Y_i = 1$. For an observation with $x_i = 0$, the probability that the individual gets classified into the middle category ($Y_i = 2$) is the largest. Finally, for an observation with $x_i = 2$, most probability mass gets assigned to the upper category ($Y_i = 3$). As a by-product, it is clear from this graph that if the thresholds α_1 and α_2 get closer to each other, and the variance of ε_i in (6.1) is not small, it may become difficult correctly to classify observations in the middle category.

When we combine the expressions in (6.3) and (6.4) we obtain the ordered regression model, that is,

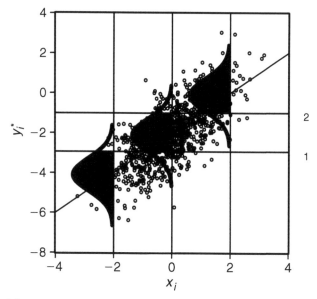

Figure 6.1 Scatter diagram of y_i^* against x_i

$$Pr[Y_i = j|X_i] = Pr[\alpha_{j-1} < y_i^* \leq \alpha_j]$$
$$= Pr[\alpha_{j-1} - (\beta_0 + \beta_1 x_i) < \varepsilon_i \leq \alpha_j - (\beta_0 + \beta_1 x_i)]$$
$$= F(\alpha_j - (\beta_0 + \beta_1 x_i)) - F(\alpha_{j-1} - (\beta_0 + \beta_1 x_i)),$$

$$(6.6)$$

for $j = 2, 3, \ldots, J - 1$, where

$$Pr[Y_i = 1|X_i] = F(\alpha_1 - (\beta_0 + \beta_1 x_i)), \tag{6.7}$$

and

$$Pr[Y_i = J|X_i] = 1 - F(\alpha_{J-1} - (\beta_0 + \beta_1 x_i)), \tag{6.8}$$

for the two outer categories. As usual, F denotes the cumulative distribution function of ε_i.

It is important to notice from (6.6)–(6.8) that the parameters α_1 to α_{J-1} and β_0 are not jointly identified. One may now opt to set one of the threshold parameters equal to zero, which is what is in effect done for the models for a binomial dependent variable in chapter 4. In practice, one usually opts to impose $\beta_0 = 0$ because this may facilitate the interpretation of the ordered regression model. Consequently, from now on we consider

$$Pr[Y_i = j|x_i] = F(\alpha_j - \beta_1 x_i) - F(\alpha_{j-1} - \beta_1 x_i). \tag{6.9}$$

Finally, notice that this model assumes no heterogeneity across individuals, that is, the parameters α_j and β_1 are the same for every individual. An extension to such heterogeneity would imply the parameters $\alpha_{j,i}$ and $\beta_{1,i}$, which depend on i.

6.1.2 The Ordered Logit and Ordered Probit models

As with the binomial and multinomial dependent variable models in the previous two chapters, one should now decide on the distribution of ε_i. Before we turn to this discussion, we need to introduce some new notation concerning the inclusion of more than a single explanatory variable. The threshold parameters and the intercept parameter in the latent variable equation are not jointly identified, and hence it is common practice to set the intercept parameter equal to zero. This is the same as assuming that the regressor vector X_i contains only K columns with explanatory variables, and no column for the intercept. To avoid notational confusion, we summarize these variables in a $1 \times K$ vector $\tilde{X}_i$, and we summarize the K unknown parameters β_1 to β_K in a $K \times 1$ parameter vector $\tilde{\beta}$. The general expression for the ordered regression model thus becomes

$$\Pr[Y_i = j|\tilde{X}_i] = F(\alpha_j - \tilde{X}_i\tilde{\beta}) - F(\alpha_{j-1} - \tilde{X}_i\tilde{\beta}), \tag{6.10}$$

for $i = 1, \ldots, N$ and $j = 1, \ldots, J$. Notice that (6.10) implies that the scale of F is not identified, and hence one also has to restrict the variance of ε_i. This model thus contains $K + J - 1$ unknown parameters. This amounts to a substantial reduction compared with the models for an unordered multinomial dependent variable in the previous chapter.

Again there are many possible choices for the distribution function F, but in practice one usually considers either the cumulative standard normal distribution or the cumulative standard logistic distribution (see section A.2 in the Appendix). In the first case, that is,

$$F(\alpha_j - \tilde{X}_i\tilde{\beta}) = \Phi(\alpha_j - \tilde{X}_i\tilde{\beta}) = \int_{-\infty}^{\alpha_j - \tilde{X}_i\tilde{\beta}} \frac{1}{\sqrt{2\pi}} \exp\left(-\frac{z^2}{2}\right) dz, \tag{6.11}$$

the resultant model is called the Ordered Probit model. The corresponding normal density function is denoted in shorthand as $\phi(\alpha_j - \tilde{X}_i\tilde{\beta})$. The second case takes

$$F(\alpha_j - \tilde{X}_i\tilde{\beta}) = \Lambda(\alpha_j - \tilde{X}_i\tilde{\beta}) = \frac{\exp(\alpha_j - \tilde{X}_i\tilde{\beta})}{1 + \exp(\alpha_j - \tilde{X}_i\tilde{\beta})}, \tag{6.12}$$

and the resultant model is called the Ordered Logit model. The corresponding density function is denoted as $\lambda(\alpha_j - \tilde{X}_i\tilde{\beta})$. These two cumulative distribution functions are standardized, which implies that the variance of ε_i is set equal to 1 in the Ordered Probit model and equal to $\frac{1}{3}\pi^2$ in the Ordered Logit model. This implies that the parameters for the Ordered Logit model are likely to be

$$\sqrt{\frac{1}{3}\pi^2}$$

times as large as those of the Probit model.

6.1.3   Model interpretation

The effects of the explanatory variables on the ordered dependent variable are not linear, because they get channeled through a nonlinear cumulative distribution function. Therefore, convenient methods to illustrate the interpretation of the model again make use of odds ratios and quasi-elasticities.

Because the outcomes on the left-hand side of an ordered regression model obey a specific sequence, it is customary to consider the odds ratio defined by

$$\frac{\Pr[Y_i \leq j|\tilde{X}_i]}{\Pr[Y_i > j|\tilde{X}_i]}, \tag{6.13}$$

where

$$\Pr[Y_i \leq j|\tilde{X}_i] = \sum_{m=1}^{j} \Pr[Y_i = m|\tilde{X}_i] \tag{6.14}$$

denotes the cumulative probability that the outcome is less than or equal to j. For the Ordered Logit model with K explanatory variables, this odds ratio equals

$$\frac{\Lambda(\alpha_j - \tilde{X}_i\tilde{\beta})}{1 - \Lambda(\alpha_j - \tilde{X}_i\tilde{\beta})} = \exp(\alpha_j - \tilde{X}_i\tilde{\beta}), \tag{6.15}$$

which after taking logs becomes

$$\log\left(\frac{\Lambda(\alpha_j - \tilde{X}_i\tilde{\beta})}{1 - \Lambda(\alpha_j - \tilde{X}_i\tilde{\beta})}\right) = \alpha_j - \tilde{X}_i\tilde{\beta}. \tag{6.16}$$

This expression clearly indicates that the explanatory variables all have the same impact on the dependent variable, that is, $\tilde{\beta}$, and that the classification into the ordered categories on the left-hand side hence depends on the values of α_j.

An ordered regression model can also be interpreted by considering the quasi-elasticity of each explanatory variable. This quasi-elasticity with respect to the k'th explanatory variable is defined as

$$\frac{\partial \Pr[Y_i = j|\tilde{X}_i]}{\partial x_{k,i}} x_{k,i} = \left(\frac{\partial F(\alpha_j - \tilde{X}_i\tilde{\beta})}{\partial x_{k,i}} - \frac{\partial F(\alpha_{j-1} - \tilde{X}_i\tilde{\beta})}{\partial x_{k,i}} \right) x_{k,i}$$

$$= \beta_k x_{k,i} (f(\alpha_{j-1} - \tilde{X}_i\tilde{\beta}) - f(\alpha_j - \tilde{X}_i\tilde{\beta})),$$

(6.17)

where $f(\cdot)$ denotes the density function. Interestingly, it can be seen from this expression that, even though β_k can be positive (negative), the quasi-elasticity of $x_{k,i}$ also depends on the value of $f(\alpha_{j-1} - \tilde{X}_i\tilde{\beta}) - f(\alpha_j - \tilde{X}_i\tilde{\beta})$. This difference between densities may take negative (positive) values, whatever the value of β_k. Of course, for a positive value of β_k the probability that individual i is classified into a higher category gets larger.

Finally, one can easily derive that

$$\frac{\partial \Pr[Y_i \leq j|\tilde{X}_i]}{\partial x_{k,i}} x_{k,i} + \frac{\partial \Pr[Y_i > j|\tilde{X}_i]}{\partial x_{k,i}} x_{k,i} = 0.$$

(6.18)

As expected, given the odds ratio discussed above, the sum of these two quasi-elasticities is equal to zero. This indicates that the ordered regression model effectively contains a sequence of $J - 1$ models for a range of binomial dependent variables. This notion will be used in section 6.3 to diagnose the validity of an ordered regression model.

6.2   Estimation

In this section we discuss the Maximum Likelihood estimation method for the ordered regression models. The models are then written in terms of the joint probability distribution for the observed variables y given the explanatory variables and the parameters. Notice again that the variance of ε_i is fixed, and hence it does not have to be estimated.

6.2.1   A general ordered regression model

The likelihood function follows directly from (6.9), that is,

$$L(\theta) = \prod_{i=1}^{N} \prod_{j=1}^{J} \Pr[Y_i = j|\tilde{X}_i]^{I[y_i=j]}$$

$$= \prod_{i=1}^{N} \prod_{j=1}^{J} (F(\alpha_j - \tilde{X}_i\tilde{\beta}) - F(\alpha_{j-1} - \tilde{X}_i\tilde{\beta}))^{I[y_i=j]},$$

(6.19)

where θ summarizes $\alpha = (\alpha_1, \ldots, \alpha_{J-1})$ and $\tilde{\beta} = (\beta_1, \ldots, \beta_K)$ and where the indicator function $I[y_i = j]$ is defined below equation (6.3). Again, the parameters are estimated by maximizing the log-likelihood, which in this case is given by

$$l(\theta) = \sum_{i=1}^{N} \sum_{j=1}^{J} I[y_i = j] \log \Pr[Y_i = j | \tilde{X}_i]$$

$$= \sum_{i=1}^{N} \sum_{j=1}^{J} I[y_i = j] \log\big(F(\alpha_j - \tilde{X}_i \tilde{\beta}) - F(\alpha_{j-1} - \tilde{X}_i \tilde{\beta})\big).$$

(6.20)

Because it is not possible to solve the first-order conditions analytically, we again opt for the familiar Newton–Raphson method. The maximum of the log-likelihood is found by applying

$$\theta_h = \theta_{h-1} - H(\theta_h)^{-1} G(\theta_h)$$

(6.21)

until convergence, where $G(\theta_h)$ and $H(\theta_h)$ are the gradient and Hessian matrix evaluated in θ_h (see also section 3.2.2). The gradient and Hessian matrix are defined as

$$G(\theta) = \frac{\partial l(\theta)}{\partial \theta},$$

$$H(\theta) = \frac{\partial^2 l(\theta)}{\partial \theta \partial \theta'}.$$

(6.22)

The gradient of the log-likelihood (6.20) can be found to be equal to

$$\frac{\partial l(\theta)}{\partial \theta} = \sum_{i=1}^{N} \sum_{j=1}^{J} \left(\frac{I[y_i = j]}{\Pr[Y_i = j | \tilde{X}_i]} \frac{\partial \Pr[Y_i = j | \tilde{X}_i]}{\partial \theta} \right)$$

(6.23)

with

$$\frac{\partial \Pr[Y_i = j | \tilde{X}_i]}{\partial \theta} = \left(\frac{\partial \Pr[Y_i = j | \tilde{X}_i]}{\partial \tilde{\beta}'} \frac{\partial \Pr[Y_i = j | \tilde{X}_i]}{\partial \alpha_1} \cdots \frac{\partial \Pr[Y_i = j | \tilde{X}_i]}{\partial \alpha_{J-1}} \right)'$$

(6.24)

and

$$\frac{\partial \Pr[Y_i = j | \tilde{X}_i]}{\partial \tilde{\beta}} = (f(\alpha_{j-1} - \tilde{X}_i \tilde{\beta}) - f(\alpha_j - \tilde{X}_i \tilde{\beta})) \tilde{X}_i'$$

$$\frac{\partial \Pr[Y_i = j | \tilde{X}_i]}{\partial \alpha_s} = \begin{cases} f(\alpha_s - \tilde{X}_i \tilde{\beta}) & \text{if } s = j \\ -f(\alpha_s - \tilde{X}_i \tilde{\beta}) & \text{if } s = j - 1 \\ 0 & \text{otherwise} \end{cases}$$

(6.25)

where $f(z)$ is $\partial F(z)/\partial z$. The Hessian matrix follows from

$$\frac{\partial^2 l(\theta)}{\partial\theta\partial\theta'} = \sum_{i=1}^{N}\sum_{j=1}^{J}\frac{I[y_i=j]}{\Pr[Y_i=j]^2}$$

$$\left(\Pr[Y_i=j]\frac{\partial^2\Pr[Y_i=j]}{\partial\theta\partial\theta'} - \frac{\partial\Pr[Y_i=j]}{\partial\theta}\frac{\Pr[Y_i=j]}{\partial\theta'}\right),$$

(6.26)

where we use the short notation $\Pr[Y_i=j]$ instead of $\Pr[Y_i=j|\tilde{X}_i]$. The second-order derivative of the probabilities to θ are summarized by

$$\frac{\partial^2\Pr[Y_i=j|\tilde{X}_i]}{\partial\theta\partial\theta'} =$$

$$\begin{pmatrix} \dfrac{\partial^2\Pr[Y_i=j|\tilde{X}_i]}{\partial\tilde{\beta}\partial\tilde{\beta}'} & \dfrac{\partial^2\Pr[Y_i=j|\tilde{X}_i]}{\partial\tilde{\beta}\partial\alpha_1} & \cdots & \dfrac{\partial^2\Pr[Y_i=j|\tilde{X}_i]}{\partial\tilde{\beta}\partial\alpha_{J-1}} \\[2ex] \dfrac{\partial^2\Pr[Y_i=j|\tilde{X}_i]}{\partial\alpha_1\partial\tilde{\beta}'} & \dfrac{\partial^2\Pr[Y_i=j|\tilde{X}_i]}{\partial\alpha_1\partial\alpha_1} & \cdots & \dfrac{\partial^2\Pr[Y_i=j|\tilde{X}_i]}{\partial\alpha_1\partial\alpha_{J-1}} \\[2ex] \vdots & \vdots & \ddots & \vdots \\[2ex] \dfrac{\partial^2\Pr[Y_i=j|\tilde{X}_i]}{\partial\alpha_{J-1}\partial\tilde{\beta}'} & \dfrac{\partial^2\Pr[Y_i=j|\tilde{X}_i]}{\partial\alpha_{J-1}\partial\alpha_1} & \vdots & \dfrac{\partial^2\Pr[Y_i=j|\tilde{X}_i]}{\partial\alpha_{J-1}\partial\alpha_{J-1}} \end{pmatrix}.$$

(6.27)

The elements of this matrix are given by

$$\frac{\partial^2\Pr[Y_i=j|\tilde{X}_i]}{\partial\tilde{\beta}\partial\tilde{\beta}'} = (f'(\alpha_j - \tilde{X}_i\tilde{\beta}) - f'(\alpha_{j-1} - \tilde{X}_i\tilde{\beta}))\tilde{X}_i'\tilde{X}_i$$

$$\frac{\partial^2\Pr[Y_i=j|\tilde{X}_i]}{\partial\tilde{\beta}\partial\alpha_s} = \frac{\partial\Pr[Y_i=j|\tilde{X}_i]}{\partial\alpha_s}\tilde{X}_i' \quad \text{for } s = 1,\ldots,J-1$$

(6.28)

$$\frac{\partial^2\Pr[Y_i=j|\tilde{X}_i]}{\partial\alpha_s\partial\alpha_l} = \begin{cases} f'(\alpha_s - \tilde{X}_i\tilde{\beta}) & \text{if } s=l=j \\ -f'(\alpha_s - \tilde{X}_i\tilde{\beta}) & \text{if } s=l=j-1 \\ 0 & \text{otherwise} \end{cases}$$

where $f'(z)$ equals $\partial f(z)/\partial z$.

Unrestricted optimization of the log-likelihood does not guarantee a feasible solution because the estimated thresholds should obey $\hat{\alpha}_1 < \hat{\alpha}_2 << \hat{\alpha}_{J-1}$. To ensure that this restriction is satisfied, one can consider the following approach. Instead of maximizing over unrestricted α's, one can maximize the log-likelihood over μ's, where these are defined by

$$\alpha_1 = \mu_1$$
$$\alpha_2 = \mu_1 + \mu_2^2 = \alpha_1 + \mu_2^2$$
$$\alpha_3 = \mu_1 + \mu_2^2 + \mu_3^2 = \alpha_2 + \mu_3^2$$

$$\vdots \qquad \vdots \qquad \vdots \qquad\qquad (6.29)$$

$$\alpha_{J-1} = \mu_1 + \sum_{j=2}^{J-1} \mu_j^2 = \alpha_{J-2} + \mu_{J-1}^2.$$

To maximize the log-likelihood one now needs the first- and second-order derivatives with respect to $\mu = (\mu_1, \ldots, \mu_{J-1})$ instead of α. These follow from

$$\frac{\partial l(\theta)}{\partial \mu_s} = \sum_{j=1}^{J-1} \frac{\partial l(\theta)}{\partial \alpha_j} \frac{\partial \alpha_j}{\partial \mu_s},$$

$$\frac{\partial l(\theta)}{\partial \mu_s \partial \mu_l} = \sum_{j=1}^{J-1} \frac{\partial l(\theta)}{\partial \alpha_j} \frac{\partial \alpha_j}{\partial \mu_s \partial \mu_l}, \quad s, l = 1, \ldots, J-1, \qquad (6.30)$$

where

$$\frac{\partial \alpha_j}{\partial \mu_s} = \begin{cases} 1 & \text{if } s = 1 \\ 2\mu_s & \text{if } 1 < s \le j \\ 0 & \text{if } s > j \end{cases} \qquad (6.31)$$

and

$$\frac{\partial \alpha_j}{\partial \mu_s \partial \mu_l} = \begin{cases} 1 & \text{if } s = l = 1 \\ 2\mu_s & \text{if } 1 < s = l \le j \\ 0 & \text{otherwise.} \end{cases} \qquad (6.32)$$

6.2.2 The Ordered Logit and Probit models

The expressions in the previous subsection hold for any ordered regression model. If one decides to use the Ordered Logit model, the above expressions can be simplified using the property of the standardized logistic distribution that implies that

$$f(z) = \lambda(z) = \frac{\partial \Lambda(z)}{\partial z} = \Lambda(z)(1 - \Lambda(z)), \qquad (6.33)$$

and

$$f'(z) = \lambda'(z) = \frac{\partial \lambda(z)}{\partial z} = \lambda(z)(1 - 2\Lambda(z)). \qquad (6.34)$$

For the Ordered Probit model, we use the property of the standard normal distribution, and therefore we have

$$f(z) = \phi(z) = \frac{\partial \Phi(z)}{\partial z}$$

$$f'(z) = \phi'(z) = \frac{\partial \phi(z)}{\partial z} = -z\phi(z).$$

(6.35)

In Pratt (1981) it is shown that the ML estimation routine for the Ordered Probit model always converges to a global maximum of the likelihood function.

6.2.3   *Visualizing estimation results*

As mentioned above, it may not be trivial to interpret the estimated parameters for the marketing problem at hand. One possibility for examining the relevance of explanatory variables is to examine graphs of

$$\hat{\Pr}[Y_i \leq j | \tilde{X}_i] = \sum_{m=1}^{j} \hat{\Pr}[Y_i = m | \tilde{X}_i]$$

(6.36)

for each j against one of the explanatory variables in $\tilde{X}_i$. To save on the number of graphs, one should fix the value of all variables in $\tilde{X}_i$ to their mean levels, except for the variable of interest. Similarly, one can depict

$$\hat{\Pr}[Y_i = j | \tilde{X}_i] = F(\hat{\alpha}_j - \tilde{X}_i \hat{\beta}) - F(\hat{\alpha}_{j-1} - \tilde{X}_i \hat{\beta})$$

(6.37)

against one of the explanatory variables, using a comparable strategy.

Finally, it may also be insightful to present the estimated quasi-elasticities

$$\frac{\partial \hat{\Pr}[Y_i = j | \tilde{X}_i]}{\partial x_{k,i}} x_{k,i}$$

(6.38)

against the k'th variable $x_{k,i}$, while setting other variables at a fixed value.

6.3   Diagnostics, model selection and forecasting

Once the parameters in ordered regression models have been estimated, it is important to check the empirical adequacy of the model. If the model is found to be adequate, one may consider deleting possibly redundant variables. Finally, one may evaluate the models on within-sample or out-of-sample forecasting performance.

6.3.1   Diagnostics

Diagnostic tests for the ordered regression models are again to be based on the residuals (see also, Murphy, 1996). Ideally one would want to be able to estimate the values of ε_i in the latent regression model $y_i^* = X_i\beta + \varepsilon_i$, but unfortunately these values cannot be obtained because y_i^* is an unobserved variable. A useful definition of residuals can now be obtained from considering the first-order conditions concerning the $\tilde{\beta}$ parameters in the ML estimation method. From (6.23) and (6.24) we can see that these first-order conditions are

$$\frac{\partial l(\theta)}{\partial \tilde{\beta}} = \sum_{i=1}^{N} \sum_{j=1}^{J} I[y_i = j]\tilde{X}_i' \left(\frac{f(\hat{\alpha}_{j-1} - \tilde{X}_i\hat{\tilde{\beta}}) - f(\hat{\alpha}_j - \tilde{X}_i\hat{\tilde{\beta}})}{F(\hat{\alpha}_j - \tilde{X}_i\hat{\tilde{\beta}}) - F(\hat{\alpha}_{j-1} - \tilde{X}_i\hat{\tilde{\beta}})} \right) = 0.$$

$$(6.39)$$

This suggests the possible usefulness of the residuals

$$\hat{e}_i = \frac{f(\hat{\alpha}_{j-1} - \tilde{X}_i\hat{\tilde{\beta}}) - f(\hat{\alpha}_j - \tilde{X}_i\hat{\tilde{\beta}})}{F(\hat{\alpha}_j - \tilde{X}_i\hat{\tilde{\beta}}) - F(\hat{\alpha}_{j-1} - \tilde{X}_i\hat{\tilde{\beta}})}.$$

$$(6.40)$$

As before, these residuals can be called the generalized residuals. Large values of $\hat{e}_i$ may indicate the presence of outlying observations. Once these have been detected, one may consider deleting these and estimating the model parameters again.

The key assumption of an ordered regression model is that the explanatory variable is discrete and ordered. An informal check of the presumed ordering can be based on the notion that

$$\Pr[Y_i \le j|\tilde{X}_i] = \sum_{m=1}^{j} \Pr[Y_i = m|\tilde{X}_i]$$

$$(6.41)$$

$$= F(\alpha_j - \tilde{X}_i\tilde{\beta}),$$

which implies that the ordered regression model combines $J - 1$ models for the binomial dependent variable $Y_i \le j$ and $Y_i > j$. Notice that these $J - 1$ binomial models all have the same parameters $\tilde{\beta}$ for the explanatory variables. The informal check amounts to estimating the parameters of these $J - 1$ models, and examining whether or not this equality indeed holds in practice. A formal Hausman-type test is proposed in Brant (1990); see also Long (1997, pp. 143–144).

6.3.2   Model selection

The significance of each explanatory variable can be based on its individual z-score, which can be obtained from the relevant parameter estimates combined with the square root of the diagonal elements of the estimated covariance matrix. The significance of a set of, say, g variables can be examined by using a Likelihood Ratio test. The corresponding test statistic can be calculated as

$$\text{LR} = -2\log\frac{L(\hat{\theta}_N)}{L(\hat{\theta}_A)} = -2(l(\hat{\theta}_N) - l(\hat{\theta}_A)), \tag{6.42}$$

where $l(\hat{\theta}_A)$ is the maximum of the log-likelihood under the alternative hypothesis that the g variables cannot be deleted and $l(\hat{\theta}_N)$ is the maximum value of the log-likelihood under the null hypothesis with the restrictions imposed. Under the null hypothesis that the g variables are redundant, it holds that

$$\text{LR} \overset{a}{\sim} \chi^2(g). \tag{6.43}$$

The null hypothesis is rejected if the value of LR is sufficiently large when compared with the critical values of the $\chi^2(g)$ distribution. If $g = K$, this LR test can be considered as a measure of the overall fit.

To evaluate the model one can also use a pseudo-R^2 type of measure. In the case of an ordered regression model, such an R^2 can be defined by

$$R^2 = 1 - \frac{l(\hat{\theta})}{l(\hat{\alpha})}, \tag{6.44}$$

where $l(\hat{\alpha})$ here denotes that an ordered regression model contains only $J - 1$ intercepts.

The R^2 proposed in McKelvey and Zavoina (1975) is particularly useful for an ordered regression model. This R^2 measures the ratio of the variance of $\hat{y}_i^*$ and the variance of y_i^*, where $\hat{y}_i^*$ equals $\tilde{X}_i\tilde{\beta}$, and it is given by

$$R^2 = \frac{\sum_{i=1}^{N}(\hat{y}_i^* - \bar{y}_i^*)^2}{\sum_{i=1}^{N}(\hat{y}_i^* - \bar{y}_i^*)^2 + N\sigma^2}, \tag{6.45}$$

where $\bar{y}_i^*$ denotes the average value of $\hat{y}_i^*$. Naturally, $\sigma^2 = \frac{1}{3}\pi^2$ in the Ordered Logit model and $\sigma^2 = 1$ in the Ordered Probit model.

If one has more than one model within the Ordered Logit or Ordered Probit class of models, one may also consider the familiar Akaike and Schwarz information criteria (see section 4.3.2).

6.3.3   Forecasting

Another way to evaluate the empirical performance of an Ordered Regression model amounts to evaluating its in-sample and out-of-sample forecasting performance. Forecasting here means that one examines the ability of the model to yield a correct classification of the dependent variable, given the explanatory variables. This classification emerges from

$$\hat{\Pr}(Y_i = j | \tilde{X}_i) = F(\hat{\alpha}_j - \tilde{X}_i \hat{\beta}) - F(\hat{\alpha}_{j-1} - \tilde{X}_i \hat{\beta}), \tag{6.46}$$

where the category with the highest probability is favored.

In principle one can use the same kind of evaluation techniques for the hit rate as were considered for the models for a multinomial dependent variable in the previous chapter. A possible modification can be given by the fact that misclassification is more serious if the model does not classify individuals to categories adjacent to the correct ones. One may choose to give weights to the off-diagonal elements of the prediction–realization table.

6.4   Modeling risk profiles of individuals

In this section we illustrate the Ordered Logit and Probit models for the classification of individuals into three risk profiles. Category 1 should be associated with individuals who do not take much risk, as they, for example, only have a savings account. In contrast, category 3 corresponds with those who apparently are willing to take high financial risk, like those who often trade in financial derivatives. The financial investment firm is of course interested as to which observable characteristics of individuals, which are contained in their customer database, have predictive value for this classification. We have at our disposal information on 2,000 clients of the investment firm, 329 of whom had been assigned (beyond our control) to the high-risk category, and 531 to the low-risk category. Additionally, we have information on four explanatory variables. Three of the four variables amount to counts, that is, the number of funds of type 2 and the number of transactions of type 1 and 3. The fourth variable, that is wealth, is a continuous variable and corresponds to monetary value. We refer to chapter 2 for a more detailed discussion of the data.

In table 6.1 we report the ML parameter estimates for the Ordered Logit and Ordered Probit models. It can be seen that several parameters have the expected sign and are also statistically significant. The wealth variable and the transactions of type 1 variable do not seem to be relevant. When we compare the parameter estimates across the two models, we observe that the Logit parameters are approximately

Table 6.1 *Estimation results for Ordered Logit and Ordered Probit models for risk profiles*

	Logit model		Probit model	
Variable	Parameter	Standard error	Parameter	Standard error
Funds of type 2	0.191***	(0.013)	0.105***	(0.008)
Transactions of type 1	−0.009	(0.016)	−0.007	(0.010)
Transactions of type 3	0.052***	(0.016)	0.008***	(0.002)
Wealth (NLG 100,000)	0.284	(0.205)	0.173	(0.110)
$\hat{\alpha}_1$	−0.645***	(0.060)	−0.420***	(0.035)
$\hat{\alpha}_2$	2.267***	(0.084)	1.305***	(0.044)
max. log-likelihood value	−1818.49		−1826.69	

Notes:
*** Significant at the 0.01 level, ** at the 0.05 level, * at the 0.10 level
The total number of observations is 2,000, of which 329 concern the high-risk profile, 1,140 the intermediate profile and 531 the low-risk profile.

$$\sqrt{\frac{1}{3}\pi^2}$$

times the Probit parameters, as expected. Notice that this of course also applies to the α parameters. Both α_1 and α_2 are significant. The confidence intervals of these threshold parameters do not overlap, and hence there seems no need to reduce the number of categories.

The McFadden R^2 (6.44) of the estimated Ordered Logit model is 0.062, while it is 0.058 for the Ordered Probit model. This does not seem very large, but the LR test statistics for the significance of the four variables, that is, only the $\tilde{\beta}$ parameters, are 240.60 for the Ordered Logit model and 224.20 for the Ordered Probit model. Hence, it seems that the explanatory variables contribute substantially to the fit. The McKelvey and Zavoina R^2 measure (6.45) equals 0.28 and 0.14 for the Logit and Probit specifications, respectively.

In table 6.2 we report on the estimation results for two binomial dependent variable models, where we confine the focus to the Logit model. In the first case the binomial variable is $Y_i \leq 1$ and $Y_i > 1$, where the first outcome gets associated with 0 and the second with 1; in the second case we consider $Y_i \leq 2$ and $Y_i > 2$. If we compare the two columns with parameter estimates in table 6.2 with those of the Ordered Logit model in table 6.1, we see that

Table 6.2 *Estimation results for two binomial Logit models for cumulative risk profiles*

	$Y_i > 1$		$Y_i > 2$	
Variables	Parameter	Standard error	Parameter	Standard error
Intercept	0.595***	(0.069)	−2.298***	(0.092)
Funds of type 2	0.217***	(0.027)	0.195***	(0.018)
Transactions of type 1	−0.001	(0.018)	−0.014	(0.029)
Transactions of type 3	0.054**	(0.024)	0.064***	(0.014)
Wealth (NLG 100,000)	0.090	(0.279)	0.414	(0.295)
max. log-likelihood value	−1100.97		−789.39	

Notes:
*** Significant at the 0.01 level, ** at the 0.05 level, * at the 0.10 level
For the model for $Y_i > 1$, 1,149 observations are 1 and 531 are 0, while, for the model for $Y_i > 2$, 329 are 1 and 1,671 are 0.

the parameters apart from the intercepts have the same sign and are roughly similar. This suggests that the presumed ordering is present and hence that the Ordered Logit model is appropriate.

We continue with an analysis of the estimation results for the Ordered Logit model. In figures 6.2 and 6.3 we depict the quasi-elasticities (6.17) of the number of type 2 funds and of transactions of type 3 for each class, respectively. The other explanatory variables are set at their mean values. Note that the three elasticities sum to zero. Figure 6.2 shows that the quasi-elasticity of the number of type 2 funds for the low-risk class is relatively close to zero. The same is true if we consider the quasi-elasticity of type 3 transactions (see figure 6.3). The shapes of the elasticities for the other classes are also rather similar. The scale, however, is different. This is not surprising because the estimated parameters for type 2 funds and type 3 transactions are both positive but different in size (see table 6.1). The quasi-elasticity for the high-risk class rises until the number of type 2 funds is about 15, after which the elasticity becomes smaller again. For the quasi-elasticity with respect to the number of type 3 transactions, the peak is at about 50. For the middle-risk class we observe the opposite pattern. The quasi-elasticity mainly decreases until the number of type 2 funds is about 15 (or the number of type 3 transactions is about 50) and increases afterwards. The figures suggest that both variables mainly explain the classification between high risk and middle risk.

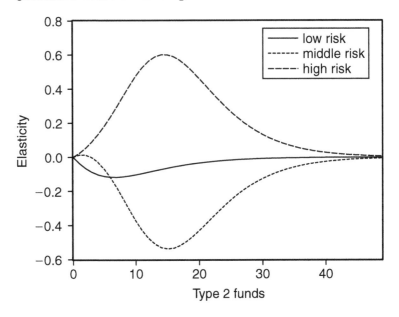

Figure 6.2   Quasi-elasticities of type 2 funds for each category

If we generate within-sample forecasts for the Ordered Logit model, we obtain that none of the individuals gets classified in the low-risk category (whereas there are 531), 1,921 are assigned to the middle category (which is much more than the true 1,140) and 79 to the top category (which has 329 observations). The corresponding forecasts for the Ordered Probit model are 0, 1,936 and 64. These results suggest that the explanatory variables do not have substantial explanatory value for the classification. Indeed, most individuals get classified into the middle category. We can also compute the prediction–realization table for the Ordered Logit model, that is,

	low	Predicted middle	high	
Observed				
low	0.000	0.266	0.001	0.266
middle	0.000	0.556	0.015	0.570
high	0.000	0.140	0.025	0.165
	0.000	0.961	0.040	1

where small inconsistencies in the table are due to rounding errors. We observe that 58% of the individuals get correctly classified.

To compare the forecasting performance of the Ordered Logit model with an unordered choice model, we calculate the same kind of table based on a Multinomial Logit model and obtain

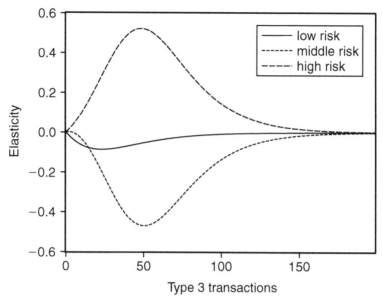

Figure 6.3 Quasi-elasticities of type 3 transactions for each category

		Predicted		
	low	middle	high	
Observed				
low	0.000	0.265	0.001	0.266
middle	0.000	0.555	0.015	0.570
high	0.000	0.137	0.028	0.165
	0.000	0.957	0.044	1

where again small inconsistencies in the table are due to rounding errors. For this model we also correctly classify about 58% of the individuals. We see that the forecasting results for the two types of model are almost the same.

6.5 Advanced topics

In this section we discuss two advanced topics for the ordered regression model. As the illustration in the previous section indicates, it may be that the common parameter $\tilde{\beta}$ for all categories is too restrictive. In the literature, alternative models have been proposed for ordered categorical data, and three of these will be mentioned in section 6.5.1. A second observation from the illustration is that there is one category with most of the observations. Suppose one has to collect data and it is known that one of the category outcomes outnumbers the others, one may decide to apply selective sampling. In section 6.5.2 we discuss how one should modify the likelihood in the case where one considers selective draws from the available data.

6.5.1 Related models for an ordered variable

Other models for an ordered variable often start with a log odds ratio. For the ordered regression models discussed so far, this is given by

$$\log\left(\frac{\Pr[Y_i \leq j|\tilde{X}_i]}{\Pr[Y_i > j|\tilde{X}_i]}\right). \tag{6.47}$$

However, one may also want to consider

$$\log\left(\frac{\Pr[Y_i = j|\tilde{X}_i]}{\Pr[Y_i = j+1|\tilde{X}_i]}\right) = \alpha_j - \tilde{X}_i\tilde{\beta}, \tag{6.48}$$

which results in the so-called Adjacent Categories model, which corresponds with a set of connected models for binomial dependent variables.

The model that is closest to a model for a multinomial dependent variable is the stereotype model, that is,

$$\log\left(\frac{\Pr[Y_i = j|\tilde{X}_i]}{\Pr[Y_i = m|\tilde{X}_i]}\right) = \alpha_j - \tilde{X}_i\tilde{\beta}_j, \tag{6.49}$$

where it is imposed that $\alpha_1 < \alpha_2 < \ldots < \alpha_{J-1}$. Through $\tilde{\beta}_j$, the explanatory variables now have different effects on the outcome categories. A recent lucid survey of some of these and other models is given in Agresti (1999).

6.5.2 Selective sampling

When a market researcher makes an endogenous selection of the available observations or the observations to be collected, the estimation method needs to be adjusted. Recall that the true probabilities in the population for customer i and category j are

$$\Pr[Y_i = j|\tilde{X}_i] = F(\alpha_j - \tilde{X}_i\tilde{\beta}) - F(\alpha_{j-1} - \tilde{X}_i\tilde{\beta}). \tag{6.50}$$

When the full sample is a random sample from the population with sampling fraction λ, the probabilities that individual i is in the observed sample and is a member of class $1, 2, \ldots J$ are $\lambda \Pr[Y_i = j|\tilde{X}_i]$. These probabilities do not sum to 1 because it is also possible that an individual is not present in the sample, which happens with probability $(1 - \lambda)$. If, however, the number of observations in class j is reduced by γ_j, where the deleted observations are selected at random, these probabilities become $\lambda \gamma_j \Pr[Y_i = j | \tilde{X}_i]$. Of course, when all observations are considered then $\gamma_j = 1$. Note that γ_j is not an unknown parameter but is set by the researcher.

To simplify notation, we write $\Pr[Y_i = j]$ instead of $\Pr[Y_i = j | \tilde{X}_i]$. The probability of observing $Y_i = j$ in the reduced sample is now given by

$$\frac{\lambda \gamma_j \Pr[Y_i = j]}{\sum_{l=1}^{J} \lambda \gamma_l \Pr[Y_i = l]} = \frac{\gamma_j \Pr[Y_i = j]}{\sum_{l=1}^{J} \gamma_l \Pr[Y_i = l]}. \tag{6.51}$$

With these adjusted probabilities, we can construct the modified log-likelihood function as

$$l(\theta) = \sum_{i=1}^{N} \sum_{j=1}^{J} I[y_i = j] \log\left(\frac{\gamma_j \Pr[Y_i = j]}{\sum_{l=1}^{J} \gamma_l \Pr[Y_i = l]}\right). \tag{6.52}$$

To optimize the likelihood we need the derivatives of the log-likelihood to the parameters β and α. The first-order derivatives are

$$\frac{\partial l(\theta)}{\partial \theta} = \sum_{i=1}^{N} \sum_{j=1}^{J} \left(\frac{I[y_i = j]}{\Pr[Y_i = j]} \frac{\partial \Pr[Y_i = j]}{\partial \theta} - \frac{I[y_i = j]}{\sum_{l=1}^{J} \gamma_l \Pr[Y_i = l]} \frac{\partial \sum_{l=1}^{J} \gamma_l \Pr[Y_i = l]}{\partial \theta}\right), \tag{6.53}$$

where we need the additional derivative

$$\frac{\partial \sum_{l=1}^{J} \gamma_l \Pr[Y_i = l]}{\partial \theta} = \sum_{l=1}^{J} \gamma_l \frac{\partial \Pr[Y_i = l]}{\partial \theta}. \tag{6.54}$$

The second-order derivatives now become

$$\frac{\partial^2 l(\theta)}{\partial \theta \partial \theta'} = \sum_{i=1}^{N} \sum_{j=1}^{J} \left(\frac{I[y_i = j]}{\Pr[Y_i = j]^2}\right.$$

$$\left(\Pr[Y_i = j] \frac{\partial^2 \Pr[Y_i = j]}{\partial \theta \partial \theta'} - \frac{\partial \Pr[Y_i = j]}{\partial \theta} \frac{\partial \Pr[Y_i = j]}{\partial \theta'}\right)$$

$$+ \frac{I[y_i = j]}{\left(\sum_{l=1}^{J} \gamma_l \Pr[Y_i = l]\right)^2}$$

$$\left(\sum_{l=1}^{J} \gamma_l \Pr[Y_i = l] \frac{\partial^2 \sum_{l=1}^{J} \gamma_l \Pr[Y_i = 1]}{\partial \theta \partial \theta'} - \frac{\partial \sum_{l=1}^{J} \gamma_l \Pr[Y_i = l]}{\partial \theta}\right.$$

$$\left.\left.\frac{\partial \sum_{l=1}^{J} \gamma_l \Pr[Y_i = l]}{\partial \theta'}\right)\right), \tag{6.55}$$

where one additionally needs that

$$\frac{\partial^2 \sum_{l=1}^{J} \gamma_l \Pr[Y_i = l]}{\partial \theta \partial \theta'} = \sum_{l=1}^{J} \gamma_l \frac{\partial^2 \Pr[Y_i = l]}{\partial \theta \partial \theta'}. \qquad (6.56)$$

A detailed account of this method, as well as an illustration, appears in Fok et al. (1999).

7 A limited dependent variable

In chapter 3 we considered the standard Linear Regression model, where the dependent variable is a continuous random variable. The model assumes that we observe all values of this dependent variable, in the sense that there are no missing observations. Sometimes, however, this is not the case. For example, one may have observations on expenditures of households in relation to regular shopping trips. This implies that one observes only expenditures that exceed, say, $10 because shopping trips with expenditures of less than $10 are not registered. In this case we call expenditure a truncated variable, where truncation occurs at $10. Another example concerns the profits of stores, where losses (that is, negative profits) are perhaps not observed. The profit variable is then also a truncated variable, where the point of truncation is now equal to 0. The standard Regression model in chapter 3 cannot be used to correlate a truncated dependent variable with explanatory variables because it does not directly take into account the truncation. In fact, one should consider the so-called Truncated Regression model.

In marketing research it can also occur that a dependent variable is censored. For example, if one is interested in the demand for theater tickets, one usually observes only the number of tickets actually sold. If, however, the theater is sold out, the actual demand may be larger than the maximum capacity of the theater, but we observe only the maximum capacity. Hence, the dependent variable is either smaller than the maximum capacity or equal to the maximum capacity of the theater. Such a variable is called censored. Another example concerns the donation behavior of individuals to charity. Individuals may donate a positive amount to charity or they may donate nothing. The dependent variable takes a value of 0 or a positive value. Note that, in contrast to a truncated variable, one does observe the donations of individuals who give nothing, which is of course 0. In practice, one may want to relate censored dependent variables to explanatory variables using a regression-type model. For example, the donation behavior may be explained by the age and income of the individual. The regression-type models to describe censored dependent variables are closely related to the Truncated Regression models. Models concerning censored dependent variables are known as Tobit models, named after Tobin (1958) by Goldberger (1964). In this chapter we will discuss the Truncated Regression model and the Censored Regression model.

   The outline of this chapter is as follows. In section 7.1 we discuss the representation and interpretation of the Truncated Regression model. Additionally, we consider two types of the Censored Regression model, the Type-1 and Type-2 Tobit models. Section 7.2 deals with Maximum Likelihood estimation of the parameters of the Truncated and Censored Regression models. In section 7.3 we consider diagnostic measures, model selection and forecasting. In section 7.4 we apply two Tobit models to describe the charity donations data discussed in section 2.2.5. Finally, in section 7.5 we consider two other types of Tobit model.

7.1   Representation and interpretation

   In this section we discuss important properties of the Truncated and Censored Regression models. We also illustrate the potential effects of neglecting the fact that observations of the dependent variable are limited.

7.1.1   Truncated Regression model

   Suppose that one observes a continuous random variable, indicated by Y_i, only if the variable is larger than 0. To relate this variable to a single explanatory variable x_i, one can use the regression model

$$Y_i = \beta_0 + \beta_1 x_i + \varepsilon_i \quad Y_i > 0, \text{ for } i = 1, \dots, N, \tag{7.1}$$

with $\varepsilon_i \sim N(0, \sigma^2)$. This model is called a Truncated Regression model, with the point of truncation equal to 0. Note that values of Y_i smaller than zero may occur, but that these are not observed by the researcher. This corresponds to the example above, where one observes only the positive profits of a store. It follows from (7.1) that the probability of observing Y_i is

$$\begin{aligned}
\Pr[Y_i > 0 | x_i] &= \Pr[\beta_0 + \beta_1 x_i + \varepsilon_i > 0] \\
&= \Pr[\varepsilon_i > -\beta_0 - \beta_1 x_i] = 1 - \Phi(-(\beta_0 + \beta_1 x_i)/\sigma),
\end{aligned}$$
$$\tag{7.2}$$

where $\Phi(\cdot)$ is again the cumulative distribution function of a standard normal distribution. This implies that the density function of the random variable Y_i is not the familiar density function of a normal distribution. In fact, to obtain the density function for positive Y_i values we have to condition on the fact that Y_i is observed. Hence, the density function reads

$$f(y_i) = \begin{cases} \dfrac{1}{\sigma} \dfrac{\phi((y_i - \beta_0 - \beta_1 x_i)/\sigma)}{1 - \Phi(-(\beta_0 + \beta_1 x_i)/\sigma)} & \text{if } y_i > 0 \\ \\ 0 & \text{if } y_i \leq 0, \end{cases} \tag{7.3}$$

where as before $\phi(\cdot)$ denotes the density function of a standard normal distribution defined as

$$\phi(z) = \frac{1}{\sqrt{2\pi}} \exp\left(-\frac{z^2}{2}\right), \tag{7.4}$$

(see also section A.2 in the Appendix).

To illustrate the Truncated Regression model, we depict in figure 7.1 a set of simulated y_i and x_i, generated by the familiar DGP, that is,

$$x_i = 0.0001i + \varepsilon_{1,i} \quad \text{with } \varepsilon_{1,i} \sim N(0, 1)$$

$$y_i = -2 + x_i + \varepsilon_{2,i} \quad \text{with } \varepsilon_{2,i} \sim N(0, 1), \tag{7.5}$$

where $i = 1, 2, \ldots, N$. In this figure we do not include the observations for which $y_i \leq 0$. The line in this graph is the estimated regression line based on OLS (see chapter 3). We readily notice that the estimated slope of the line $(\hat{\beta}_1)$ is smaller than 1, whereas (7.5) implies that it should be approximately equal to 1. Additionally, the estimated intercept parameter $(\hat{\beta}_0)$ is larger than -2.

The regression line in figure 7.1 suggests that neglecting the truncation can lead to biased estimators. To understand this formally, consider the expected value of Y_i for $Y_i > 0$. This expectation is not equal to $\beta_0 + \beta_1 x_i$ as in the standard Regression model, but is

$$E[Y_i | Y_i > 0, x_i] = \beta_0 + \beta_1 x_i + E[\varepsilon_i | \varepsilon_i > -\beta_0 - \beta_1 x_i]$$

$$= \beta_0 + \beta_1 x_i + \sigma \frac{\phi(-(\beta_0 + \beta_1 x_i)/\sigma)}{1 - \Phi(-(\beta_0 + \beta_1 x_i)/\sigma)}, \tag{7.6}$$

where we have used that $E[Z|Z > 0]$ for a normal random variable Z with mean μ and variance σ^2 equals $\mu + \sigma\phi(-\mu/\sigma)/(1 - \Phi(-\mu/\sigma))$ (see Johnson and Kotz, 1970, p. 81, and section A.2 in the Appendix). The term

$$\lambda(z) = \frac{\phi(z)}{1 - \Phi(z)} \tag{7.7}$$

is known in the literature as the inverse Mills ratio. In chapter 8 we will return to this function when we discuss models for a duration dependent variable. The expression in (7.6) indicates that a standard Regression model for y_i on x_i neglects the variable $\lambda(-(\beta_0 + \beta_1 x_i)/\sigma)$, and hence it is misspecified, which in turn leads to biased estimators for β_0 and β_1.

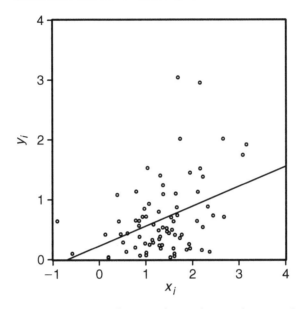

Figure 7.1   Scatter diagram of y_i against x_i given $y_i > 0$

For the case of no truncation, the β_1 parameter in (7.1) represents the partial derivative of Y_i to x_i and hence it describes the effect of the explanatory variable x_i on Y_i. Additionally, if $x_i = 0$, β_0 represents the mean of Y_i in the case of no truncation. Hence, we can use these β parameters to draw inferences for all (including the non-observed) y_i observations. For example, the β_1 parameter measures the effect of the explanatory variable x_i if one considers all stores. In contrast, if one is interested only in the effect of x_i on the profit of stores with only positive profits, one has to consider the partial derivative of the expectation of Y_i given that $Y_i > 0$ with respect to x_i, that is,

$$\frac{\partial E[Y_i | Y_i > 0, x_i]}{\partial x_i} = \beta_1 + \sigma \frac{\partial \lambda(-(\beta_0 + \beta_1 x_i)/\sigma)}{\partial x_i}$$
$$= \beta_1 + \sigma(\lambda_i^2 - (-(\beta_0 + \beta_1 x_i)/\sigma)\lambda_i)(-\beta_1/\sigma) \quad (7.8)$$
$$= \beta_1(1 - \lambda_i^2 + (-(\beta_0 + \beta_1 x_i)/\sigma)\lambda_i)$$
$$= \beta_1 w_i,$$

where $\lambda_i = \lambda(-(\beta_0 + \beta_1 x_i)/\sigma)$ and we use $\partial\lambda(z)/\partial z = \lambda(z)^2 - z\lambda(z)$. It turns out that the variance of Y_i given $Y_i > 0$ is equal to $\sigma^2 w_i$ (see, for example, Johnson and Kotz, 1970, p. 81, or section A.2 in the Appendix). Because the variance of Y_i given $Y_i > 0$ is smaller than σ^2 owing to truncation, w_i is smaller than 1. This in turn implies that the partial derivative is smaller than β_1 in absolute value for any value of x_i. Hence, for the truncated data the effect of x_i is smaller than for all data.

In this subsection we have assumed so far that the point of truncation is 0. Sometimes the point of truncation is positive, as in the example on regular shopping trips, or negative. If the point of truncation is c instead of 0, one just has to replace $\beta_0 + \beta_1 x_i$ by $c + \beta_0 + \beta_1 x_i$ in the discussion above. It is also possible to have a sample of observations truncated from above. In that case Y_i is observed only if it is smaller than a threshold c. One may also encounter situations where the data are truncated from both below and above. Similar results for the effects of x_i can now be derived.

7.1.2 Censored Regression model

The Truncated Regression model concerns a dependent variable that is observed only beyond a certain threshold level. It may, however, also occur that the dependent variable is censored. For example, the dependent variable Y_i can be 0 or a positive value. To illustrate the effects of censoring we consider again the DGP in (7.5). Instead of deleting observations for which y_i is smaller than zero, we set negative y_i observations equal to 0.

Figure 7.2 displays such a set of simulated y_i and x_i observations. The straight line in the graph denotes the estimated regression line using OLS (see chapter 3). Again, the intercept of the regression is substantially larger than the -2 in the data generating process because the intersection of the regression line with the y-axis is about -0.5. The slope of the regression line is clearly smaller than 1, which is of course due to the censored observations, which take the value 0. This graph illustrates that including censored observations in a standard Regression model may lead to a bias in the OLS estimator of its parameters.

To describe a censored dependent variable, several models have been proposed in the literature. In this subsection we discuss two often applied Censored Regression models. The first model is the basic Type-1 Tobit model introduced by Tobin (1958). This model consists of a single equation. The second model is the Type-2 Tobit model, which more or less describes the censored and non-censored observations in two separate equations.

Type-1 Tobit model

The idea behind the standard Tobit model is related to the Probit model for a binary dependent variable discussed in chapter 4. In section 4.1.1 it was shown that the Probit model assumes that the binary dependent variable Y_i is 0 if an unobserved latent variable y_i^* is smaller than or equal to zero and 1 if this latent variable is positive. For the latent variable one considers a

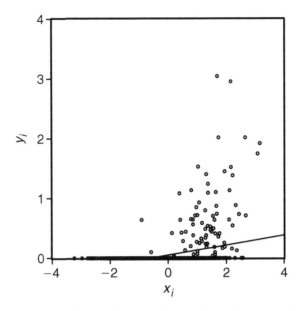

Figure 7.2　Scatter diagram of y_i against x_i for censored y_i

standard Linear Regression model $y_i^* = X_i\beta + \varepsilon_i$ with $\varepsilon_i \sim N(0, 1)$, where X_i contains $K + 1$ explanatory variables including an intercept. The extension to a Tobit model for a censored dependent variable is now straightforward. The censored variable Y_i is 0 if the unobserved latent variable y_i^* is smaller than or equal to zero and $Y_i = y_i^*$ if y_i^* is positive, which in short-hand notation is

$$Y_i = X_i\beta + \varepsilon_i \quad \text{if } y_i^* = X_i\beta + \varepsilon_i > 0$$
$$Y_i = 0 \qquad\quad \text{if } y_i^* = X_i\beta + \varepsilon_i \leq 0, \tag{7.9}$$

with $\varepsilon_i \sim N(0, \sigma^2)$.

For the observations y_i that are zero, we know only that

$$\Pr[Y_i = 0|X_i] = \Pr[X_i\beta + \varepsilon_i \leq 0|X_i] = \Pr[\varepsilon_i \leq -X_i\beta|X_i]$$
$$= \Phi(-X_i\beta/\sigma). \tag{7.10}$$

This probability is the same as in the Probit model. Likewise, the probability that $Y_i = y_i^* > 0$ corresponds with $\Pr[Y_i = 1|X_i]$ in the Probit model (see (4.12)). Note that, in contrast to the Probit model, we do not have to impose the restriction $\sigma = 1$ in the Tobit model because the positive observations of the dependent variable y_i identify the variance of ε_i. If we consider the charity donation example, probability (7.10) denotes the probability that individual i does not give to charity.

The expected donation of an individual, to stick to the charity example, follows from the expected value of Y_i given X_i, that is,

$$
\begin{aligned}
\mathrm{E}[Y_i|X_i] &= \mathrm{Pr}[Y_i = 0|X_i]\mathrm{E}[Y_i|Y_i = 0, X_i] \\
&\quad + \mathrm{Pr}[Y_i > 0|X_i]\mathrm{E}[Y_i|Y_i > 0, X_i] \\
&= 0 + (1 - \Phi(-X_i\beta/\sigma))\left(X_i\beta + \sigma\frac{\phi(-X_i\beta/\sigma)}{(1 - \Phi(-X_i\beta/\sigma))}\right) \\
&= (1 - \Phi(-X_i\beta/\sigma))X_i\beta + \sigma\phi(-X_i\beta/\sigma),
\end{aligned}
$$

(7.11)

where $\mathrm{E}[Y_i|Y_i > 0, X_i]$ is given in (7.6). The explanatory variables X_i affect the expectation of the dependent variable Y_i in two ways. First of all, from (7.10) it follows that for a positive element of β an increase in the corresponding component of X_i increases the probability that Y_i is larger than 0. In terms of our charity donation example, a larger value of X_i thus results in a larger probability of donating to charity. Secondly, an increase in X_i also affects the conditional mean of the positive observations. Hence, for individuals who give to charity, a larger value of X_i also implies that the expected donated amount is larger.

The total effect of a change in the k'th explanatory variable $x_{k,i}$ on the expectation of Y_i follows from

$$
\begin{aligned}
\frac{\partial\mathrm{E}[Y_i|X_i]}{\partial x_{k,i}} &= (1 - \Phi(-X_i\beta/\sigma))\beta_k - X_i\beta\phi(-X_i\beta/\sigma)\beta_k/\sigma \\
&\quad + \sigma\phi(-X_i\beta/\sigma)(-X_i\beta/\sigma)(-\beta_k/\sigma) \\
&= (1 - \Phi(-X_i\beta/\sigma))\beta_k.
\end{aligned}
$$

(7.12)

Because $(1 - \Phi(-X_i\beta/\sigma))$ is always positive, the direction of the effect of an increase in $x_{k,i}$ on the expectation of Y_i is completely determined by the sign of the β parameter.

The Type-1 Tobit model assumes that the parameters for the effect of the explanatory variables on the probability that an observation is censored and the effect on the conditional mean of the non-censored observations are the same. This may be true if we consider for example the demand for theater tickets, but may be unrealistic if we consider charity donating behavior. In the remainder of this subsection we discuss the Type-2 Tobit model, which relaxes this assumption.

Type-2 Tobit model

The standard Tobit model presented above can be written as a combination of two already familiar models. The first model is a Probit model, which determines whether the y_i variable is zero or positive, that is,

$$Y_i = 0 \quad \text{if } X_i\beta + \varepsilon_i \leq 0$$
$$Y_i > 0 \quad \text{if } X_i\beta + \varepsilon_i > 0$$
(7.13)

(see chapter 4), and the second model is a Truncated Regression model for the positive values of Y_i, that is,

$$Y_i = y_i^* = X_i\beta + \varepsilon_i \quad Y_i > 0.$$
(7.14)

The difference from the Probit model is that in the Probit specification we never observe y_i^*, whereas in the Tobit model we observe y_i^* if y_i^* is larger than zero. In that case y_i^* is equal to y_i.

The two models in the Type-1 Tobit model contain the same explanatory variables X_i with the same β parameters and the same error term ε_i. It is of course possible to relax this assumption and allow for different parameters and error terms in both models. An example is

$$Y_i = 0 \qquad\quad \text{if } y_i^* = X_i\alpha + \varepsilon_{1,i} \leq 0$$
$$Y_i = X_i\beta + \varepsilon_{2,i} \quad \text{if } y_i^* = X_i\alpha + \varepsilon_{1,i} > 0,$$
(7.15)

where $\alpha = (\alpha_0, \ldots, \alpha_K)$, where $\varepsilon_{1,i} \sim N(0, 1)$ because it concerns the Probit part, and where $\varepsilon_{2,i} \sim N(0, \sigma_2^2)$. Both error terms may be correlated and hence $E[\varepsilon_{1,i}\varepsilon_{2,i}] = \sigma_{12}$. This model is called the Type-2 Tobit model (see Amemiya, 1985, p. 385). It consists of a Probit model for y_i being zero or positive and a standard Regression model for the positive values of y_i. The Probit model may, for example, describe the influence of explanatory variables X_i on the decision whether or not to donate to charity, while the Regression model measures the effect of the explanatory variables on the size of the amount for donating individuals.

The Type-2 Tobit model is more flexible than the Type-1 model. Owing to potentially different α and β parameters, it can for example describe situations where older individuals are more likely to donate to charity than are younger individuals, but, given a positive donation, younger individuals perhaps donate more than older individuals. The explanatory variable age then has a positive effect on the donation decision but a negative effect on the amount donated given a positive donation. This phenomenon cannot be described by the Type-1 Tobit model.

The probability that an individual donates to charity is now given by the probability that $Y_i = 0$ given X_i, that is,

$$\Pr[Y_i = 0|X_i] = \Pr[X_i\alpha + \varepsilon_{1,i} \leq 0|X_i] = \Pr[\varepsilon_{1,i} \leq -X_i\alpha|X_i]$$
$$= \Phi(-X_i\alpha).$$
(7.16)

The interpretation of this probability is the same as for the standard Probit model in chapter 4. For individuals who donate to charity, the expected value of the donated amount equals the expectation of Y_i given X_i and $y_i^* > 0$, that is

$$
\begin{aligned}
E[Y_i|y_i^* > 0, X_i] &= E[X_i\beta + \varepsilon_{2,i}|\varepsilon_{1,i} > -X_i\alpha] \\
&= X_i\beta + E[\varepsilon_{2,i}|\varepsilon_{1,i} > -X_i\alpha] \\
&= X_i\beta + E[E[\varepsilon_{2,i}|\varepsilon_{1,i}]|\varepsilon_{1,i} > -X_i\alpha] \\
&= X_i\beta + E[\sigma_{12}\varepsilon_{1,i}|\varepsilon_{1,i} > -X_i\alpha] \\
&= X_i\beta + \sigma_{12}\frac{\phi(-X_i\alpha)}{1 - \Phi(-X_i\alpha)}.
\end{aligned}
\tag{7.17}
$$

Notice that the expectation is a function of the covariance between the error terms in (7.15), that is, σ_{12}. The conditional mean of Y_i thus gets adjusted owing to the correlation between the decision to donate and the donated amount. A special case concerns what is called the two-part model, where the covariance between the Probit and the Regression equation σ_{12} is 0. In that case the expectation simplifies to $X_i\beta$. The advantage of a two-part model over a standard Regression model for only those observations with non-zero value concerns the possibility of computing the unconditional expectation of Y_i as shown below.

The effect of a change in the k'th explanatory variable $x_{k,i}$ on the expectation of non-censored Y_i for the Type-2 Tobit model is given by

$$
\frac{\partial E[Y_i|y_i^* > 0, X_i]}{\partial x_{k,i}} = \beta_k - \sigma_{12}(\lambda_i^2 - (-X_i\alpha)\lambda_i)\alpha_k,
\tag{7.18}
$$

where $\lambda_i = \lambda(-X_i\alpha)$ and we use the result below equation (7.8). Note again that it represents the effect of $x_{k,i}$ on the expected donated amount given a positive donation. If one wants to analyze the effect of $x_{k,i}$ on the expected donation without conditioning on the decision to donate to charity, one has to consider the unconditional expectation of Y_i. This expectation can be constructed in a straightforward way, and it equals

$$
\begin{aligned}
E[Y_i|X_i] &= E[Y_i|y_i^* \le 0, X_i]\Pr[y_i^* \le 0|X_i] \\
&\quad + E[Y_i|y_i^* > 0, X_i]\Pr[y_i^* > 0|X_i] \\
&= 0 + \left(X_i\beta + \sigma_{12}\frac{\phi(-X_i\alpha)}{1 - \Phi(-X_i\alpha)}\right)(1 - \Phi(-X_i\alpha)) \\
&= X_i\beta(1 - \Phi(-X_i\alpha)) + \sigma_{12}\phi(-X_i\alpha).
\end{aligned}
\tag{7.19}
$$

It follows from the second line of (7.19) that the expectation of Y_i is always smaller than the expectation of y_i given that $y_i^* > 0$. For our charity donation example, this means that the expected donated amount of individual i is always smaller than the expected donated amount given that individual i donates to charity.

To determine the effect of the k'th explanatory variable $x_{k,i}$ on the expectation (7.19), we consider the partial derivative of $E[Y_i|X_i]$ with respect to $x_{k,i}$, that is,

$$\frac{\partial E[Y_i|X_i]}{\partial x_{k,i}} = (1 - \Phi(-X_i\alpha))\beta_k + X_i\beta\phi(-X_i\alpha)\alpha_k$$

$$- \sigma_{12}(X_i\alpha)\phi(-X_i\alpha)\alpha_k.$$

(7.20)

Again, this partial derivative captures both the changes in probability that an observation is not censored and the changes in the conditional mean of positive y_i observations.

7.2   Estimation

The parameters of the Truncated and Censored Regression models can be estimated using the Maximum Likelihood method. For both types of model, the first-order conditions cannot be solved analytically. Hence, we again have to use numerical optimization algorithms such as the Newton–Raphson method discussed in section 3.2.2.

7.2.1   Truncated Regression model

The likelihood function of the Truncated Regression model follows directly from the density function of y_i given in (7.3) and reads

$$L(\theta) = \prod_{i=1}^{N}\left((1 - \Phi(-X_i\beta/\sigma))^{-1}\frac{1}{\sigma\sqrt{2\pi}}\exp(-\frac{1}{2\sigma^2}(y_i - X_i\beta)^2)\right)$$

(7.21)

where $\theta = (\beta, \sigma)$. Again we consider the log-likelihood function

$$l(\theta) = \sum_{i=1}^{N}\left(-\log(1 - \Phi(-X_i\beta/\sigma)) - \frac{1}{2}\log 2\pi - \log\sigma\right.$$

(7.22)

$$\left. - \frac{1}{2\sigma^2}(y_i - X_i\beta)^2\right).$$

To estimate the model using ML it is convenient to reparametrize the model (see Olsen, 1978). Define $\gamma = \beta/\sigma$ and $\xi = 1/\sigma$. The log-likelihood function in terms of $\theta^* = (\gamma, \xi)$ now reads

$$l(\theta^*) = \sum_{i=1}^{N}\left(-\log(1 - \Phi(-X_i\gamma)) - \frac{1}{2}\log 2\pi + \log\xi\right.$$

(7.23)

$$\left. - \frac{1}{2}(\xi y_i - X_i\gamma)^2\right).$$

The first-order derivatives of the log-likelihood function with respect to γ and ξ are simply

$$\frac{\partial l(\theta^*)}{\partial \gamma} = \sum_{i=1}^{N} (-\lambda(-X_i\gamma) + (\xi y_i - X_i\gamma))X_i'$$

$$\frac{\partial l(\theta^*)}{\partial \xi} = \sum_{i=1}^{N} (1/\xi - (\xi y_i - X_i\gamma)y_i),$$

(7.24)

where $\lambda(\cdot)$ again denotes the inverse Mills ratio. The second-order derivatives read

$$\frac{\partial l(\theta^*)}{\partial \gamma \partial \gamma'} = \sum_{i=1}^{N} (\lambda(-X_i\gamma)^2 + X_i\gamma\lambda(-X_i\gamma) - 1)X_i'X_i$$

$$\frac{\partial l(\theta^*)}{\partial \gamma \partial \xi} = \sum_{i=1}^{N} y_i X_i'$$

(7.25)

$$\frac{\partial l(\theta^*)}{\partial \xi \partial \xi} = \sum_{i=1}^{N} (-1/\xi^2 - y_i^2).$$

It can be shown that the log-likelihood is globally concave in θ^* (see Olsen, 1978), and hence that the Newton–Raphson algorithm converges to the unique maximum, that is, the ML estimator.

The ML estimator $\hat{\theta}^*$ is asymptotically normally distributed with the true value θ^* as mean and with the inverse of the information matrix as the covariance matrix. This matrix can be estimated by evaluating minus the inverse of the Hessian $H(\theta^*)$ in the ML estimates. Hence, we can use for inference that

$$\hat{\theta}^* \overset{a}{\sim} N(\theta^*, -H(\hat{\theta}^*)^{-1}).$$

(7.26)

Recall that we are interested in the ML estimates of θ instead of θ^*. It is easy to see that $\hat{\beta} = \hat{\gamma}\hat{\xi}$ and $\hat{\sigma} = 1/\hat{\xi}$ maximize the log-likelihood function (7.22) over θ. The resultant ML estimator $\hat{\theta} = (\hat{\beta}, \hat{\sigma})$ is asymptotically normally distributed with the true parameter θ as mean and the inverse of the information matrix as covariance matrix. For practical purposes, one can transform the estimated covariance matrix of $\hat{\theta}^*$ and use that

$$\hat{\theta} \overset{a}{\sim} N(\theta, -J(\hat{\theta}^*)H(\hat{\theta}^*)^{-1}J(\hat{\theta}^*)'),$$

(7.27)

where $J(\theta^*)$ denotes the Jacobian of the transformation from θ^* to θ given by

$$J(\theta^*) = \begin{pmatrix} \partial\beta/\partial\gamma' & \partial\beta/\partial\xi \\ \partial\sigma/\partial\gamma' & \partial\sigma/\partial\xi \end{pmatrix} = \begin{pmatrix} \xi^{-1}I_{K+1} & -\xi^{-2}\gamma \\ 0' & \xi^{-2} \end{pmatrix}, \tag{7.28}$$

where $0'$ denotes a $1 \times (K+1)$ vector with zeroes.

7.2.2 Censored Regression model

In this subsection we first outline parameter estimation for the Type-1 Tobit model and after that we consider the Type-2 Tobit model.

Type-1 Tobit

Maximum likelihood estimation for the Type-1 Tobit model proceeds in a similar way as for the Truncated Regression model. The likelihood function consists of two parts. The probability that an observation is censored is given by (7.10) and the density of the non-censored observations is a standard normal density. The likelihood function is

$$L(\theta) = \prod_{i=1}^{N} \Phi\left(\frac{-X_i\beta}{\sigma}\right)^{I[y_i=0]} \left(\frac{1}{\sigma\sqrt{2\pi}}\exp(-\frac{1}{2\sigma^2}(y_i - X_i\beta)^2)\right)^{I[y_i>0]},$$

$$\tag{7.29}$$

where $\theta = (\beta, \sigma)$. Again it is more convenient to reparametrize the model according to $\gamma = \beta/\sigma$ and $\xi = 1/\sigma$. The log-likelihood function in terms of $\theta^* = (\gamma, \xi)$ reads

$$l(\theta^*) = \sum_{i=1}^{N}(I[y_i = 0]\log\Phi(-X_i\gamma) + I[y_i > 0](\log\xi - \frac{1}{2}\log(2\pi)$$

$$-\frac{1}{2}(\xi y_i - X_i\gamma)^2)). \tag{7.30}$$

The first-order derivatives of the log-likelihood function with respect to γ and ξ are

$$\frac{\partial l(\theta^*)}{\partial\gamma} = \sum_{i=1}^{N}(-I[y_i = 0]\lambda(X_i\gamma)X_i' + I[y_i > 0](\xi y_i - X_i\gamma)X_i')$$

$$\tag{7.31}$$

$$\frac{\partial l(\theta^*)}{\partial\xi} = \sum_{i=1}^{N}I[y_i > 0](1/\xi - (\xi y_i - X_i\gamma)y_i)$$

and the second-order derivatives are

$$\frac{\partial l(\theta^*)}{\partial \gamma \partial \gamma'} = \sum_{i=1}^{N} (I[y_i = 0](-\lambda(X_i\gamma)^2 + X_i\gamma\lambda(X_i\gamma))X_i'X_i - I[y_i > 0]X_i'X_i)$$

$$\frac{\partial l(\theta^*)}{\partial \gamma \partial \xi} = \sum_{i=1}^{N} I[y_i > 0]y_i X_i'$$

$$\frac{\partial l(\theta^*)}{\partial \xi \partial \xi} = \sum_{i=1}^{N} I[y_i > 0](-1/\xi^2 - y_i^2).$$

$$(7.32)$$

Again, Olsen (1978) shows that the log-likelihood function is globally concave and hence the Newton–Raphson converges to a unique maximum,
which corresponds to the ML estimator for γ and ξ. Estimation and inference on β and σ proceed in the same way as for the Truncated Regression
model discussed above.

Type-2 Tobit

The likelihood function of the Type-2 Tobit model also contains
two parts. For the censored observations, the likelihood function equals the
probability that $Y_i = 0$ or $y_i^* \leq 0$ given in (7.16). For the non-censored
observations one uses the density function of y_i given that $y_i^* > 0$ denoted
by $f(y_i|y_i^* > 0)$ times the probability that $y_i^* > 0$. Hence, the likelihood func-
tion is given by

$$L(\theta) = \prod_{i=1}^{N} \left(\Pr[y_i^* < 0]^{I[y_i=0]} (f(y_i|y_i^* > 0) \Pr[y_i^* > 0])^{I[y_i=1]} \right), \quad (7.33)$$

where $\theta = (\alpha, \beta, \sigma_2^2, \sigma_{12})$. To express the second part of the likelihood function (7.33) as density functions of univariate normal distributions, we write

$$f(y_i|y_i^* > 0) \Pr[y_i^* > 0] = \int_0^\infty f(y_i, y_i^*) dy_i^*$$

$$(7.34)$$

$$= \int_0^\infty f(y_i^*|y_i) f(y_i) dy_i^*,$$

where $f(y_i, y_i^*)$ denotes the joint density of y_i^* and y_i which is in fact the
density function of a bivariate normal distribution (see section A.2 in the
Appendix). We now use that, if (y_i, y_i^*) are jointly normally distributed, y_i^*
given y_i is also normally distributed with mean $X_i\alpha + \sigma_{12}\sigma_2^{-2}(y_i - X_i\beta)$ and
variance $\tilde{\sigma}^2 = 1 - \sigma_{12}^2\sigma_2^{-2}$ (see section A.2 in the Appendix). We can thus
write the log-likelihood function as

$$l(\theta) = \sum_{i=1}^{N} \Big(I[y_i = 0]\Phi(-X_i\alpha) + I[y_i = 1](1 - \Phi(-(X_i\alpha + \sigma_{12}\sigma_2^{-2}$$

$$(y_i - X_i\beta))/\tilde{\sigma})) + I[y_i = 1]$$

$$(-\log \sigma_2 - \frac{1}{2}\log 2\pi - \frac{1}{2\sigma_2^2}(y_i - X_i\beta)^2) \Big).$$

$$(7.35)$$

This log-likelihood function can be maximized using the Newton–Raphson method discussed in section 3.2.2. This requires the first- and second-order derivatives of the log-likelihood function. In this book we will abstain from a complete derivation and refer to Greene (1995) for an approach along this line.

Instead of the ML method, one can also use a simpler but less efficient method to obtain parameter estimates, known as the Heckman (1976) two-step procedure. In the first step one estimates the parameters of the Probit model, where the dependent variable is 0 if $y_i = 0$ and 1 if $y_i > 0$. This can be done using the ML method as discussed in section 4.2. This yields $\hat{\alpha}$ and an estimate of the inverse Mills ratio, that is, $\lambda(-X_i\hat{\alpha})$, $i = 1, \ldots, N$. For the second step we use that the expectation of Y_i given that $Y_i > 0$ equals (7.17) and we estimate the β parameters in the regression model

$$y_i = X_i\beta + \omega\lambda(-X_i\hat{\alpha}) + \eta_i \qquad (7.36)$$

using OLS, where we add the inverse Mills ratio $\lambda(-X_i\hat{\alpha})$ to correct the conditional mean of Y_i, thereby relying on the result in (7.17). It can be shown that the Heckman two-step estimation method provides consistent estimates of β. The two-step estimator is, however, not efficient because the variance of the error term η_i in (7.36) is not homoskedastic. In fact, it can be shown that the variance of η_i is $\sigma_2^2 - \sigma_{12}^2(X_i\alpha\lambda(-X_i\alpha) + \lambda(-X_i\alpha)^2)$. Hence we cannot rely on the OLS standard errors. The asymptotic covariance matrix of the two-step estimator was first derived in Heckman (1979). It is, however, also possible to use White's (1980) covariance estimator to deal with the heterogeneity in the error term. The White estimator of the covariance matrix for the regression model $y_i = X_i\beta + \varepsilon_i$ equals

$$\frac{N}{N-K-1} \left(\sum_{i=1}^{N} X_i'X_i \right)^{-1} \left(\sum_{i=1}^{N} \hat{\varepsilon}_i X_i'X_i \right) \left(\sum_{i=1}^{N} X_i'X_i \right)^{-1}. \qquad (7.37)$$

This estimator is nowadays readily available in standard packages. In the application below we also opt for this approach. A recent survey of the Heckman two-step procedure can be found in Puhani (2000).

7.3   Diagnostics, model selection and forecasting

In this section we discuss diagnostics, model selection and forecasting for the Truncated and Censored Regression models. Because model selection is not much different from that for the standard regression model, that particular subsection contains a rather brief discussion.

7.3.1   Diagnostics

In this subsection we first discuss the construction of residuals, and then do some tests for misspecification.

Residuals

The simplest way to construct residuals in a Truncated Regression model is to consider

$$\hat{\varepsilon}_i = y_i - X_i\hat{\beta}. \tag{7.38}$$

However, in this way one does not take into account that the dependent variable is censored. The expected value of these residuals is therefore not equal to 0. An alternative approach to define residuals is

$$\hat{\varepsilon}_i = y_i - \mathrm{E}[Y_i|Y_i > 0, X_i], \tag{7.39}$$

where $\mathrm{E}[Y_i|Y_i > 0, X_i]$ is given in (7.6), and where β and σ are replaced by their ML estimates. The residuals in (7.39) are however heteroskedastic, and therefore one often considers the standardized residuals

$$\hat{\varepsilon} = \frac{y_i - \mathrm{E}[Y_i|Y_i > 0, X_i]}{\sqrt{\mathrm{V}[Y_i|Y_i > 0, X_i]}}, \tag{7.40}$$

where $\mathrm{V}[Y_i|Y_i > 0, X_i]$ is the variance of Y_i given that Y_i is larger than 0. This variance equals $\sigma^2(1 - (X_i\beta/\sigma)\lambda(-X_i\beta/\sigma) - \lambda(-X_i\beta/\sigma)^2)$ (see Johnson and Kotz, 1970, pp. 81–83, and section A.2 in the Appendix).

In a similar way we can construct residuals for the Type-1 Tobit model. Residuals with expectation zero follow from

$$\hat{\varepsilon}_i = y_i - \mathrm{E}[Y_i|X_i], \tag{7.41}$$

where $\mathrm{E}[Y_i|X_i]$ is given in (7.11). The standardized version of these residuals is given by

$$\hat{\varepsilon}_i = \frac{y_i - \mathrm{E}[Y_i|X_i]}{\sqrt{\mathrm{V}[Y_i|X_i]}}, \tag{7.42}$$

where

$$\mathrm{V}[Y_i|X_i] = \sigma^2(1 - \Phi(-X_i\beta/\sigma)) + X_i\beta\mathrm{E}[Y_i|X_i] - \mathrm{E}[Y_i|X_i]^2$$

(see Gourieroux and Monfort, 1995, p. 483).

An alternative approach to construct residuals in a Censored Regression model is to consider the residuals of the regression $y_i^* = X_i\beta + \varepsilon_i$ in (7.9). These residuals turn out to be useful in the specification tests as discussed below. For the non-censored observations $y_i = y_i^*$, one can construct residuals as in the standard Regression model (see section 3.3.1). For the censored observations one considers the expectation of ε_i in (7.9) for $y_i^* < 0$. Hence, the residuals are defined as

$$\hat{\varepsilon}_i = (y_i - X_i\hat{\beta})I[y_i > 0] + E[(y_i^* - X_i\hat{\beta})|y_i^* < 0]I[y_i = 0]. \qquad (7.43)$$

Along similar lines to (7.6) one can show that

$$E[(y_i^* - X_i\hat{\beta})|y_i^* < 0] = -\hat{\sigma}\frac{\phi(X_i\hat{\beta}/\hat{\sigma})}{1 - \Phi(X_i\hat{\beta}/\hat{\sigma})} = -\hat{\sigma}\lambda(X_i\hat{\beta}/\hat{\sigma}). \qquad (7.44)$$

Specification tests

There exist a number of specification tests for the Tobit model (see Pagan and Vella, 1989, and Greene, 2000, section 20.3.4, for more references). Some of these tests are Lagrange multiplier tests. For example, Greene (2000, p. 912) considers an LM test for heteroskedasticity. The construction of this test involves the derivation of the first-order conditions under the alternative specification and this is not pursued here. Instead, we will follow a more general and simpler approach to construct tests for misspecification. The resultant tests are in fact conditional moment tests.

We illustrate the conditional moment test by analyzing whether the error terms in the latent regression $y_i^* = X_i\beta + \varepsilon_i$ of the Type-1 Tobit model are homoskedastic. If the disturbances are indeed homoskedastic, a variable z_i should not have explanatory power for σ^2 and hence there is no correlation between z_i and $(E[\varepsilon_i^2] - \sigma^2)$, that is,

$$E[z_i(E[\varepsilon_i^2] - \sigma^2)] = 0. \qquad (7.45)$$

The expectation of ε_i^2 is simply $(y_i - X_i\beta)^2$ in the case of no censoring. In the case of censoring we use that $E[\varepsilon_i^2|y_i = 0] = \sigma^2 + \sigma(X_i\beta)\lambda(X_i\beta/\sigma)$ (see Lee and Maddala, 1985, p. 4). To test the moment condition (7.45) we consider the sample counterpart of $z_i(E[\varepsilon_i^2] - \sigma^2)$, which equals

$$m_i = z_i((y_i - X_i\hat{\beta})^2 - \hat{\sigma}^2)I[y_i > 0] + z_i\left(\hat{\sigma}^2\frac{X_i\hat{\beta}}{\hat{\sigma}}\lambda(X_i\hat{\beta}/\hat{\sigma})\right)I[y_i = 0].$$

$$(7.46)$$

The idea behind the test is now to check whether the difference between the theoretical moment and the empirical moment is zero. The test for homoskedasticity of the error terms turns out to be a simple F- or t-test for the significance of the constant ω_0 in the following regression

$$m_i = \omega_0 + G_i'\omega_1 + \eta_i,\qquad(7.47)$$

where G_i is a vector of first-order derivatives of the log-likelihood function per observation evaluated in the maximum likelihood estimates (see Pagan and Vella, 1989, for details). The vector of first-order derivatives G_i is contained in (7.31) and equals

$$G_i = \begin{pmatrix} I[y_i = 0]\lambda(X_i\gamma)X_i' - I[y_i > 0](\xi y_i - X_i\gamma)X_i' \\ I[y_i > 0](1/\xi - (\xi y_i - X_i\gamma)y_i) \end{pmatrix}.\qquad(7.48)$$

Note that the first-order derivatives are expressed in terms of $\theta^* = (\gamma, \xi)$ and hence we have to evaluate G_i in the ML estimate $\hat{\theta}^*$.

If homoskedasticity is rejected, one may consider a Censored Regression model (7.9) where the variance of the disturbances is different across observations, that is,

$$\sigma_i^2 = \exp(\alpha_0 + \alpha_1 z_i)\qquad(7.49)$$

(see Greene, 2000, pp. 912–914, for an example).

The conditional moment test can also be used to test, for example, whether explanatory variables have erroneously been omitted from the model or whether the disturbances ε_i are normally distributed (see Greene, 2000, pp. 917–919, and Pagan and Vella, 1989).

7.3.2 Model selection

We can be fairly brief about model selection because, as far as we know, the choice of variables and a comparison of models can be performed along similar lines to those discussed in section 3.3.2. Hence, one can use the z-scores for individual parameters, LR tests for joint significance of variables and the AIC and BIC model selection criteria.

In Laitila (1993) a pseudo-R^2 measure is proposed for a limited dependent variable model. If we define $\hat{y}_i^*$ as $X_i\hat{\beta}$ and $\hat{\sigma}^2$ as the ML estimate of σ^2, this pseudo-R^2 is defined as

$$R^2 = \frac{\sum_{i=1}^N (\hat{y}_i^* - \bar{y}_i^*)^2}{\sum_{i=1}^N (\hat{y}_i^* - \bar{y}_i^*)^2 + N\hat{\sigma}^2},\qquad(7.50)$$

where $\bar{y}_i^*$ denotes the average value of $\hat{y}_i^*$; see also the R^2 measure of McKelvey and Zavoina (1975), which was used in previous chapters for an ordered dependent variable.

7.3.3   Forecasting

One of the purposes of using Truncated and Censored Regression models is to predict the outcomes of out-of-sample observations. Additionally, using within-sample predictions one can evaluate the model. In contrast to the standard Regression model of chapter 3, there is not a unique way to compute predicted values in the Truncated and Censored Regression models. In our opinion, the type of the prediction depends on the research question. In the remainder of this subsection we therefore provide several types of prediction generated by Truncated and Censored Regression models and their interpretation.

Truncated Regression model

To illustrate forecasting using Truncated Regression models, we consider again the example in the introduction to this chapter, where we model the positive profits of stores. The prediction of the profit of a store i with a single characteristic x_i is simply $\hat{\beta}_0 + \hat{\beta}_1 x_i$. Note that this prediction can obtain a negative value, which means that the Truncated Regression model can be used to forecast outside the range of the truncated dependent variable in the model. If one does not want to allow for negative profits because one is certain that this store has a positive profit, one should consider computing the expected value of Y_i given that $Y_i > 0$ given in (7.6).

Censored Regression model

Several types of forecasts can be made using Censored Regression models depending on the question of interest. To illustrate some possibilities, we consider again the example of donating to charity. If, for example, one wants to predict the probability that an individual i with characteristics X_i does not donate to charity, one has to use (7.10) if one is considering a Type-1 Tobit model. If one opts for a Type-2 Tobit model, one should use (7.16). Of course, the unknown parameters have to be replaced by their ML estimates.

To forecast the donation of an individual i with characteristics X_i one uses the expectation in equation (7.19) for the Type-2 Tobit model. For the Type-1 Tobit model we take expectation (7.11). If, however, one knows for sure that this individual donates to charity, one has to take the expectation in (7.6) and (7.17) for the Type-1 and Type-2 Tobit models, respectively. The first type of prediction is not conditional on the fact that the individual donates to charity, whereas the second type of prediction is conditional on the fact that the individual donates a positive amount of money. The choice between the two possibilities depends of course on the goal of the forecasting exercise.

7.4 Modeling donations to charity

To illustrate a model of a censored dependent variable, we consider a sample of donations to charity. The data have already been discussed in section 2.2.5. Our sample contains 4,268 individuals who received a mailing from a charitable institution. We use the first 4,000 individuals to estimate various models and the remaining 268 observations to evaluate the estimated models in a forecasting exercise. Of these 4,000 individuals, about 59% do not donate and 41% donate amount y_i.

As explanatory variables to describe the response and donation behavior we consider the Recency Frequency and Monetary Value (RFM) variables discussed in section 2.2.5, that is, a 0/1 dummy indicating whether the individual responded to the previous mailing, the number of weeks since the last response, the average number of mailings received per year, the proportion of response in the past, the average donation in the past and the amount donated in the last response. The correlation between the last two explanatory variables is extremely high (> 0.99) and to avoid multicollinearity we do not consider the amount donated in the last response. Additionally, our preliminary analysis reveals, upon using the residuals in (7.42), that there is a huge outlier (observation 678). For this observation we include a 0/1 dummy variable.

First, we relate the amount donated (including the zero observations) to the RFM explanatory variables using a standard Regression model that does not take censoring into account. The first two columns of table 7.1 show the least squares parameter estimates and their corresponding standard errors. All RFM variables turn out to be significant.

The last two columns of table 7.1 show the estimation results of a Type-1 Tobit model. The Laitila pseudo-R^2 measure (7.50) equals 0.28. All the Tobit parameter estimates turn out to be larger in absolute value. Note that a similar phenomenon could be observed in figure 7.2, where the OLS parameter estimates were substantially smaller in absolute value than the true DGP parameters. All parameters are significant except the one modeling the effect of the response to the previous mailing. The number of weeks since last response has a negative effect on expected donation, while the other variables have a positive effect. Note that the Type-1 Tobit model imposes that the parameters modeling the effect of the explanatory variables on the probability of donating to charity and the expected donation are the same. To see whether these effects are different we now consider a Type-2 Tobit model.

Table 7.2 shows the parameter estimates and corresponding standard errors of this Type-2 Tobit model. The parameters are estimated using Heckman's two-step procedure. The first two columns show the parameter

Table 7.1 *Estimation results for a standard Regression model (including the 0 observations) and a Type-1 Tobit model for donation to charity*

Variables	Standard regression		Tobit model	
	Parameter	Standard error	Parameter	Standard error
Constant	−5.478***	(1.140)	−29.911***	(2.654)
Response to previous mailing	1.189**	(0.584)	1.328	(1.248)
Weeks since last response	−0.019***	(0.007)	−0.122***	(0.017)
No. of mailings per year	1.231***	(0.329)	3.102***	(0.723)
Proportion response	12.355***	(1.137)	32.604***	(2.459)
Average donation (NLG)	0.296***	(0.011)	0.369***	(0.021)
max. log-likelihood value	−15928.03		−8665.53	

Notes:
*** Significant at the 0.01 level, ** at the 0.05 level, * at the 0.10 level
The total number of observations is 3,999, of which 1,626 correspond to donations larger than 0.

Table 7.2 *Estimation results for a Type-2 Tobit model for the charity donation data*

Variables	Probit part		Regression part	
	Parameter	Standard error	Parameter	Standard error[a]
Constant	−1.299***	(0.121)	26.238***	(10.154)
Response to previous mailing	0.139**	(0.059)	−1.411**	(0.704)
Weeks since last response	−0.004***	(0.001)	0.073***	(0.027)
No. of mailings per year	0.164***	(0.034)	1.427**	(0.649)
Proportion response	1.779***	(0.117)	−17.239**	(6.905)
Average donation (NLG)	0.000	(0.001)	1.029***	(0.053)
Inverse Mills ratio			−17.684***	(6.473)
max. log-likelihood value	−2252.86		−5592.61	

Notes:
*** Significant at the 0.01 level, ** at the 0.05 level, * at the 0.10 level
[a]White heteroskedasticity-consistent standard errors.
The total number of observations is 3,999, of which 1,626 correspond to donations larger than 0.

estimates of a binomial Probit model for the decision whether or not to respond to the mailing and donate to charity. The last two columns show the estimates of the regression model for the amount donated for the individuals who donate to charity. The inverse Mills ratio is significant at the 1% level, and hence we do not have a two-part model here. We can see that some parameter estimates are quite different across the two components of this Type-2 Tobit model, which suggests that a Type-2 Tobit model is more appropriate than a Type-1 Tobit model.

Before we turn to parameter interpretation, we first discuss some diagnostics for the components of the Type-2 Tobit model. The McFadden R^2 (4.53) for the Probit model equals 0.17, while the McKelvey and Zavoina R^2 measure (4.54) equals 0.31. The Likelihood Ratio statistic for the significance of the explanatory variables is 897.71, which is significant at the 1% level. The R^2 of the regression model is 0.83. To test for possible heteroskedasticity in the error term of the Probit model, we consider the LM test for constant variance versus heteroskedasticity of the form (4.48) as discussed in section 4.3.1. One may include several explanatory variables in the variance equation (4.48). Here we perform five LM tests where each time we include a single explanatory variable in the variance equation. It turns out that constant variance cannot be rejected except for the case where we include weeks since last response. The LM test statistics equal 0.05, 0.74, 10.09, 0.78 and 0.34, where we use the same ordering as in table 7.1. Hence, the Type-2 Tobit model may be improved by allowing for heteroskedasticity in the Probit equation, but this extension is too difficult to pursue in this book.

As the Type-2 model does not seem to be seriously misspecified, we turn to parameter interpretation. Interesting variables are the response to the previous mailing and the proportion of response. If an individual did respond to the previous mailing, it is likely that he or she will respond again, but also donate less. A similar conclusion can be drawn for the proportion of response. The average donation does not have an impact on the response, whereas it matters quite substantially for the current amount donated. The differences across the parameters in the two components of the Type-2 Tobit model also suggest that a Type-1 Tobit model is less appropriate here. This notion is further supported if we consider out-of-sample forecasting.

To compare the forecasting performance of the models, we consider first whether or not individuals will respond to a mailing by the charitable organization. For the 268 individuals in the hold-out sample we compute the probability that the individual, given the value of his or her RFM variables, will respond to the mailing using (7.10). We obtain the following prediction–realization table, which is based on a cut-off point of $1626/3999 = 0.4066$,

	Predicted		
	no donation	donation	
Observed			
no donation	0.616	0.085	0.701
donation	0.153	0.146	0.299
	0.769	0.231	1

The hit rate is 76% . The prediction–realization table for the Probit model contained in the Type-2 Tobit model is

	Predicted		
	no donation	donation	
Observed			
no donation	0.601	0.101	0.701
donation	0.127	0.172	0.299
	0.728	0.272	1

where small inconsistencies in the table are due to rounding errors. The hit rate is 77%, which is only slightly higher than for the Type-1 Tobit model. If we compute the expected donation to charity for the 268 individuals in the hold-out sample using the Type-1 and Type-2 Tobit models as discussed in section 7.3.3, we obtain a Root Mean Squared Prediction Error (RMSPE) of 14.36 for the Type-1 model and 12.34 for the Type-2 model. Hence, although there is little difference in forecasting performance as regards whether or not individuals will respond to the mailing, the forecasting performance for expected donation is better for the Type-2 Tobit model.

The proposed models in this section can be used to select individuals who are likely to respond to a mailing and donate to charity. This is known as target selection. Individuals may be ranked according to their response probability or according to their expected donation. To compare different selection strategies, we consider again the 268 individuals in the hold-out sample. For each individual we compute the expected donation based on the Type-1 Tobit model and the Type-2 Tobit model. Furthermore, we compute the probability of responding based on the estimated Probit model in table 7.2. These forecasts are used to divide the individuals into four groups A, B, C, D according to the value of the expected donation (or the probability of responding). Group A corresponds to the 25% of individuals with the largest expected donation (or probability of responding). Group D contains the 25% of individuals with the smallest expected donation (or probability of responding). This is done for each of the three forecasts, hence we obtain three subdivisions in the four groups.

Table 7.3 *A comparison of target selection strategies based on the Type-1 and Type-2 Tobit models and the Probit model*

Group	Model	Total revenue	Response rate
A	Type-1 Tobit	904	0.61
	Type-2 Tobit	984	0.66
	Probit	945	0.69
B	Type-1 Tobit	340	0.28
	Type-2 Tobit	370	0.30
	Probit	224	0.18
C	Type-1 Tobit	310	0.28
	Type-2 Tobit	200	0.22
	Probit	360	0.30
D	Type-1 Tobit	10	0.01
	Type-2 Tobit	10	0.01
	Probit	35	0.03

Table 7.3 shows the total revenue and the response rate for each group and for each model. If we consider the total revenue, we can see that selection based on the Type-2 Tobit model results in the best target selection. The total revenues for groups A and B are larger than for the other models and as a result smaller for groups C and D. The response rate for group A is largest for the Probit model. This is not surprising because this model is designed to model response rate. Note further that the total revenue for group A based on selection with the Type-1 Tobit model is smaller than that based on selection with the Probit model.

7.5 Advanced topics

A possible extension to the standard Tobit model is to include unobserved heterogeneity as in the advanced topics sections in chapters 4 and 6. Because this can be done in a similar way to those chapters, we will not pursue this in this section and refer the reader to DeSarbo and Choi (1999) and Jonker et al. (2000) for some examples. In this section we briefly discuss two alternative types of Tobit model, which might be useful for marketing research.

In our illustration in this chapter we considered the case where one can donate to only one charitable organization. This can of course be extended to the case where an individual may donate amount y_A to charity A and amount y_B to charity B. Assuming the availability of explanatory variables

$X_{A,i}$ and $X_{B,i}$, which may differ because of different RFM variables, one can then consider the model

$$y_{A,i} = \begin{cases} X_{A,i}\beta_A + \varepsilon_{A,i} & \text{if } y_i^* = X_i\alpha + \varepsilon_i > 0 \\ 0 & \text{if } y_i^* = X_i\alpha + \varepsilon_i \le 0 \end{cases} \tag{7.51}$$

and

$$y_{B,i} = \begin{cases} X_{B,i}\beta_B + \varepsilon_{B,i} & \text{if } y_i^* = X_i\alpha + \varepsilon_i > 0 \\ 0 & \text{if } y_i^* = X_i\alpha + \varepsilon_i \le 0, \end{cases} \tag{7.52}$$

where $\varepsilon_{A,i} \sim N(0, \sigma_A^2)$, $\varepsilon_{B,i} \sim N(0, \sigma_B^2)$ and $\varepsilon_i \sim N(0, 1)$. Just as in the Type-2 Tobit model, it is possible to impose correlations between the error terms. Estimation of the model parameters can be done in a similar way to that for the Type-2 Tobit model.

Another extension concerns the case where an individual always donates to charity, but can choose between charity A or B. Given this binomial choice, the individual then decides to donate $y_{A,i}$ or $y_{B,i}$. Assuming again the availability of explanatory variables $X_{A,i}$ and $X_{B,i}$, one can then consider the model

$$y_{A,i} = \begin{cases} X_{A,i}\beta_A + \varepsilon_{A,i} & \text{if } y_i^* = X_i\alpha + \varepsilon_i > 0 \\ 0 & \text{if } y_i^* = X_i\alpha + \varepsilon_i \le 0 \end{cases} \tag{7.53}$$

and

$$y_{B,i} = \begin{cases} 0 & \text{if } y_i^* = X_i\alpha + \varepsilon_i > 0 \\ X_{B,i}\beta_B + \varepsilon_{B,i} & \text{if } y_i^* = X_i\alpha + \varepsilon_i \le 0, \end{cases} \tag{7.54}$$

where $\varepsilon_{A,i} \sim N(0, \sigma_A^2)$, $\varepsilon_{B,i} \sim N(0, \sigma_B^2)$ and $\varepsilon_i \sim N(0, 1)$. Again, it is possible to impose correlations between ε_i and the other two error terms (see Amemiya, 1985, p. 399, for more details). Note that the model does not allow an individual to donate to both charities at the same time.

The y_i^* now measures the unobserved willingness to donate to charity A instead of to B. The probability that an individual i donates to charity A is of course $1 - \Phi(-X_i\alpha)$. Likewise, the probability that an individual donates to charity B is $\Phi(-X_i\alpha)$. If we assume no correlation between the error terms, the log-likelihood function is simply

$$
L(\theta) = \sum_{i=1}^{N} I[y_{A,i} > 0]\left(\log(1 - \Phi(-X_i\alpha)) - \frac{1}{2}\log 2\pi \right.
$$

$$
\left. - \log \sigma_A - \frac{1}{2\sigma_A^2}(y_{A,i} - X_i\beta_A)^2 \right) + I[y_{B,i} > 0]
$$

$$
\left(\log \Phi(-X_i\alpha) - \frac{1}{2}\log 2\pi - \log \sigma_B - \frac{1}{2\sigma_B^2}(y_{B,i} - X_i\beta_B)^2 \right)
$$

$$(7.55)$$

where θ summarizes the model parameters. The Probit model and the two Regression models can be estimated separately using the ML estimators discussed in chapters 3 and 4. If one wants to impose correlation between the error terms, one can opt for a similar Heckman two-step procedure to that for the Type-2 Tobit model (see Amemiya, 1985, section 10.10).

8   A duration dependent variable

In the previous chapters we have discussed econometric models for ordered and unordered discrete choice dependent variables and continuous dependent variables, which may be censored or truncated. In this chapter we deal with models for duration as the dependent variable. Duration data often occur in marketing research. Some examples concern the time between two purchases, the time until a customer becomes inactive or cancels a subscription or service contract, and the time it takes to respond to a direct mailing (see Helsen and Schmittlein, 1993, table 1, for more examples).

Models for duration data receive special attention in the econometric literature. This is because standard regression models cannot be used. In fact, standard regression models are used to correlate a dependent variable with explanatory variables that are all measured at the same point in time. In contrast, if one wants to relate a duration variable to explanatory variables, it is likely that the duration will also depend on the path of the values of the explanatory variables during the period of duration. For example, the timing of a purchase may depend on the price of the product at the time of the purchase but also on the price in the weeks or days before the purchase. During these weeks a household may have considered the price of the product to be too high, and therefore it postponed its purchase. Hence, the focus of modeling of duration is often not on explaining duration directly but merely on the probability that the duration will end this week given that it lasted until this week.

A second important feature of duration data is censoring. If one collects duration data it is likely that at the beginning of the measurement period some durations will already be in progress. Also, at the end of the measurement period, some durations may not have been completed. It is, for example, unlikely that all households in the sample purchased a product exactly at the end of the observation period. To deal with these properties of duration variables, so-called duration models, have been proposed and used. For an extensive theoretical discussion of duration models, we refer to Kalbfleisch and Prentice (1980), Kiefer (1988) and Lancaster (1990), among others.

The outline of this chapter is as follows. In section 8.1 we discuss the representation and interpretation of two commonly considered duration models, which are often used to analyze duration data in marketing. Although the discussion starts off with a simple model for discrete duration variables, we focus in this section on duration models with continuous dependent variables. We discuss the Accelerated Lifetime specification and the Proportional Hazard specification in detail. Section 8.2 deals with Maximum Likelihood estimation of the parameters of the two models. In section 8.3 we discuss diagnostics, model selection and forecasting with duration models. In section 8.4 we illustrate models for interpurchase times in relation to liquid detergents (see section 2.2.6 for more details on the data). Finally, in section 8.5 we again deal with modeling unobserved heterogeneity as an advanced topic.

8.1   Representation and interpretation

Let T_i be a discrete random variable for the length of a duration observed for individual i and t_i the actual length, where T_i can take the values $1, 2, 3, \ldots$ for $i = 1, \ldots, N$. It is common practice in the econometric literature to refer to a duration variable as a *spell*. Suppose that the probability that the spell ends is equal to λ at every period t in time, where $t = 1, \ldots, t_i$. The probability that the spell ends after two periods is therefore $\lambda(1 - \lambda)$. In general, the probability that the spell ends after t_i duration periods is then

$$\Pr[T_i = t_i] = \lambda(1 - \lambda)^{(t_i - 1)}. \tag{8.1}$$

In other words, the random variable T_i has a geometric distribution with parameter λ (see section A.2 in the Appendix).

In many cases one wants to relate the probability that a spell ends to explanatory variables. Because λ is a probability, one can, for example, consider

$$\lambda = F(\beta_0 + \beta_1 x_i), \tag{8.2}$$

where F is again a function that maps the explanatory variable x_i on the unit interval $[0, 1]$ (see also section 4.1). The function F can, for example, be the logistic function.

If x_i is a variable that takes the same value over time (for example, gender), the probability that the spell ends does not change over time. This may be an implausible assumption. If we consider, for example, purchase timing, we may expect that the probability that a household will buy detergent is higher if the relative price of detergent is low and lower if the relative price is high. In other words, the probability that a spell will end can be time dependent. In this case, the probability that the spell ends after t_i periods is given by

$$\Pr[T_i = t_i] = \lambda_{t_i} \prod_{t=1}^{t_i-1} (1 - \lambda_t), \tag{8.3}$$

where λ_t is the probability that the spell will end at time t given that it has lasted until t for $t = 1, \ldots, t_i$. This probability may be related to explanatory variables that stay the same over time, x_i, and explanatory variables that change over time, $w_{i,t}$, according to

$$\lambda_t = F(\beta_0 + \beta_1 x_i + \gamma w_{i,t}). \tag{8.4}$$

The variable $w_{i,t}$ can be the price of detergent in week t, for example.

Additionally it is likely that the probability that a household will buy detergent is higher if it had already bought detergent four weeks ago, rather than two weeks ago. To allow for an increase in the purchase probability over time, one may include (functions of) the variable t as an explanatory variable with respect to λ_t, as in

$$\lambda_t = F(\beta_0 + \beta_1 x_i + \gamma w_{i,t} + \alpha t). \tag{8.5}$$

The functions λ_t, which represent the probability that the spell will end at time t given that it has lasted until t, are called hazard functions.

In practice, duration data are often continuous variables (or treated as continuous variables) instead of discrete variables. This means that T_i is a continuous random variable that can take values on the interval $[0, \infty)$. In the remainder of this chapter we will focus the discussion on modeling such continuous duration data. The discussion concerning discrete duration data turns out to be a good basis for the interpretation of the models for continuous duration data. The distribution of the continuous random variable T_i for the length of a spell of individual i is described by the density function $f(t_i)$. The density function $f(t_i)$ is the continuous-time version of (8.3). Several distributions have been proposed to describe duration (see table 8.1 for some examples and section A.2 in the Appendix for more details). The normal distribution, which is frequently used in econometric models, is however not a good option because duration has to be positive. The log-normal distribution can be used instead.

The probability that the continuous random variable T_i is smaller than t is now given by

$$\Pr[T_i < t] = F(t) = \int_0^t f(s)ds, \tag{8.6}$$

where $F(t)$ denotes the cumulative distribution function of T_i. It is common practice in the duration literature to use the survival function, which is

Table 8.1 *Some density functions with expressions for their corresponding hazard functions*

	Density $f(t)$	Survival $S(t)$	Hazard $\lambda(t)$
Exponential	$\gamma \exp(-\gamma t)$	$\exp(-\gamma t)$	γ
Weibull	$\gamma \alpha (\gamma t)^{\alpha-1} \exp(-(\gamma t)^{\alpha})$	$\exp(-(\gamma t)^{\alpha})$	$\gamma \alpha (\gamma t)^{\alpha-1}$
Loglogistic	$\gamma \alpha (\gamma t)^{\alpha-1} (1+(\gamma t)^{\alpha})^{-2}$	$(1+(\gamma t)^{\alpha})^{-1}$	$\gamma \alpha (\gamma t)^{\alpha-1} (1+(\gamma t)^{\alpha})^{-1}$
Lognormal	$(\alpha/t)\phi(\alpha \log(\gamma t))$	$\Phi(-\alpha \log(\gamma t))$	$(\alpha/t)\phi(\alpha \log(\gamma t))(\Phi(-\alpha \log(\gamma t)))^{-1}$

Notes: In all cases $\alpha > 0$ and $\gamma > 0$. Φ and ϕ are the cumulative distribution function and the density function of a standard normal distribution defined as the probability that the random variable T_i will equal or exceed t, that is,

$$S(t) = 1 - F(t) = \Pr[T_i \geq t]. \tag{8.7}$$

Using the survival function we can define the continuous-time analogue of the hazard functions λ_t in (8.2) and (8.5), that is,

$$\lambda(t) = \frac{f(t)}{S(t)}, \tag{8.8}$$

where we now use $\lambda(t)$ to indicate that t is a continuous variable. The function $\lambda(t)$ is called the hazard function of a distribution. Roughly speaking, it denotes the rate at which spells will be completed at time t given that they have lasted until t. In terms of purchases, $\lambda(t)$ measures the probability that a purchase will be made at time t given that it has not yet been purchased. More precisely, the hazard function is defined as

$$\lambda(t) = \lim_{h \to 0} \frac{\Pr[t \leq T_i < t + h | T \geq t]}{h}. \tag{8.9}$$

The hazard function is not a density function for the random variable T_i because $\int_0^\infty \lambda(t)dt$ is in general not equal to 1. Because $dS(t)/dt = -f(t)$ (see (8.7)), the hazard function equals the derivative of minus the log of the survival function with respect to t, that is,

$$\lambda(t) = -\frac{d \log S(t)}{dt}. \tag{8.10}$$

This expression is useful to determine the hazard function if one has an expression for the survival function (see below).

Table 8.1 shows the density function, the survival function and the hazard function for four familiar distributions: the exponential, the Weibull, the loglogistic and the lognormal distribution. The simplest distribution to describe duration is the exponential distribution. Its hazard function is constant and hence the rate at which a spell ends does not depend on time. Because there is no duration dependence for this distribution it is often called memoryless. The hazard function of the Weibull distribution depends on time unless $\alpha = 1$, in which case the distribution simplifies to the exponential distribution. For $\alpha > 1$ the hazard function is increasing in t and we have positive duration dependence, and for $0 < \alpha < 1$ we have negative duration dependence; see also figure 8.1, which shows the hazard function for different values of α and γ. The graph also shows that the γ parameter is just a scale parameter because the shape of the density functions does not change with changing values for γ. The loglogistic and the lognormal distributions allow for hazard functions that increase for small values of t and decrease for large values of t (see figure 8.2).

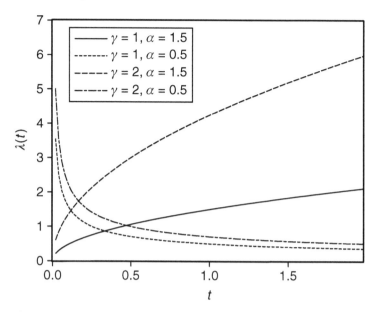

Figure 8.1   Hazard functions for a Weibull distribution

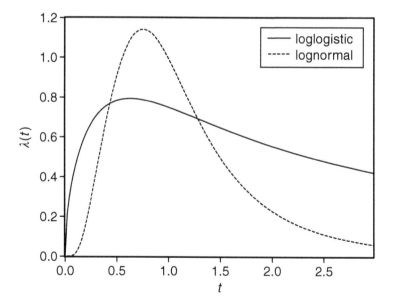

Figure 8.2   Hazard functions for the loglogistic and the lognormal distributions with $\alpha = 1.5$ and $\gamma = 1$

In practice, for many problems we are interested not particularly in the density of the durations but in the shape of the hazard functions. For example, we are interested in the probability that a household will buy detergent now given that it last purchased detergent four weeks ago. Another example concerns the probability that a contract that started three months ago will be canceled today. It is therefore more natural to think in terms of hazard functions, and hence the analysis of duration data often starts with the specification of the hazard function $\lambda(t)$ instead of the density function $F(t)$.

Because the hazard function is not a density function, any non-negative function of time t can be used as a hazard function. A flexible form for the hazard function, which can describe different shapes for various values of the parameters, is, for example,

$$\lambda(t) = \exp(\alpha_0 + \alpha_1 t + \alpha_2 \log(t) + \alpha_3 t^2), \tag{8.11}$$

where the exponential transformation ensures positiveness of $\lambda(t)$ (see, for example, Jain and Vilcassim, 1991, and Chintagunta and Prasad, 1998, for an application). Often, and also in case of (8.11), it is difficult to find the density function $f(t)$ that belongs to a general specified hazard function. This should, however, not be considered a problem because one is usually interested only in the hazard function and not in the density function.

For the estimation of the model parameters via Maximum Likelihood it is not necessary to know the density function $f(t)$. It suffices to know the hazard function $\lambda(t)$ and the integrated hazard function defined as

$$\Lambda(t) = \int_0^t \lambda(s)ds. \tag{8.12}$$

This function has no direct interpretation, however, but is useful to link the hazard function and the survival function. From (8.10) it is easy to see that the survival function equals

$$S(t) = \exp(-\Lambda(t)). \tag{8.13}$$

So far, the models for continuous duration data have not included much information from explanatory variables. Two ways to relate duration data to explanatory variables are often applied. First of all, one may scale (or accelerate) t by a function of explanatory variables. The resulting model is called an Accelerated Lifetime (or Failure Time) model. The other possibility is to scale the hazard function, which leads to a Proportional Hazard model. In the following subsections we discuss both specifications.

8.1.1   Accelerated Lifetime model

The hazard and survival functions that involve only t are usually called the baseline hazard and baseline survival functions, denoted by $\lambda_0(t)$ and $S_0(t)$, respectively. In the Accelerated Lifetime model the explanatory variables are used to scale time in a direct way. This means that the survival function for an individual i, given a single explanatory variable x_i, equals

$$S(t_i|x_i) = S_0(\psi(x_i)t_i), \tag{8.14}$$

where the duration t_i is scaled through the function $\psi(\cdot)$. We assume now for simplicity that the x_i variable has the same value during the whole duration. Below we will discuss how time-varying explanatory variables may be incorporated in the model. Applying (8.10) to (8.14) provides the hazard function

$$\lambda(t_i|x_i) = \psi(x_i)\lambda_0(\psi(x_i)t_i), \tag{8.15}$$

and differentiating (8.14) with respect to t provides the corresponding density function

$$f(t_i|x_i) = \psi(x_i)f_0(\psi(x_i)t_i), \tag{8.16}$$

where $f_0(\cdot)$ is the density function belonging to $S_0(\cdot)$.

The function $\psi(\cdot)$ naturally has to be nonnegative and it is usually of the form

$$\psi(x_i) = \exp(\beta_0 + \beta_1 x_i). \tag{8.17}$$

If we consider the distributions in table 8.1, we see that the parameter γ in these distributions also scales time. Hence, the parameters β_0 and γ are not jointly identified. To identify the parameters we may set either $\gamma = 1$ or $\beta_0 = 0$. In practice one usually opts for the first restriction. To interpret the parameter β_1 in (8.17), we linearize the argument of (8.14), that is, $\exp(\beta_0 + \beta_1 x_i)t_i$, by taking logarithms. This results in the linear representation of the Accelerated Lifetime model

$$-\log t_i = \beta_0 + \beta_1 x_i + u_i. \tag{8.18}$$

The distribution of the error term u_i follows from the probability that u_i is smaller than U:

$$
\begin{aligned}
\Pr[u_i < U] &= \Pr[-\log t_i < U + \beta_0 + \beta_1 x_i] \\
&= \Pr[t_i > \exp(-U - \beta_0 - \beta_1 x_i)] \\
&= S_0(\exp(\beta_0 + \beta_1 x_i)\exp(-U - \beta_0 - \beta_1 x_i)) \\
&= S_0(\exp(-U))
\end{aligned}
\tag{8.19}
$$

and hence the density of u_i is given by $\exp(-u_i)f_0(\exp(-u_i))$, which does not depend on x_i. Recall that this is an important condition of the standard

Regression model. The parameter β_1 therefore measures the effect of x_i on the log duration as

$$\frac{\partial \log t_i}{\partial x_i} = -\beta_1. \tag{8.20}$$

Additionally, if x_i is a log transformed variable, β_1 can be interpreted as an elasticity.

8.1.2 Proportional Hazard model

A second way to include explanatory variables in a duration model is to scale the hazard function by the function $\psi(\cdot)$, that is,

$$\lambda(t_i|x_i) = \psi(x_i)\lambda_0(t_i), \tag{8.21}$$

where $\lambda_0(t_i)$ denotes the baseline hazard. Again, because the hazard function has to be nonnegative, one usually specifies $\psi(\cdot)$ as

$$\psi(x_i) = \exp(\beta_0 + \beta_1 x_i). \tag{8.22}$$

If the intercept β_0 is unequal to 0, the baseline hazard in (8.21) is identified upon a scalar. Hence, if one opts for a Weibull or an exponential baseline hazard one again has to restrict γ to 1 to identify the parameters.

The interpretation of the parameters β_1 for the proportional hazard specification is different from that for the Accelerated Lifetime model. This parameter describes the constant proportional effect of x_i on the conditional probability of completing a spell, which can be observed from

$$\frac{\partial \log \lambda(t_i|x_i)}{\partial x_i} = \frac{\partial \log \psi(x_i)}{\partial x_i} = \beta_1. \tag{8.23}$$

This suggests that one can linearize the model as follows:

$$-\log \Lambda_0(t_i) = \beta_0 + \beta_1 x_i + u_i, \tag{8.24}$$

where $\Lambda_0(t_i)$ denotes the integrated baseline hazard defined as $\int_0^{t_i} \lambda_0(s)ds$. The distribution of u_i follows from

$$\begin{aligned}
\Pr[u_i < U] &= \Pr[-\log \Lambda_0(t_i) < U + \beta_0 + \beta_1 x_i] \\
&= \Pr[\Lambda_0(t_i) > \exp(-U - \beta_0 - \beta_1 x_i)] \\
&= \Pr[t_i > \Lambda_0^{-1}[\exp(-U - \beta_0 - \beta_1 x_i)]] \\
&= S(\Lambda_0^{-1}[\exp(-U - \beta_0 - \beta_1 x_i)]) \\
&= \exp(-\exp(-U)),
\end{aligned} \tag{8.25}$$

where we use that $S(t) = \exp(-\Lambda(t))$ (see (8.13)). Hence, u_i has a type-I extreme value distribution.

Note that, in contrast to the Accelerated Lifetime specification, the dependent variable in (8.24) may depend on unknown parameters. For example, it is easy to show that the integrated baseline hazard for a Weibull distribution with $\gamma = 0$ is $\Lambda_0(t) = t^\alpha$ and hence (8.24) simplifies to $-\alpha \ln t_i = \beta_0 + \beta_1 x_i + u_i$. This suggests that, if we divide both β parameters by α, we obtain the Accelerated Lifetime model with a Weibull specification for the baseline hazard. This is in fact the case and an exact proof of this equivalence is straightforward. For other distributions it is in general not possible to write (8.24) as a linear model for the log duration variable.

So far, we have considered only one explanatory variable. In general, one may include K explanatory variables such that the $\psi(\cdot)$ function becomes

$$\psi(X_i) = \exp(X_i \beta), \tag{8.26}$$

where X_i is the familiar $(1 \times (K + 1))$ vector containing the K explanatory variables and an intercept term and β is now a $(K + 1)$-dimensional parameter vector.

Finally, until now we have assumed that the explanatory variables summarized in X_i have the same value over the complete duration. In practice it is often the case that the values of the explanatory variables change over time. For example, the price of a product may change regularly between two purchases of a household. The inclusion of time-varying explanatory variables is far from trivial (see Lancaster, 1990, pp. 23–32, for a discussion). The simplest case corresponds to the situation where the explanatory variables change a finite number of times over the duration; for example, the price changes every week but is constant during the week. Denote this time-varying explanatory variable by $w_{i,t}$ and assume that the value of $w_{i,t}$ changes at $\tau_0, \tau_1, \tau_2, \ldots, \tau_n$ where $\tau_0 = 0$ corresponds to the beginning of the spell. Hence, $w_{i,t}$ equals w_{i,τ_i} for $t \in [\tau_i, \tau_{i+1})$. The corresponding hazard function is then given by $\lambda(t_i | w_{i,t_i})$ and the integrated hazard function equals

$$\Lambda(t_i | w_{i,t}) = \sum_{i=0}^{n-1} \int_{\tau_i}^{\tau_{i+1}} \lambda(u | w_{i,\tau_i}) \, du \tag{8.27}$$

(see also Gupta, 1991, for an example in marketing). To derive the survival and density functions we can use the relation (8.13). Fortunately, we do not need expressions for these functions for the estimation of the model parameters, as will become clear in the next section. For convenience, in the remainder of this chapter we will however assume that the explanatory variables are time invariant for simplicity of notation.

8.2 Estimation

Estimation of duration models can be done via Maximum Likelihood. The likelihood function is simply the product of the individual density functions. As already discussed in the introduction to this chapter, we are often faced with spells that started before the beginning of the measurement period or with spells that have not yet ended at the end of the observation period. This results in left-censored and right-censored data, respectively. A possible solution to the censoring problem is to ignore these censored data. This solution may, however, introduce a bias in the estimated length of duration because censored data will usually correspond to long durations. To deal with censoring, one therefore has to include the censoring information in the likelihood function. The only information we have on left- and right-censored observations is that the spell lasted for at least the duration during the observation sample denoted by t_i. The probability of this event is simply $S(t_i|X_i)$. If we define d_i as a 0/1 dummy that is 1 if the observation is not censored and 0 if the observation is censored, the likelihood function is

$$L(\theta) = \prod_{i=1}^{N} f(t_i|X_i)^{d_i} S(t_i|X_i)^{(1-d_i)}, \qquad (8.28)$$

where θ is a vector of the model parameters consisting of β and the distribution-specific parameters (see again table 8.1). The log-likelihood function is given by

$$l(\theta) = \sum_{i=1}^{N} (d_i \log f(t_i|x_i) + (1 - d_i) \log S(t_i|x_i)). \qquad (8.29)$$

If we use $f(t_i|X_i) = \lambda(t_i|X_i)S(t_i|X_i)$ as well as (8.13), we can write the log-likelihood function as

$$l(\theta) = \sum_{i=1}^{N} (d_i \log \lambda(t_i|X_i) - \Lambda(t_i|X_i)) \qquad (8.30)$$

because $\Lambda(t_i|X_i)$ equals $-\log S(t_i|x_i)$. Hence, we can express the full log-likelihood function in terms of the hazard function.

The ML estimator $\hat{\theta}$ is again the solution of the equation

$$\frac{\partial l(\theta)}{\partial \theta} = 0. \qquad (8.31)$$

In general, there are no closed-form expressions for this estimator and we have to use numerical optimization algorithms such as Newton–Raphson to maximize the log-likelihood function. Remember that the ML estimates can be found by iterating over

$$\theta_h = \theta_{h-1} - H(\theta_{h-1})^{-1}G(\theta_{h-1}) \tag{8.32}$$

until convergence, where $G(\theta)$ and $H(\theta)$ denote the first- and second-order derivatives of the log-likelihood function.

The analytical form of the first- and second-order derivatives of the log-likelihood depends on the form of the baseline hazard. In the remainder of this section, we will derive the expression of both derivatives for an Accelerated Lifetime model and a Proportional Hazard model for a Weibull-type baseline hazard function. Results for other distributions can be obtained in a similar way.

8.2.1   Accelerated Lifetime model

The hazard function of an Accelerated Lifetime model with a Weibull specification reads as

$$\begin{aligned}
\lambda(t_i|X_i) &= \exp(X_i\beta)\lambda_0(\exp(X_i\beta)t_i) \\
&= \exp(X_i\beta)\alpha(\exp(X_i\beta)t_i)^{\alpha-1},
\end{aligned} \tag{8.33}$$

where we put $\gamma = 1$ for identification. The survival function is then given by

$$S(t_i|X_i) = \exp(-(\exp(X_i\beta)t_i)^{\alpha}). \tag{8.34}$$

To facilitate the differentiation of the likelihood function in an Accelerated Lifetime model, it is convenient to define

$$z_i = \alpha\ln(\exp(X_i\beta)t_i) = \alpha(\ln t_i + X_i\beta). \tag{8.35}$$

Straightforward substitution in (8.34) results in the survival function and the density function of t_i expressed in terms of z_i, that is,

$$S(t_i|X_i) = \exp(-\exp(z_i)). \tag{8.36}$$

$$f(t_i|X_i) = \alpha\exp(z_i - \exp(z_i)), \tag{8.37}$$

(see also Kalbfleisch and Prentice, 1980, chapter 2, for similar results for other distributions than the Weibull). The log-likelihood function can be written as

$$\begin{aligned}
l(\theta) &= \sum_{i=1}^{N}(d_i\log f(t_i|X_i) + (1-d_i)\log S(t_i|X_i)) \\
&= \sum_{i=1}^{N}(d_i(z_i + \log(\alpha)) - \exp(z_i)),
\end{aligned} \tag{8.38}$$

where $\theta = (\beta, \alpha)$.

The first-order derivative of the log-likelihood equals $G(\theta) = (\partial l(\theta)/\partial\beta'$, $\partial l(\theta)/\partial\alpha)'$ with

$$\frac{\partial l(\theta)}{\partial \beta} = \sum_{i=1}^{N} \alpha(d_i - \exp(z_i))X_i'$$

$$\frac{\partial l(\theta)}{\partial \alpha} = \sum_{i=1}^{N} \frac{d_i(z_i + 1) - \exp(z_i)z_i}{\alpha},$$

$$(8.39)$$

where we use that $\partial z_i / \partial \alpha = z_i / \alpha$ and $\partial z_i / \partial \beta = \alpha X_i$. The Hessian equals

$$H(\theta) = \begin{pmatrix} \frac{\partial^2 l(\theta)}{\partial \beta \partial \beta'} & \frac{\partial^2 l(\theta)}{\partial \alpha \partial \beta} \\ \frac{\partial^2 l(\theta)}{\partial \alpha \partial \beta'} & \frac{\partial^2 l(\theta)}{\partial \alpha \partial \alpha} \end{pmatrix}, \tag{8.40}$$

where

$$\frac{\partial^2 l(\theta)}{\partial \beta \partial \beta'} = -\sum_{i=1}^{N} \alpha^2 \exp(z_i)X_i'X_i$$

$$\frac{\partial^2 l(\theta)}{\partial \alpha \partial \beta} = \sum_{i=1}^{N} (d_i - \exp(z_i))X_i' \tag{8.41}$$

$$\frac{\partial^2 l(\theta)}{\partial \alpha \partial \alpha} = -\sum_{i=1}^{N} \frac{d_i + \exp(z_i)z_i^2}{\alpha^2}.$$

The ML estimates are found by iterating over (8.32) for properly chosen starting values for β and α. One may, for example, use OLS estimates of β in (8.18) as starting values and set α equal to 1. In section 8.A.1 we provide the EViews code for estimating an Accelerated Lifetime model with a Weibull specification.

8.2.2   *Proportional Hazard model*

The log-likelihood function for the Proportional Hazard model

$$\lambda(t_i|X_i) = \exp(X_i\beta)\lambda_0(t_i) \tag{8.42}$$

is given by

$$l(\theta) = \sum_{i=1}^{N}(d_iX_i\beta + d_i \log \lambda_0(t_i) - \exp(X_i\beta)\Lambda_0(t_i)), \tag{8.43}$$

which allows for various specifications of the baseline hazard. If we assume that the parameters of the baseline hazard are summarized in α, the first-order derivatives of the log-likelihood are given by

$$\frac{\partial l(\theta)}{\partial \beta} = \sum_{i=1}^{N} (d_i - \exp(X_i\beta)\Lambda_0(t_i))X_i'$$

$$\frac{\partial l(\theta)}{\partial \alpha} = \sum_{i=1}^{N} \left(\frac{d_i}{\lambda_0(t_i)} \frac{\partial \lambda_0(t_i)}{\partial \alpha} - \exp(X_i\beta) \frac{\partial \Lambda_0(t_i)}{\partial \alpha} \right).$$

(8.44)

The second-order derivatives are given by

$$\frac{\partial^2 l(\theta)}{\partial \beta \partial \beta'} = - \sum_{i=1}^{N} \exp(X_i\beta)\Lambda_0(t_i)X_i'X_i$$

$$\frac{\partial^2 l(\theta)}{\partial \alpha \partial \beta} = \sum_{i=1}^{N} \exp(X_i\beta) \frac{\partial \Lambda_0(t_i)}{\partial \alpha'} X_i'$$

$$\frac{\partial^2 l(\theta)}{\partial \alpha \partial \alpha'} = - \sum_{i=1}^{N} \left(\frac{d_i}{\lambda_0(t_i)} \frac{\partial^2 \lambda_0(t_i)}{\partial \alpha \partial \alpha'} - \frac{d_i}{\lambda_0(t_i)^2} \frac{\partial \lambda_0(t_i)}{\partial \alpha} \frac{\partial \lambda_0(t_i)}{\partial \alpha'} \right.$$

$$\left. - \exp(X_i\beta) \frac{\partial^2 \Lambda_0(t_i)}{\partial \alpha \partial \alpha'} \right),$$

(8.45)

which shows that we need the first- and second-order derivatives of the baseline hazard and the integrated baseline hazard. If we assume a Weibull baseline hazard with $\gamma = 1$, the integrated baseline hazard equals $\Lambda_0(t) = t^\alpha$. Straightforward differentiation gives

$$\frac{\partial \lambda_0(t_i)}{\partial \alpha} = (1 + \alpha \log(t))t^\alpha \qquad \frac{\partial^2 \lambda_0(t_i)}{\partial \alpha^2} = (2\log(t) + \alpha(\log(t))^2)t^{\alpha-1}$$

(8.46)

$$\frac{\partial \Lambda_0(t_i)}{\partial \alpha} = t^\alpha \log(t) \qquad \frac{\partial^2 \Lambda_0(t_i)}{\partial \alpha^2} = t^\alpha(\log(t))^2 \qquad (8.47)$$

The ML estimates are found by iterating over (8.32) for properly chosen starting values for β and α. In section 8.A.2 we provide the EViews code for estimating a Proportional Hazard model with a log-logistic baseline hazard specification.

For both specifications, the ML estimator $\hat{\theta}$ is asymptotically normally distributed with the true parameter vector θ as mean and the inverse of the information matrix as covariance matrix. The covariance matrix can be estimated by evaluating minus the inverse of the Hessian $H(\theta)$ in $\hat{\theta}$, and hence we use for inference that

$$\hat{\theta} \overset{a}{\sim} N(\theta, -H(\hat{\theta})^{-1}). \qquad (8.48)$$

This means that we can rely on z-scores to examine the relevance of individual explanatory variables.

8.3 Diagnostics, model selection and forecasting

Once the parameters of the duration model have been estimated, it is important to check the validity of the model before we can turn to the interpretation of the estimation results. In section 8.3.1 we will discuss some useful diagnostic tests for this purpose. If the model is found to be adequate, one may consider deleting possibly redundant variables or compare alternative models using selection criteria. This will be addressed in section 8.3.2. Finally, one may want to compare models on their forecasting performance. In section 8.3.3 we discuss several ways to use the model for prediction.

8.3.1 Diagnostics

Just as for the standard regression model, the analysis of the residuals is the basis for checking the empirical adequacy of the estimated model. They display the deviations from the model and may suggest directions for model improvement. As we have already discussed, it is possible to choose from among many distributions which lead to different forms of the hazard function. It is therefore convenient for a general diagnostic checking procedure to employ errors, which do not depend on the specification of the hazard function. Because the distribution of the error of (8.24) is the same for all specifications of the baseline hazard, one may opt for $u_i = -\log \Lambda_0 (t_i) - X_i\beta$ to construct residuals. In practice, however, one tends to consider $\exp(-u_i) = \Lambda_0(t_i)\exp(X_i\beta) = \Lambda(t_i|X_i)$. Hence,

$$e_i = \Lambda(t_i|X_i) = -\log S(t_i|X_i) \quad \text{for } i = 1, \ldots, N \qquad (8.49)$$

is defined as the generalized error term. The distribution of e_i follows from

$$\begin{aligned}
\Pr[e_i < E] &= \Pr[\Lambda(t_i|X_i) < E] \\
&= \Pr[t_i < \Lambda^{-1}(E|X_i)] \\
&= S(\Lambda^{-1}(E|X_i)) \\
&= 1 - \exp(-E),
\end{aligned} \qquad (8.50)$$

where we use that $S(t) = \exp(-\Lambda(t))$. Hence, the distribution of the generalized error terms is an exponential distribution with $\gamma = 1$ (see table 8.1). It therefore does not depend on the functional form of the hazard function.

The generalized residuals are obtained by evaluating the integrated hazard in the ML estimates. For the Accelerated Lifetime model with a Weibull distribution, the generalized residuals are given by

$$\hat{e}_i = (\exp(X_i\hat{\beta})t_i)^{\hat{\alpha}}, \qquad (8.51)$$

while for the Proportional Hazard specification we obtain

$$\hat{e}_i = \exp(X_i\hat{\beta})t_i^{\hat{\alpha}}. \tag{8.52}$$

To check the empirical adequacy of the model, one may analyze whether the residuals are drawings from an exponential distribution. One can make a graph of the empirical cumulative distribution function of the residuals minus the theoretical cumulative distribution function where the former is defined as

$$F_{\hat{e}}(x) = \frac{\#[\hat{e}_i < x]}{N}, \tag{8.53}$$

where $\#[\hat{e}_i < x]$ denotes the number of generalized residuals smaller than x. This graph should be approximately a straight horizontal line on the horizontal axis (see Lawless, 1982, ch. 9, for more discussion). The integrated hazard function of an exponential distribution with $\gamma = 1$ is $\int_0^t 1du = t$. We may therefore also plot the empirical integrated hazard function, evaluated at x, against x. The relevant points should approximately lie on a 45 degree line (see Lancaster, 1990, ch. 11, and Kiefer, 1988, for a discussion).

In this chapter we will consider a general test for misspecification of the duration model using the conditional moment test discussed in section 7.3.1. We compare the empirical moments of the generalized residuals with their theoretical counterparts using the approach of Newey (1985) and Tauchen (1985) (see again Pagan and Vella, 1989). The theoretical moments of the exponential distribution with $\gamma = 1$ are given by

$$E[e_i^r] = r! \tag{8.54}$$

Because the expectation of e_i and the sample mean of $\hat{e}_i$ are both 1, one sometimes defines the generalized residuals as $\hat{e}_i - 1$ to obtain zero mean residuals. In this section we will continue with the definition in (8.49).

Suppose that one wants to test whether the third moment of the generalized residuals equals 6, that is, we want to test whether

$$E[e_i^3] - 6 = 0. \tag{8.55}$$

Again, we check whether the difference between the theoretical moment and the empirical moment is zero, that is, we test whether the sample averages of

$$m_i = \hat{e}_i^3 - 6 \tag{8.56}$$

differ significantly from zero. To compute the test we again need the first-order derivative of the log density function of each observation, that is,

$$G_i = \frac{\partial \log f(t_i|X_i)}{\partial \theta} \quad \text{for } i = 1, \dots, N. \tag{8.57}$$

These derivatives are contained in the gradient of the log-likelihood functions (see section 8.2). The test statistic is now an F-test or Likelihood Ratio test for the significance of the intercept ω_0 in the following auxiliary regression model

$$m_i = \omega_0 + G_i \omega_1 + \eta_i \tag{8.58}$$

(see Pagan and Vella, 1989, for details). If the test statistic is too large, we reject the null hypothesis that the empirical moment of the generalized residuals is equal to the theoretical moment, which in turn indicates misspecification of the model. In that case one may decide to change the baseline hazard of the model. If one has specified a monotone baseline hazard, one may opt for a non-monotone hazard, such as, for example, the hazard function of a loglogistic distribution or the flexible baseline hazard specification in (8.11). Note that the test as described above is valid only for uncensored observations. If we want to apply the test for censored observations, we have to adjust the moment conditions.

Finally, there exist several other tests for misspecification in duration models. The interested reader is referred to, for example, Kiefer (1985), Lawless (1982, ch. 9), Lancaster (1990, ch. 11).

8.3.2 Model selection

Once one or some models have been considered empirically adequate, one may compare the different models or examine whether or not certain explanatory variables can be deleted.

The significance of the individual parameters can be analyzed using z-scores, which are defined as the parameter estimates divided by their estimated standard errors (see (8.48)). If one wants to test for the redundancy of more than one explanatory variable, one can use a Likelihood Ratio test as before (see chapter 3). The LR test statistic is asymptotically χ^2 distributed with degrees of freedom equal to the number of parameter restrictions.

To compare different models we may consider the pseudo-R^2 measure, which is often used in non-linear models. If we denote $l(\hat{\theta}_0)$ as the value of the log-likelihood function if the model contains only intercept parameters, that is $\exp(X_i\beta) = \exp(\beta_0)$, the pseudo-$R^2$ measure is

$$R^2 = 1 - \frac{l(\hat{\theta})}{l(\hat{\theta}_0)}. \tag{8.59}$$

This measure provides an indication of the contribution of the explanatory variables to the fit of the model. Indeed, one may also perform a Likelihood Ratio test for the significance of the β parameters except for β_0.

Finally, if one wants to compare models with different sets of explanatory variables, one may use the familiar AIC and BIC as discussed in section 4.3.2.

8.3.3 Forecasting

The duration model can be used to generate several types of prediction, depending on the interest of the researcher. If one is interested in the duration of a spell for an individual, one may use

$$E[T_i|X_i] = \int_0^\infty t_i \, f(t_i|X_i)dt_i. \tag{8.60}$$

If the model that generates this forecast is an Accelerated Lifetime model with a Weibull distribution, this simplifies to $\exp(-X_i\beta)\Gamma(1 + 1/\alpha)$, where Γ denotes the Gamma function defined as $\Gamma(\kappa) = \int_0^\infty x^{\kappa-1} \exp(-x)dx$ (see also section A.2 in the Appendix). For the Proportional Hazard specification, the expectation equals $\exp(-X_i\beta)^{1/\alpha}\Gamma(1 + 1/\alpha)$. To evaluate the forecasting performance of a model, one may compare the forecasted durations with the actual durations within-sample or for a hold-out-sample.

Often, however, one is interested in the probability that the spell will end in the next Δt period given that it lasted until t. For individual i this probability is given by

$$\Pr[T_i \leq t + \Delta t | T_i > t, X_i] = 1 - \Pr[T_i > t + \Delta t | T_i > t, X_i]$$

$$= 1 - \frac{\Pr[T_i > t + \Delta t | X_i]}{\Pr[T > t | X_i]} \tag{8.61}$$

$$= 1 - \frac{S(t + \Delta t | X_i)}{S(t | X_i)}.$$

To evaluate this forecast one may compare the expected number of ended spells in period Δt with the true number of ended spells. This may again be done within-sample or for a hold-out sample.

8.4 Modeling interpurchase times

To illustrate the analysis of duration data, we consider the purchase timing of liquid detergents of households. This scanner data set has already been discussed in section 2.2.6. To model the interpurchase times we first consider an Accelerated Lifetime model with a Weibull distribution (8.33). As explanatory variables we consider three 0/1 dummy variables which indicate whether the brand was only on display, only featured or displayed as well as featured at the time of the purchase. We also include the difference of

Table 8.2 *Parameter estimates of a Weibull Accelerated Lifetime model for purchase timing of liquid detergents*

Variables	Parameter	Standard error
Intercept	−4.198***	0.053
Household size	0.119***	0.011
Non-detergent expenditure	0.008	0.034
Volume previous occasion	−0.068***	0.017
Log price difference	−0.132***	0.040
Display only	0.004	0.105
Feature only	−0.180***	0.066
Display and feature	−0.112**	0.051
Shape parameter $\hat{\alpha}$	1.074***	0.017
max. log-likelihood value	−3257.733	

Notes:
*** Significant at the 0.01 level, ** at the 0.05 level, * at the 0.10 level
The total number of observations is 2,257.

the log of the price of the purchased brand on the current purchase occasion and on the previous purchase occasion. Additionally, we include household size, the volume of liquid detergent purchased on the previous purchase occasion (divided by 32 oz.) and non-detergent expenditure (divided by 100). The last two variables are used as a proxy for "regular" and "fill-in" trips and to take into account the effects of household inventory behavior on purchase timing, respectively (see also Chintagunta and Prasad, 1998). We have 2,657 interpurchase times. As we have to construct log price differences, we lose the first observation of each household and hence our estimation sample contains 2,257 observations.

Table 8.2 shows the ML estimates of the model parameters. The model parameters are estimated using EViews 3.1. The EViews code is provided in section 8.A.1. The LR test statistic for the significance of the explanatory variables (except for the intercept parameter) equals 99.80, and hence these variables seem to have explanatory power for the interpurchase times. The pseudo-R^2 is, however, only 0.02.

To check the empirical validity of the hazard specification we consider the conditional moment tests on the generalized residuals as discussed in section 8.3.1. We test whether the second, third and fourth moments of the generalized residuals equal 2, 6 and 24, respectively. The *LR* test statistics for the

Table 8.3 *Parameter estimates of a loglogistic Proportional Hazard model for purchase timing of liquid detergents*

Variables	Parameter	Standard error
Intercept	0.284**	0.131
Household size	0.127***	0.014
Non-detergent expenditure	0.007	0.041
Volume previous occasion	−0.090***	0.022
Log price difference	−0.103*	0.054
Display only	0.006	0.134
Feature only	−0.143*	0.085
Display and feature	−0.095	0.063
Shape parameter $\hat{\alpha}$	1.579***	0.054
Scale parameter $\hat{\gamma}$	−0.019***	0.002
max. log-likelihood value	−11148.52	

Notes:
*** Significant at the 0.01 level, ** at the 0.05 level, * at the 0.10 level
The total number of observations is 2,257.

significance of the intercepts in the auxiliary regression (8.58) are 84.21, 28.90 and 11.86, respectively. This suggests that the hazard function is misspecified and that we need a more flexible hazard specification.

In a second attempt we estimate a Proportional Hazard model (8.21) with a loglogistic baseline hazard (see table 8.1). Hence, the hazard function is specified as

$$\lambda(t_i|X_i) = \exp(X_i\beta)\frac{\gamma\alpha(\gamma t_i)^{\alpha-1}}{(1+(\gamma t_i)^{\alpha})}. \tag{8.62}$$

We include the same explanatory variables as in the Accelerated Lifetime model.

Table 8.3 shows the ML estimates of the model parameters. The model parameters are estimated using EViews 3.1. The EViews code is provided in section 8.A.2. To check the empirical validity of this hazard specification we consider again the conditional moment tests on the generalized residual as discussed in section 8.3.1. The generalized residuals are given by

$$\hat{e}_i = \exp(X_i\hat{\beta})\log(1+(\hat{\gamma}t_i)^{\hat{\alpha}}). \tag{8.63}$$

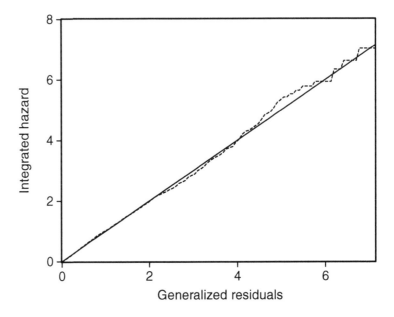

Figure 8.3   Empirical integrated hazard function for generalized residuals

We perform the same test for the second, third and fourth moments of the generalized residuals as before. The *LR* test statistics for the significance of the intercepts in the auxiliary regression (8.58) now equal 0.70, 0.35 and 1.94, respectively, and hence the hazard specification now does not seem to be misspecified. To illustrate this statement, we show in figure 8.3 the graph of the empirical integrated hazard versus the generalized residuals. If the model is well specified this graph should be approximately a straight 45 degree line. We see that the graph is very close to the straight line, indicating an appropriate specification of the hazard function.

As the duration model does not seem to be misspecified we can continue with parameter interpretation. The first panel of table 8.3 shows the effects of the non-marketing mix variables on interpurchase times. Remember that the β parameters of the Proportional Hazard model correspond to the partial derivatives of the hazard function with respect to the explanatory variables. A positive coefficient therefore implies that an increase in the explanatory variable leads to an increase in the probability that detergent will be purchased given that it has not been purchased so far. As expected, household size has a significantly positive effect; hence for larger households the interpurchase time will be longer. The same is true for non-detergent expenditures. Households appear to be more inclined to buy liquid detergents on regular shopping trips than on fill-in trips (see also Chintagunta and Prasad,

1998, for similar results). Note, however, that in our case this effect is not significant. Not surprisingly, the volume purchased on the previous purchase occasion has a significant negative effect on the conditional probability that detergent is purchased.

The second panel of table 8.3 shows the effects of the marketing mix variables. The log price difference has a negative effect on the conditional probability that detergent is purchased. Display has a positive effect, but this effect is not significant. Surprisingly, feature has a negative effect but this effect is just significant at the 10% level. The effects of combined display and feature are not significant.

8.5   Advanced topics

In the final section of this chapter we consider the modeling of unobserved heterogeneity in the two duration model specifications.

To capture differences in duration across individuals, one may include individual-specific explanatory variables in the model. For example, in the illustration in the previous section we included household size to capture differences in interpurchase times across households. In many cases, individual-specific explanatory variables are not available or are not informative enough to describe the differences in duration across individuals, leading to a misspecification of the duration model. To capture this unobserved heterogeneity one may include an individual-specific parameter in the model, resulting in a conditional hazard specification

$$\lambda(t_i|X_i, v_i), \tag{8.64}$$

where v_i denotes the individual-specific effect. Because it is usually impossible, owing to a lack of observations, to estimate individual-specific parameters, one tends to assume that v_i is a draw from a population distribution (see also some of the previous Advanced Topics sections).

Given (8.64), the conditional integrated hazard function is

$$\Lambda(t_i|X_i, v_i) = \int_0^{t_i} \lambda(u|X_i, v_i)du \tag{8.65}$$

such that the conditional survival and density functions are

$$S(t_i|X_i, v_i) = \exp(-\Lambda(t_i|X_i, v_i))$$

$$f(t_i|X_i, v_i) = -\frac{\partial \log S(t_i|X_i, v_i)}{\partial t_i}, \tag{8.66}$$

respectively. The unconditional density function results from

$$f(t_i|X_i) = \int_{v_i} f(t_i|X_i, v_i)f(v_i)dv_i, \tag{8.67}$$

where $f(t_i|X_i, v_i)$ is the conditional density function of t_i and $f(v_i)$ the density function of distribution describing the unobserved heterogeneity. Likewise,

$$S(t_i|X_i) = \int_{v_i} S(t_i|X_i, v_i)f(v_i)dv_i, \tag{8.68}$$

and hence the unconditional hazard function is defined as the ratio of (8.67) and (8.68).

In the remainder of this section, we will illustrate the inclusion of hetero-geneity in an Accelerated Lifetime and a Proportional Hazard model with a Weibull distribution, where we assume a normalized Gamma distribution for the unobserved heterogeneity. The Gamma distribution has mean 1 and variance $1/\kappa$ and its density function reads

$$f(v_i) = \frac{\kappa^\kappa}{\Gamma(\kappa)} \exp(-\kappa v_i)v_i^{\kappa-1} \tag{8.69}$$

(see also section A.2 in the Appendix).

Accelerated Lifetime model

To incorporate heterogeneity in the Accelerated Lifetime model, we adjust the survival function (8.34) to obtain the conditional survival function

$$S(t_i|X_i, v_i) = \exp((-v_i \exp(X_i\beta)t_i)^\alpha). \tag{8.70}$$

The unconditional survival function is given by

$$\begin{aligned} S(t_i|X_i) &= \int_0^\infty f(v_i)S(t_i|X_i, v_i)dv_i \\ &= \int_0^\infty \frac{\kappa^\kappa}{\Gamma(\kappa)} \exp(-\kappa v_i)v_i^{\kappa-1} \exp((-v_i \exp(X_i\beta)t_i)^\alpha)dv_i \\ &= (1 + \frac{1}{\kappa}(\exp(X_i\beta)t_i)^\alpha)^{-\kappa}. \end{aligned} \tag{8.71}$$

Differentiating with respect to t_i provides the unconditional density function

$$f(t_i|X_i) = \exp(X_i\beta)\alpha(\exp(X_i\beta)t_i)^{\alpha-1}\left(1 + \frac{1}{\kappa}(\exp(X_i\beta)t_i)^\alpha\right)^{-\kappa-1} \tag{8.72}$$

and hence the hazard function equals

$$\lambda(t_i|X_i) = \frac{\exp(X_i\beta)\alpha(\exp(X_i\beta)t_i)^{\alpha-1}}{\left(1+\frac{1}{\kappa}(\exp(X_i\beta)t_i)^{\alpha}\right)}. \tag{8.73}$$

For $\kappa \to \infty$, we obtain the hazard function of the Weibull distribution (8.33) because in that case the variance of v_i is zero. For $\kappa = 1$, we obtain the hazard function of a loglogistic distribution. This shows that it is difficult to distinguish between the distribution of the baseline hazard and the distribution of the unobserved heterogeneity. In fact, the Accelerated Lifetime model is not identified in the presence of heterogeneity, in the sense that we cannot uniquely determine the separate effects due to the explanatory variables, the duration distribution and the unobserved heterogeneity, given knowledge of the survival function. The Proportional Hazard model, however, is identified under mild assumptions (see Elbers and Ridder, 1982). In the remainder of this section, we will illustrate an example of modeling unobserved heterogeneity in a Proportional Hazard model.

Proportional Hazard model
        To incorporate unobserved heterogeneity in the Proportional Hazard model we adjust (8.42) as follows

$$\lambda(t_i|X_i, v_i) = \exp(X_i\beta)\lambda_0(t_i)v_i. \tag{8.74}$$

From (8.66) it follows that conditional integrated hazard and survival functions are given by

$$\Lambda(t_i|X_i, v_i) = \int_0^{t_i} v_i \exp(X_i\beta)\lambda_0(u)du = v_i \exp(X_i\beta)\Lambda_0(t_i)$$

$$S(t_i|X_i, v_i) = \exp(-v_i \exp(X_i\beta)\Lambda_0(t_i)). \tag{8.75}$$

For a Weibull distribution the integrated baseline hazard is t_i^{α} and hence the unconditional survival function is

$$S(t_i|X_i) = \int_0^{\infty} \exp(-v_i \exp(X_i\beta)t^{\alpha})\frac{\kappa^{\kappa}}{\Gamma(\kappa)}\exp(-\kappa v_i)v_i^{\kappa-1}dv_i$$

$$= \left(1+\frac{1}{\kappa}\exp(X_i\beta)t^{\alpha}\right)^{-\kappa}. \tag{8.76}$$

Differentiating with respect to t_i gives the unconditional density function

$$f(t_i|X_i) = \exp(X_i\beta)\alpha t^{\alpha-1}\left(1+\frac{1}{\kappa}\exp(X_i\beta)t^{\alpha}\right)^{-\kappa-1} \tag{8.77}$$

and hence the unconditional hazard function equals

$$\lambda(t_i|X_i) = \frac{\exp(X_i\beta)\alpha t^{\alpha-1}}{\left(1 + \dfrac{1}{\kappa}\exp(X_i\beta)t^{\alpha}\right)}. \tag{8.78}$$

For $\kappa \to \infty$, the hazard function simplifies to the proportional hazard function of a Weibull distribution. The variance of v_i is in that case zero. In contrast to the Accelerated Lifetime specification, the hazard function does not simplify to the hazard function of a Proportional Hazard model with loglogistic baseline hazard for $\kappa = 1$, which illustrates the differences in identification in Accelerated Lifetime and proportional hazard specifications.

8.A EViews code

This appendix provides the EViews code we used to estimate the models in section 8.4. In the code the following abbreviations are used for the variables:

- interpurch denotes the interpurchase time. The dummy variable censdum is 1 if the corresponding interpurchase time observation is not censored and 0 if it is censored.
- hhsize, nondexp and prevpurch denote household size, nondetergent expenditure and volume purchased on the previous purchase occasion, respectively.
- dlprice, displ, feat and dispfeat denote the log price difference of the purchased product, a 0/1 display only dummy, 0/1 feature only dummy and a 0/1 display and feature dummy, respectively.

8.A.1   Accelerated Lifetime model (Weibull distribution)

```
load c:\data\deterg.wf1

' Declare coefficient vectors to use in Maximum Likelihood estimation
coef(8) b = 0
coef(1) a = 1

' Specify log-likelihood for Accelerated Lifetime Weibull model
logl llal
llal.append @logl loglal

' Define exponent part
llal.append xb=b(1)+b(2)*hhsize+b(3)*nondexp/100+b(4)*prevpurch/32
                   +b(5)*dlprice+b(6)*displ+b(7)*feat+b(8)*dispfeat
```

```
' Define z
llal.append z=a(1)*(log(interpurch)+xb)

llal.append loglal = censdum*(z+log(a(1)))-exp(z)

' Estimate by Maximum Likelihood
smpl 1 2257
llal.ml(d,m=1000)
show llal.output

' Generate generalized residuals
genr res=(exp(xb)*interpurch)^a(1)
```

8.A.2 Proportional Hazard model (loglogistic distribution)

```
load c:\data\deterg\deterg.wf1

' Declare coefficient vectors to use in Maximum Likelihood Estimation
coef(1) a = 1
coef(1) g = 1

' Specify log-likelihood for log-logistic Proportional Hazard model
logl llph
llph.append @logl loglph

' Define exponent part
llph.append xb=b(1)+b(2)*hhsize+b(3)*nondexp/100+b(4)*prevpurch/32
                    +b(5)*dlprice+b(6)*displ+b(7)*feat+b(8)*dispfeat

' Define log hazard and integrated hazard function
llph.append lhaz=log(a(1))+log(g(1))+(a(1)-1)*log(g(1)*interpurch)
                -log(1+(g(1)*interpurch)^(a(1)))
llph.append ihaz=log(1+(g(1)*interpurch)^(a(1)))

llph.append loglph = censdum*(xb+lhaz)-exp(xb)*ihaz

' Estimate by Maximum Likelihood
smpl 1 2257
llph.ml(d,m=1000)
show llph.output

' Generate generalized residuals
genr res=exp(xb)*log(1+(g(1)*interpurch)^a(1))
```

Appendix

A.1 Overview of matrix algebra

In this appendix we provide a short overview of the matrix algebra we use in this book. We first start with some notation. For simplicity we assume that the dimension of the vectors is 3 or 4, because this also matches with several examples considered in the book. Generalization to higher dimensions is straightforward.

A 3-dimensional column vector β with elements $\beta_1, \beta_2, \beta_3$ is defined as

$$\beta = \begin{pmatrix} \beta_1 \\ \beta_2 \\ \beta_3 \end{pmatrix}. \tag{A.1}$$

If we transpose the column vector β, we obtain a 3-dimensional row vector β' defined as

$$\beta' = (\beta_1, \beta_2, \beta_3). \tag{A.2}$$

A 4×3 matrix X with elements $x_{i,j}$ is defined as

$$X = \begin{pmatrix} x_{1,1} & x_{1,2} & x_{1,3} \\ x_{2,1} & x_{2,2} & x_{2,3} \\ x_{3,1} & x_{3,2} & x_{3,3} \\ x_{4,1} & x_{4,2} & x_{4,3} \end{pmatrix}. \tag{A.3}$$

The transpose of this matrix X is the 3×4 matrix denoted by X', that is,

$$X' = \begin{pmatrix} x_{1,1} & x_{2,1} & x_{3,1} & x_{4,1} \\ x_{1,2} & x_{2,2} & x_{3,2} & x_{4,2} \\ x_{1,3} & x_{2,3} & x_{3,3} & x_{4,3} \end{pmatrix}. \tag{A.4}$$

An identity matrix is a symmetric matrix with a value of 1 on the diagonal and zeros elsewhere. For example, the 3×3 identity matrix denoted by I_3, is

$$I_3 = \begin{pmatrix} 1 & 0 & 0 \\ 0 & 1 & 0 \\ 0 & 0 & 1 \end{pmatrix}. \tag{A.5}$$

One can add and subtract matrices (or vectors) of the same format in the same way as scalar variables. For example, the difference between two 3×4 matrices X and Y is simply

$$
X - Y = \begin{pmatrix} x_{1,1} & x_{1,2} & x_{1,3} \\ x_{2,1} & x_{2,2} & x_{2,3} \\ x_{3,1} & x_{3,2} & x_{3,3} \\ x_{4,1} & x_{4,2} & x_{4,3} \end{pmatrix} - \begin{pmatrix} y_{1,1} & y_{1,2} & y_{1,3} \\ y_{2,1} & y_{2,2} & y_{2,3} \\ y_{3,1} & y_{3,2} & y_{3,3} \\ y_{4,1} & y_{4,2} & y_{4,3} \end{pmatrix}
$$

$$
= \begin{pmatrix} x_{1,1} - y_{1,1} & x_{1,2} - y_{1,2} & x_{1,3} - y_{1,3} \\ x_{2,1} - y_{2,1} & x_{2,2} - y_{2,2} & x_{2,3} - y_{2,3} \\ x_{3,1} - y_{3,1} & x_{3,2} - y_{3,2} & x_{3,3} - y_{3,3} \\ x_{4,1} - y_{4,1} & x_{4,2} - y_{4,2} & x_{4,3} - y_{4,3} \end{pmatrix}.
$$

(A.6)

It is also possible to multiply two vectors. For example, the so-called inner product of the 3-dimensional row vector β is defined as

$$
\beta' \beta = (\beta_1, \beta_2, \beta_3) \begin{pmatrix} \beta_1 \\ \beta_2 \\ \beta_3 \end{pmatrix} = \beta_1^2 + \beta_2^2 + \beta_3^2 = \sum_{k=1}^{3} \beta_k^2.
$$

(A.7)

Hence the outcome is a scalar. Another multiplication concerns the outer product. The outer product of the same vector β is defined as

$$
\beta \beta' = \begin{pmatrix} \beta_1 \\ \beta_2 \\ \beta_3 \end{pmatrix} (\beta_1, \beta_2, \beta_3) = \begin{pmatrix} \beta_1^2 & \beta_1\beta_2 & \beta_1\beta_3 \\ \beta_2\beta_1 & \beta_2^2 & \beta_2\beta_3 \\ \beta_3\beta_1 & \beta_3\beta_2 & \beta_3^2 \end{pmatrix},
$$

(A.8)

which is a 3×3 matrix.

The matrix product of a 3×4 matrix Y and a 4×3 matrix X is defined as

$$
YX = \begin{pmatrix} y_{1,1} & y_{1,2} & y_{1,3} & y_{1,4} \\ y_{2,1} & y_{2,2} & y_{2,3} & y_{2,4} \\ y_{3,1} & y_{3,2} & y_{3,3} & y_{3,4} \end{pmatrix} \begin{pmatrix} x_{1,1} & x_{1,2} & x_{1,3} \\ x_{2,1} & x_{2,2} & x_{2,3} \\ x_{3,1} & x_{3,2} & x_{3,3} \\ x_{4,1} & x_{4,2} & x_{4,3} \end{pmatrix}
$$

(A.9)

$$
= \begin{pmatrix} y_{1,1}x_{1,1} + y_{1,2}x_{2,1} + y_{1,3}x_{3,1} + y_{1,4}x_{4,1} \\ y_{2,1}x_{1,1} + y_{2,2}x_{2,1} + y_{2,3}x_{3,1} + y_{2,4}x_{4,1} \\ y_{3,1}x_{1,1} + y_{3,2}x_{2,1} + y_{3,3}x_{3,1} + y_{3,4}x_{4,1} \end{pmatrix}
$$

$$
\begin{matrix} \cdots & y_{1,1}x_{1,3} + y_{1,2}x_{2,3} + y_{1,3}, x_{3,3} + y_{1,4}x_{4,3} \\ \cdots & y_{2,1}x_{1,3} + y_{2,2}x_{2,3} + y_{2,3}, x_{3,3} + y_{2,4}x_{4,3} \\ \cdots & y_{3,1}x_{1,3} + y_{3,2}x_{2,3} + y_{3,3}, x_{3,3} + y_{3,4}x_{4,3} \end{matrix}
$$

which is a 3×3 matrix. In general, multiplying an $N \times K$ matrix with a $K \times M$ matrix results in an $N \times M$ matrix. Hence, one multiplies each row of the matrix Y with each column of the matrix X.

The inverse of a 3×3 matrix X, denoted by the 3×3 matrix X^{-1}, is defined by

$$XX^{-1} = I_3 \tag{A.10}$$

such that the matrix product of X and X^{-1} results in the 3×3 identity matrix I_3 defined in (A.5). This inverse is defined only for squared matrices.

Next, we consider derivatives. If X is a 3-dimensional column vector and β a 3-dimensional row vector, the first-order derivative of $X\beta = x_1\beta_1 + x_2\beta_2 + x_3\beta_3$ with respect to the vector β is defined as

$$\frac{\partial(X\beta)}{\partial\beta} = X', \tag{A.11}$$

which is a 3-dimensional column vector containing

$$\begin{pmatrix} \dfrac{\partial X\beta}{\partial\beta_1} \\ \dfrac{\partial X\beta}{\partial\beta_2} \\ \dfrac{\partial X\beta}{\partial\beta_3} \end{pmatrix}. \tag{A.12}$$

Likewise, the first-order derivative of $X\beta$ with respect to the vector β' is

$$\frac{\partial(X\beta)}{\partial\beta'} = X, \tag{A.13}$$

which is now a row vector. Just like differentiating to a scalar, we can use the chain rule. The first-order derivative of $(X\beta)^2$ with respect to β is therefore

$$\frac{\partial(X\beta)^2}{\partial\beta} = 2(X\beta)\frac{\partial(X\beta)}{\partial\beta} = 2(X\beta)X' = 2X'(X\beta), \tag{A.14}$$

which is again a 3-dimensional column vector. Hence, the second-order derivative of $(X\beta)^2$ is

$$\frac{\partial(X\beta)^2}{\partial\beta\partial\beta'} = 2X'\frac{\partial(X\beta)}{\partial\beta'} = 2X'X, \tag{A.15}$$

which is a symmetric 3×3 matrix. This matrix is in fact

$$
\begin{pmatrix}
\dfrac{(\partial X\beta)^2}{\partial^2\beta_1} & \dfrac{\partial(X\beta)^2}{\partial\beta_1\partial\beta_2} & \dfrac{\partial(X\beta)^2}{\partial\beta_1\partial\beta_3} \\[2ex]
\dfrac{\partial(X\beta)^2}{\partial\beta_2\partial\beta_1} & \dfrac{\partial(X\beta)^2}{\partial^2\beta_2} & \dfrac{\partial(X\beta)^2}{\partial\beta_2\partial\beta_3} \\[2ex]
\dfrac{\partial(X\beta)^2}{\partial\beta_3\partial\beta_1} & \dfrac{\partial(X\beta)^2}{\partial\beta_3\partial\beta_2} & \dfrac{\partial(X\beta)^2}{\partial^2\beta_3}
\end{pmatrix}. \tag{A.16}
$$

The symmetry occurs as

$$
\frac{(\partial X\beta)^2}{\partial\beta_j\partial\beta_i} = \frac{(\partial X\beta)^2}{\partial\beta_i\partial\beta_j}. \tag{A.17}
$$

A.2 Overview of distributions

In this section we give an overview of the key properties of the distributions used in various chapters of this book. Table A.1 displays the density functions, the means and variances of the relevant univariate discrete distributions. These are the binomial, the Bernoulli, the negative binomial and the geometric distributions. Table A.2 displays similar results for relevant multivariate discrete distributions, which are the multinomial and the multivariate Bernoulli distribution. Important properties of various other relevant continuous distributions are displayed in tables A.3 and A.4. For further reference and more details, we refer the interested reader to Johnson and Kotz (1969, 1970, 1972).

In chapter 7 we need the mean and the variance of truncated distributions. Suppose that $Y \sim N(\mu, \sigma^2)$. The expectation and variance of Y given that Y is larger than c equal

$$
\begin{aligned}
E[Y|Y > c] &= \mu + \sigma\frac{\phi((c-\mu)/\sigma)}{1-\Phi((c-\mu)/\sigma)} \\
V[Y|Y > c] &= \sigma^2(1 + ((c-\mu)/\sigma)\lambda((c-\mu)/\sigma) - \lambda((c-\mu)/\sigma)^2),
\end{aligned} \tag{A.18}
$$

where $\phi(\cdot)$ and $\Phi(\cdot)$ are the pdf and cdf of a standard normal distribution and where $\lambda(\cdot) = \phi(\cdot)/(1 - \Phi(\cdot))$ (see table A.3). Likewise, the expectation and variance of Y given that Y is smaller than c equal

$$
\begin{aligned}
E[Y|Y < c] &= \mu + \sigma\frac{-\phi((c-\mu)/\sigma)}{\Phi((c-\mu)/\sigma)} \\
V[Y|Y < c] &= \sigma^2(1 - ((c-\mu)/\sigma)\lambda(-(c-\mu)/\sigma) - \lambda(-(c-\mu)/\sigma)^2)
\end{aligned} \tag{A.19}
$$

Table A.1 *Density functions (pdf), cumulative distribution functions (cdf), means and variances of the univariate discrete distributions used in this book*

Notation	pdf	cdf	Mean	Variance
Binomial distribution				
$Y \sim \text{BIN}(N, \pi)$	$\binom{N}{y}\pi^y(1-\pi)^{N-y}$	$\sum_{x=0}^{y}\binom{N}{x}\pi^i(1-\pi)^{N-x}$	$N\pi$	$N\pi(1-\pi)$
$0 < \pi < 1, N \in \mathbb{N}$	$y = 0, 1, \ldots, n$			
Bernoulli distribution				
$Y \sim \text{BIN}(1, \pi)$	$\pi^y(1-\pi)^{1-y}$	$(1-\pi)^{1-y}$	π	$\pi(1-\pi)$
$0 < \pi < 1$	$y = 0, 1$			
Negative binomial distribution				
$Y \sim \text{NB}(r, \pi)$	$\binom{y-1}{r-1}\pi^r(1-\pi)^{y-r}$	$\sum_{x=r}^{y}\binom{x-1}{r-1}\pi^r(1-\pi)^{x-r}$	r/π	$r(1-\pi)/\pi^2$
$0 < \pi < 1, r \in \mathbb{N}$	$y = r, r+1, \ldots$			
Geometric distribution				
$Y \sim \text{NB}(1, \pi)$	$\pi(1-\pi)^{y-1}$	$\sum_{x=1}^{y}\pi(1-\pi)^{x-1}$	$1/\pi$	$(1-\pi)/\pi^2$
$0 < \pi < 1$	$y = 1, 2, \ldots$			

Notes:

The pdf denotes $\Pr[Y = y]$ and the cdf refers to $\Pr[Y \le y]$. The first two distributions are mainly used in chapter 4 and the last two distributions are used in chapter 8.

Table A.2 *Density functions, means and variances of J-dimensional discrete distributions used in this book*

Notation	pdf	Mean	Variance
Multinomial distribution			
$Y \sim \mathrm{MN}(N, \pi_1, \ldots, \pi_J)$	$\dfrac{N!}{y_1! \cdots y_J!} \displaystyle\prod_{i=1}^{J} \pi_i^{y_i}$	$N\pi_i$	$N\pi_i(1 - \pi_i)$
$0 < \pi_i < 1 \wedge \displaystyle\sum_{i=1}^{J} \pi_i = 1$	$y_i = 0, 1, \ldots, N \wedge \displaystyle\sum_{i=1}^{J} y_i = N$		
$N \in \mathbb{N}$			
Multivariate Bernoulli distribution			
$Y \sim \mathrm{MN}(1, \pi_1, \ldots, \pi_J)$	$\pi_1^{y_1} \cdots \pi_J^{y_J}$	π_i	$\pi_i(1 - \pi_i)$
$0 < \pi_i < 1 \wedge \displaystyle\sum_{i=1}^{J} \pi_i = 1$	$y_i = 0, 1 \wedge \displaystyle\sum_{i=1}^{J} y_i = 1$		

Notes:
The pdf denotes $\Pr[Y_1 = y_1, \ldots, Y_J = y_J]$. The distributions are used in chapter 5.

Table A.3 *Density functions (pdf), cumulative distribution functions (cdf), means and variances of continuous distributions used in this book*

Notation	pdf	cdf	Mean	Variance
Standard logistic distribution				
$Y \sim \mathbf{LOG}(0,1)$ $Y \in \mathbb{R}$	$\dfrac{\exp(y)}{(1+\exp(y))^2}$	$\dfrac{\exp(y)}{1+\exp(y)}$	0	$\pi^2/3$
Logistic distribution				
$Y \sim \mathbf{LOG}(\mu,\sigma^2)$ $Y \in \mathbb{R}$	$\dfrac{1}{\sigma}\dfrac{\exp((y-\mu)/\sigma)}{(1+\exp((y-\mu)/\sigma))^2}$	$\dfrac{\exp((y-\mu)/\sigma)}{1+\exp((y-\mu)/\sigma)}$	μ	$\sigma^2\pi^2/3$
Loglogistic distribution				
$Y \sim \mathbf{LLOG}(\gamma,\alpha)$ $\gamma,\alpha > 0$	$\dfrac{\gamma\alpha(\gamma y)^{\alpha-1}}{(1+(\gamma y)^\alpha)^2}$	$\dfrac{(\gamma y)^\alpha}{1+(\gamma y)^\alpha}$	$\dfrac{\alpha\Gamma\!\left(\dfrac{\alpha-1}{\alpha}\right)\Gamma\!\left(\dfrac{2\alpha+1}{\alpha}\right)}{\gamma(\alpha+1)}$	$\dfrac{\alpha\Gamma\!\left(\dfrac{\alpha-2}{\alpha}\right)\Gamma\!\left(\dfrac{2\alpha+2}{\alpha}\right)}{\gamma^2(2\alpha+1)} - E[Y]^2$
Standard normal distribution				
$Y \sim \mathbf{N}(0,1)$ $y \in \mathbb{R}$	$\dfrac{1}{\sqrt{2\pi}}e^{-\frac{1}{2}y^2}$	$\displaystyle\int_{-\infty}^{y}\dfrac{1}{\sqrt{2\pi}}e^{-\frac{1}{2}x^2}\,dx$	0	1

Normal distribution

$Y \sim N(\mu, \sigma^2)$

$\dfrac{1}{\sqrt{2\pi}} e^{-\frac{(y-\mu)^2}{2\sigma^2}}$

$\displaystyle\int_{-\infty}^{y} \dfrac{1}{\sigma\sqrt{2\pi}} e^{-\frac{(x-\mu)^2}{2\sigma^2}} dx$

μ

σ^2

$\mu \in \mathbb{R}, \sigma > 0$

$y \in \mathbb{R}$

Lognormal distribution

$Y \sim LN(\gamma, \alpha)$

$\dfrac{\alpha}{\sqrt{2\pi}y} e^{-\frac{\alpha^2}{2}(\log \gamma y)^2}$

$\displaystyle\int_{-\infty}^{y} \dfrac{\alpha}{\sqrt{2\pi}x} e^{-\frac{\alpha^2}{2}(\log \gamma x)^2} dx$

$\gamma e^{-\frac{1}{2}\alpha^{-2}}$

$\gamma^2 (e^{2\alpha^{-2}} - e^{-\alpha^{-2}})$

$\gamma, \alpha > 0$

$y > 0$

Notes:

The (standard) logistic distribution appears in chapters 4 and 6. The (standard) normal distribution is key to chapters 3–7. The loglogistic and lognormal distributions appear in chapter 8.

The pdf and cdf of a standard logistic distribution are denoted in this book by $\lambda(y)$ and $\Lambda(y)$, respectively.

The pdf and cdf of a standard normal distribution are denoted in this book by $\phi(y)$ and $\Phi(y)$, respectively. The pdf and cdf of the normal distribution equal $1/\sigma((y - \mu)/\sigma)$ and $\Phi((y - \mu)/\sigma)$, while for the lognormal distribution the pdf and cdf are $\alpha/y\phi(\log(\gamma y))$ and $\Phi(\alpha \log(\gamma y))$.

Table A.4 *Density functions, cumulative distribution functions, means and variances of continuous distributions used in chapter 8*

Name	pdf	cdf	Mean	Variance
Standard exponential distribution				
$Y \sim \mathbf{EXP}(1)$	$\exp(-y)$ $y > 0$	$1 - \exp(-y)$	1	1
Exponential distribution				
$Y \sim \mathbf{EXP}(\gamma)$ $\gamma > 0$	$\gamma \exp(-\gamma y)$ $y > 0$	$1 - \exp(-\gamma y)$	$1/\gamma$	$1/\gamma^2$
Gamma distribution				
$Y \sim \mathbf{GAM}(\theta, \kappa)$ $\kappa > 0, \theta > 0$	$\dfrac{\exp(-y/\theta)y^{\kappa-1}}{\Gamma(\kappa)\theta^{\kappa}}$ $y > 0$	$\displaystyle\int_0^y \dfrac{\exp(-x/\theta)x^{\kappa-1}}{\Gamma(\kappa)\theta^{\kappa}}\,dx$	$\kappa\theta$	$\kappa\theta^2$
Normalized Gamma distribution				
$Y \sim \mathbf{GAM}(\kappa^{-1}, \kappa)$ $\kappa > 0$	$\dfrac{\kappa^{\kappa}\exp(-\kappa y)y^{\kappa-1}}{\Gamma(\kappa)}$ $y > 0$	$\displaystyle\int_0^y \dfrac{\kappa^{\kappa}\exp(-\kappa x)x^{\kappa-1}}{\Gamma(\kappa)}\,dx$	1	$1/\kappa$
Weibull distribution				
$Y \sim \mathbf{WEI}(\gamma, \alpha)$ $\gamma, \alpha > 0$	$\gamma\alpha(\gamma y)^{\alpha-1}e^{-(\gamma y)^{\alpha}}$ $y > 0$	$1 - \exp(-(\gamma y)^{\alpha})$	$\dfrac{\Gamma(1 + 1/\alpha)}{\gamma}$	$\dfrac{\Gamma(1 + 2/\alpha) - \Gamma(1 + 1/\alpha)^2}{\gamma^2}$

(see Johnson and Kotz, 1970, pp. 81–83, and Gourieroux and Monfort, 1995, p. 483).

In many chapters we rely on the multivariate normal distribution. To illustrate some of its properties, consider the bivariate random variable $Y = (Y_1, Y_2)$, which is normally distributed with mean $\mu = (\mu_1, \mu_2)$ and covariance matrix

$$\Sigma = \begin{pmatrix} \sigma_1^2 & \sigma_{12} \\ \sigma_{12} & \sigma_2^2 \end{pmatrix}, \tag{A.20}$$

or, in shorthand, $Y \sim N(\mu, \Sigma)$. The term σ_{12} denotes the covariance between Y_1 and Y_2, that is, $E[(Y_1 - \mu_1)(Y_2 - \mu_2)]$. The correlation between Y_1 and Y_2 is defined as $\rho = \sigma_{12}/(\sigma_1 \sigma_2)$. The density function of this bivariate normal distribution is

$$f(y_1, y_2) = \frac{1}{\left(\sqrt{2\pi}\right)^2} \frac{1}{\sigma_1 \sigma_2 \sqrt{1 - \rho^2}}$$

$$\exp\left(\frac{-1}{2(1 - \rho^2)}((y_1 - \mu_1)^2/\sigma_1^2 - 2\rho(y_1 - \mu_1)(y_2 - \mu_2)/\right.$$

$$\left.(\sigma_1 \sigma_2) + (y_2 - \mu_2)^2/\sigma_2^2)\right). \tag{A.21}$$

An important property of the bivariate (or multivariate) normal distribution is that the marginal and conditional distributions of Y_1 and Y_2 are again normal, that is,

$$\begin{aligned}
Y_1 &\sim N(\mu_1, \sigma_1^2) \\
Y_2 &\sim N(\mu_2, \sigma_2^2) \\
Y_1|y_2 &\sim N(\mu_1 + \sigma_{12}/\sigma_2^2(y_2 - \mu_2), \sigma_1^2 - \sigma_{12}^2/\sigma_2^2) \\
Y_2|y_1 &\sim N(\mu_2 + \sigma_{12}/\sigma_1^2(y_1 - \mu_1), \sigma_2^2 - \sigma_{12}^2/\sigma_1^2).
\end{aligned} \tag{A.22}$$

The results in (A.22) can be extended to a J-dimensional normally distributed random variable in a straightforward way (see Johnson and Kotz, 1972).

A.3   Critical values

In this section we provide some important critical values for the test statistics used in the book. Table A.5 provides the critical values for normally distributed test statistics, while table A.6 displays the critical values for χ^2 distributed test statistics, and table A.7 gives some critical values for the $F(k, n)$ distribution.

Table A.5 *Some critical values for a normally distributed test statistic*

Significance level			
20%	10%	5%	1%
1.282	1.645	1.960	2.576

Note: The critical values are for a two-sided test.

Table A.6 *Some critical values for a $\chi^2(v)$ distributed test statistic*

Degrees of freedom of the $\chi^2(v)$ distribution	Significance level			
	20%	10%	5%	1%
1	1.642	2.706	3.841	6.635
2	3.219	4.605	5.991	9.210
3	4.642	6.251	7.814	11.345
4	5.989	7.779	9.488	13.278
5	7.289	9.236	11.071	15.086
6	8.558	10.645	12.592	16.812
7	9.803	12.017	14.067	18.475
8	11.030	13.362	15.508	20.090
9	12.242	14.684	16.919	21.667
10	13.442	15.987	18.307	23.209

Table A.7 *Some critical values for an F(k, n) distributed test statistic*

Degrees of freedom of denominator n	s.l.	Degrees of freedom for numerator k									
		1	2	3	4	5	6	7	8	9	10
10	10%	3.29	2.92	2.73	2.61	2.52	2.46	2.41	2.38	2.35	2.32
	5%	4.96	4.10	3.71	3.48	3.33	3.22	3.14	3.07	3.02	2.98
	1%	10.04	7.56	6.55	5.99	5.64	5.39	5.20	5.06	4.94	4.85
20	10%	2.97	2.59	2.38	2.25	2.16	2.09	2.04	2.00	1.96	1.94
	5%	4.35	3.49	3.10	2.87	2.71	2.60	2.51	2.45	2.39	2.35
	1%	8.10	5.85	4.94	4.43	4.10	3.87	3.70	3.56	3.46	3.37
30	10%	2.88	2.49	2.28	2.14	2.05	1.98	1.93	1.88	1.85	1.82
	5%	4.17	3.32	2.92	2.69	2.53	2.42	2.33	2.27	2.21	2.16
	1%	7.56	5.39	4.51	4.02	3.70	3.30	3.30	3.17	3.07	2.98
40	10%	2.84	2.44	2.23	2.09	2.00	1.93	1.87	1.83	1.79	1.76
	5%	4.08	3.23	2.84	2.61	2.45	2.34	2.25	2.18	2.12	2.08
	1%	7.31	5.18	4.51	4.02	3.70	3.47	3.30	3.17	3.07	2.98
60	10%	2.79	2.39	2.18	2.04	1.95	1.87	1.82	1.77	1.74	1.71
	5%	4.00	3.15	2.76	2.53	2.37	2.35	2.17	2.10	2.04	1.99
	1%	7.08	4.98	4.13	3.83	3.51	3.29	3.12	2.99	2.89	2.80
120	10%	2.75	2.35	2.13	1.99	1.90	1.82	1.77	1.72	1.68	1.65
	5%	3.92	3.07	2.68	2.45	2.29	2.17	2.09	2.02	1.96	1.91
	1%	6.85	4.79	3.95	3.48	3.17	2.96	2.79	2.66	2.56	2.47
200	10%	2.73	2.33	2.11	1.97	1.88	1.80	1.75	1.70	1.66	1.63
	5%	3.89	3.04	2.65	2.42	2.26	2.14	2.06	1.98	1.93	1.88
	1%	6.76	4.71	3.88	3.41	3.11	2.89	2.73	2.60	2.50	2.41
∞	10%	2.71	2.30	2.08	1.94	1.85	1.77	1.72	1.67	1.63	1.60
	5%	3.84	3.00	2.60	2.37	2.21	2.10	2.01	1.94	1.88	1.83
	1%	6.63	4.61	3.78	3.32	3.32	2.80	2.64	2.51	2.41	2.32

Note:
s.l. = significance level

Bibliography

Agresti, A. (1999), Modelling Ordered Categorical Data: Recent Advances and Future Challenges, *Statistics in Medicine*, **18**, 2191–2207.

Akaike, H. (1969), Fitting Autoregressive Models for Prediction, *Annals of the Institute of Statistical Mathematics*, **21**, 243–247.

Allenby, G. M. and P. E. Rossi (1999), Marketing Models of Consumer Heterogeneity, *Journal of Econometrics*, **89**, 57–78.

Allenby, G. M., R. P. Leone, and L. Jen (1999), A Dynamic Model of Purchase Timing with Application to Direct Marketing, *Journal of the American Statistical Association*, **94**, 365–374.

Amemiya, T. (1981), Qualitative Response Models: A Survey, *Journal of Economic Literature*, **19**, 483–536.

(1985), *Advanced Econometrics*, Blackwell, Oxford.

Ben-Akiva, M. and S. R. Lerman (1985), *Discrete Choice Analysis: Theory and Application to Travel Demand*, vol. 9 of MIT Press Series in Transportation Studies, MIT Press, Cambridge, MA.

Bera, A. K. and C. M. Jarque (1982), Model Specification Tests: A Simultaneous Approach, *Journal of Econometrics*, **20**, 59–82.

Berndt, E. K., B. H. Hall, E. Hall, and J. A. Hausman (1974), Estimation and Inference in Non-linear Structural Models, *Annals of Economic and Social Measurement*, **3**, 653–665.

Bolduc, D. (1999), A Practical Technique to Estimate Multinomial Probit Models, *Transportation Research B*, **33**, 63–79.

Bolton, R. N. (1998), A Dynamic Model of the Duration of the Customer's Relationship with a Continuous Service Provider: The Role of Satisfaction, *Marketing Science*, **17**, 45–65.

Börsch-Supan, A. and V. A. Hajivassiliou (1993), Smooth Unbiased Multivariate Probability Simulators for Maximum Likelihood Estimation of Limited Dependent Variable Models, *Journal of Econometrics*, **58**, 347–368.

Bowman, K. O. and L. R. Shenton (1975), Omnibus Test Contours for Departures from Normality Based on $b_1^{1/2}$ and b_2, *Biometrika*, **62**, 243–250.

Brant, R. (1990), Assessing Proportionality in the Proportional Odds Model for Ordinal Logistic Regression, *Biometrika*, **46**, 1171–1178.

Bult, J. R. (1993), Semiparametric versus Parametric Classification Models: An Application to Direct Marketing, *Journal of Marketing Research*, **30**, 380–390.

Bunch, D. S. (1991), Estimatibility in the Multinomial Probit Model, *Transportation Research B*, **25B**, 1–12.

Chintagunta, P. K. and A. R. Prasad (1998), An Empirical Investigation of the "Dynamic McFadden" Model of Purchase Timing and Brand Choice: Implications for Market Structure, *Journal of Business & Economic Statistics*, **16**, 2–12.

Chintagunta, P. K., D. C. Jain, and N. J. Vilcassim (1991), Investigating Heterogeneity in Brand Preferences in Logit Models for Panel Data, *Journal of Marketing Research*, **28**, 417–428.

Cooper, L. G. (1993), Market-Share Models, in J. Eliashberg and G. L. Lilien (eds.), *Handbooks in Operations Research and Management Science*, vol. 5, ch. 6, North-Holland, Amsterdam, pp. 259–314.

Cooper, L. G. and M. Nakanishi (1988), *Market Share Analysis: Evaluating Competitive Marketing Effectiveness*, Kluwer Academic Publishers, Boston.

Cramer, J. S. (1991), *The Logit Model: An Introduction for Economists*, Edward Arnold, New York.

Cramer, J. S. and G. Ridder (1991), Pooling States in the Multinomial Logit Model, *Journal of Econometrics*, **47**, 267–272.

Cramer, J. S., P. H. Franses, and E. Slagter (1999), Censored Regression Analysis in Large Samples with Many Zero Observations, Econometric Institute Report 9939/A, Erasmus University Rotterdam.

Daganzo, C. (1979), *Multinomial Probit: The Theory and Its Application to Demand Forecasting*, Academic Press, New York.

Davidson, R. and J. G. MacKinnon (1993), *Estimation and Inference in Econometrics*, Oxford University Press, Oxford.

Dekimpe, M. G. and D. M. Hanssens (1995), The Persistence of Marketing Effects on Sales, *Marketing Science*, **14**, 1–21.

DeSarbo, W. S. and J. Choi (1999), A Latent Structure Double Hurdle Regression Model for Exploring Heterogeneity in Consumer Search Patterns, *Journal of Econometrics*, **89**, 423–455.

Doney, P. M. and J. P. Cannon (1997), An Examination of the Nature of Trust in Buyer–Seller Relationships, *Journal of Marketing*, **61**, 35–51.

Elbers, E. and G. Ridder (1982), True and Spurious Duration Dependence: The Identifiability of the Proportional Hazard Model, *Review of Economic Studies*, **49**, 403–411.

Erdem, T. and M. P. Keane (1996), Decision-making under Uncertainty: Capturing Dynamic Brand Choice Processes in Turbulent Consumer Good Markets, *Marketing Science*, **15**, 1–20.

Fok, D., P. H. Franses, and J. S. Cramer (1999), Ordered Logit Analysis for Selectively Sampled Data, Econometric Institute Report 9933/A, Erasmus University Rotterdam.

Franses, P. H. (1998), *Time Series Models for Business and Economic Forecasting*, Cambridge University Press, Cambridge.

Geweke, J. F., M. P. Keane, and D. E. Runkle (1994), Alternative Computation Approaches to Statistical Inference in the Multinomial Probit Model, *Review of Economic Studies*, **76**, 609–632.

(1997), Statistical Inference in the Multinomial Multiperiod Probit Model, *Journal of Econometrics*, **80**, 125–165.

Goldberger, A. S. (1964), *Econometric Theory*, Wiley, New York.

Gönül, F. and K. Srinivasan (1993), Modeling Multiple Sources of Heterogeneity in Multinomial Logit Models: Methodological and Managerial Issues, *Marketing Science*, **12**, 213–229.

Gönül, F., B.-D. Kim, and M. Shi (2000), Mailing Smarter to Catalog Customers, *Journal of Interactive Marketing*, **14**, 2–16.

Gourieroux, C. and A. Monfort (1995), *Statistics and Econometric Models*, vol. 2, Cambridge University Press, Cambridge.

Greene, W. H. (1995), *LIMDEP, Version 7.0: User's Manual*, Econometric Software, Bellport, New York.

   (2000), *Econometric Analysis*, 4th edn., Prentice Hall, New Jersey.

Guadagni, P. E. and J. D. C. Little (1983), A Logit Model of Brand Choice Calibrated on Scanner Data, *Marketing Science*, **2**, 203–238.

Gupta, S. (1991), Stochastic Models of Interpurchase Time with Time-Dependent Covariates, *Journal of Marketing Research*, **28**, 1–15.

Hausman, J. A. and D. McFadden (1984), Specification Tests for the Multinomial Logit Model, *Econometrica*, **52**, 1219–1240.

Hausman, J. A. and D. Wise (1978), A Conditional Probit Model for Qualitative Choice: Discrete Decisions Recognizing Interdependence and Heterogenous Preferences, *Econometrica*, **45**, 319–339.

Hausman, J. A., A. W. Lo, and A. C. MacKinlay (1992), An Ordered Probit Analysis of Transaction Stock-Prices, *Journal of Financial Economics*, **31**, 319–379.

Heckman, J. J. (1976), The Common Structure of Statistical Models of Truncation, Sample Selection and Limited Dependent Variables and a Simple Estimator for Such Models, *Annals of Economic and Social Measurement*, **5**, 475–492.

   (1979), Sample Selection Bias as a Specification Error, *Econometrica*, **47**, 153–161.

Helsen, K. and D. C. Schmittlein (1993), Analyzing Duration Times in Marketing: Evidence for the Effectiveness of Hazard Rate Models, *Marketing Science*, **11**, 395–414.

Hensher, D., J. Louviere, and J. Swait (1999), Combining Sources of Preference Data, *Journal of Econometrics*, **89**, 197–222.

Jain, D. C. and N. J. Vilcassim (1991), Investigating Household Purchase Timing Decisions: A Conditional Hazard Function Approach, *Marketing Science*, **10**, 1–23.

Jain, D. C., N. J. Vilcassim, and P. K. Chintagunta (1994), A Random-Coefficients Logit Brand-Choice Model Applied to Panel Data, *Journal of Business & Economic Statistics*, **12**, 317–328.

Johnson, N. L. and S. Kotz (1969), *Distributions in Statistics: Discrete Distributions*, Houghton Mifflin, Boston.

   (1970), *Distributions in Statistics: Continuous Univariate Distributions*, Houghton Mifflin, Boston.

   (1972), *Distributions in Statistics: Continuous Multivariate Distributions*, Wiley, New York.

Johnson, R. A. and D. W. Wichern (1998), *Applied Multivariate Statistical Analysis*, 4th edn., Prentice Hall, New Jersey.

Jonker, J.-J. J., R. Paap, and P. H. Franses (2000), Modeling Charity Donations: Target Selection, Response Time and Gift Size, Econometric Institute Report 2000-07/A, Erasmus University Rotterdam.

Jöreskog, K. G. and D. Sörbom (1993), *LISREL 8: Structural Equation Modeling with the SIMPLIS Command Language*, Erlbaum, Hillsdale, NJ.

Judge, G. G., W. E. Griffiths, R. C. Hill, H. Lütkepohl, and T.-C. Lee (1985), *The Theory and Practice of Econometrics*, 2nd edn., John Wiley, New York.

Kalbfleisch, J. D. and R. L. Prentice (1980), *The Statistical Analysis of Failure Time Data*, John Wiley, New York.

Kamakura, W. A. and G. J. Russell (1989), A Probabilistic Choice Model for Market Segmentation and Elasticity Structure, *Journal of Marketing Research*, **26**, 379–390.

Katahira, H. (1990), Perceptual Mapping Using Ordered Logit Analysis, *Marketing Science*, **9**, 1–17.

Keane, M. P. (1992), A Note on Identification in the Multinomial Probit Model, *Journal of Business & Economic Statistics*, **10**, 193–200.

Kekre, S., M. S. Khrishnan, and K. Srinivasan (1995), Drivers of Customer Satisfaction for Software Products – Implications for Design and Service Support, *Management Science*, **41**, 1456–1470.

Kiefer, N. M. (1985), Specification Diagnostics Based on Laguerre Alternatives for Econometric Models of Duration, *Journal of Econometrics*, **28**, 135–154.

(1988), Economic Duration Data and Hazard Functions, *Journal of Economic Literature*, **26**, 646–679.

Knapp, L. and T. Seaks (1992), An Analysis of the Probability of Default on Federally Guaranteed Student Loans, *Review of Economics and Statistics*, **74**, 404–411.

Laitila, T. (1993), A Pseudo-R^2 Measure for Limited and Quantitative Dependent Variable Models, *Journal of Econometrics*, **56**, 341–356.

Lancaster, T. (1990), *The Econometric Analysis of Transition Data*, vol. 17 of Econometric Society Monographs, Cambridge University Press, Cambridge.

Lawless, J. F. (1982), *Statistical Models and Methods for Lifetime Data*, Wiley, New York.

Lee, L.-F. and G. S. Maddala (1985), The Common Structure Test for Selectivity Bias, Serial Correlation, Heteroscedasticity and Non-normality in the Tobit Model, *International Economic Review*, **26**.

Leeflang, P. S. H., D. R. Wittink, M. Wedel, and P. A. Naert (2000), *Building Models for Marketing Decisions*, International Series in Quantitative Marketing, Kluwer Academic Publishers, Boston.

Lehmann, D. R., S. Gupta, and J. H. Steckel (1998), *Marketing Research*, Addison-Wesley, Reading, MA.

Long, J. S. (1997), *Regression Models for Categorical and Limited Dependent Variables*, Sage, Thousand Oaks, CA.

Lütkepohl, H. (1993), *Introduction to Multiple Time Series Analysis*, 2nd edn., Springer Verlag, Berlin.

McCulloch, R. and P. E. Rossi (1994), An Exact Likelihood Analysis of the Multinomial Probit Model, *Journal of Econometrics*, **64**, 207–240.

McFadden, D. (1973), Conditional Logit Analysis of Qualitative Choice Behavior, in P. Zarembka (ed.), *Frontiers in Econometrics*, ch. 4, Academic Press, New York, pp. 105–142.

(1974), The Measurement of Urban Travel Demand, *Journal of Public Economics*, **3**, 303–328.

(1984), Econometric Analysis of Qualitative Response Models, in Z. Griliches and M. Intriligator (eds.), *Handbook of Econometrics*, vol. 2, ch. 18, North-Holland, Amsterdam, pp. 1395–1457.

(1989), A Method of Simulated Moments for Estimation of Discrete Response Models without Numerical Integration, *Econometrica*, **57**, 995–1026.

McFadden, D., C. Puig, and D. Kirschner (1977), Determinants of the Long-run Demand for Electricity, *Proceedings of the American Statistical Association* (Business and Economics Section), 109–117.

McKelvey, R. D. and W. Zavoina (1975), A Statistical Model for the Analysis of Ordinal Level Dependent Variables, *Journal of Mathematical Sociology*, **4**, 103–120.

Maddala, G. S. (1983), *Limited Dependent and Qualitative Variables in Econometrics*, vol. 3 of Econometric Society Monographs, Cambridge University Press, Cambridge.

Mahajan, V., E. Muller, and F. M. Bass (1993), New-Product Diffusion Models, in J Eliashberg and G. L. Lilien (eds.), *Handbooks in Operations Research and Management Science*, vol. 5, ch. 8, North-Holland, Amsterdam, pp. 349–408.

Malhotra, N. K. (1984), The Use of Linear Logit Models in Marketing Research, *Journal of Marketing Research*, **21**, 20–31.

Manski, C. and S. R. Lerman (1977), The Estimation of Choice Probabilities from Choice-Based Samples, *Econometrica*, **45**, 1977–1988.

Murphy, A. (1996), Simple LM Tests of Mis-specification for Ordered Logit Models, *Economics Letters*, **52**, 137–141.

Newey, W. K. (1985), Maximum Likelihood Specification Testing and Conditional Moment Tests, *Econometrica*, **53**, 1047–1070.

Olsen, R. (1978), A Note on the Uniqueness of the Maximum Likelihood Estimator for the Tobit Model, *Econometrica*, **46**, 1211–1215.

Paap, R. and P. H. Franses (2000), A Dynamic Multinomial Probit Model for Brand Choice with Different Long-run and Short-run Effects of Marketing-Mix Variables, *Journal of Applied Econometrics*, **15**, 717–744.

Pagan, A. and F. Vella (1989), Diagnostic Tests for Models Based on Individual Data: A Survey, *Journal of Applied Econometrics*, **4**, S29–S59.

Pratt, J. W. (1981), Concavity of the Log-Likelihood, *Journal of the American Statistical Association*, **76**, 137–159.

Pregibon, D. (1981), Logistic Regression Diagnostics, *Annals of Statistics*, **9**, 705–724.

Puhani, P. A. (2000), The Heckman Correction for Sample Selection and Its Critique, *Journal of Economic Surveys*, **14**, 53–67.

Rossi, P. E. and G. M. Allenby (1993), A Bayesian Approach to Estimating Household Parameters, *Journal of Marketing Research*, **30**, 171–182.

Roy, R., P. K. Chintagunta, and S. Haldar (1996), A Framework for Investigating Habits, "The Hand of the Past" and Heterogeneity in Dynamic Brand Choice, *Marketing Science*, **15**, 208–299.

Schwarz, G. (1978), Estimating the Dimension of a Model, *Annals of Statistics*, **6**, 461–464.

Sinha, I. and W. S. DeSarbo (1998), An Integrated Approach toward the Spatial Modeling of Perceived Customer Value, *Journal of Marketing Research*, **35**, 236–249.

Tauchen, G. E. (1985), Diagnostic Testing and Evaluation of Maximum Likelihood Methods, *Journal of Econometrics*, **30**, 415–443.

Tobin, J. (1958), Estimation of Relationships for Limited Dependent Variables, *Econometrica*, **26**, 24–36.

van Heerde, H. J., P. S. H. Leeflang, and D. R. Wittink (2000), The Estimation of Pre- and Postpromotion Dips with Store-Level Scanner Data, *Journal of Marketing Research*, **37**, 383–395.

Veall, M. R. and K. F. Zimmermann (1992), Performance Measures from Prediction–Realization Tables, *Economics Letters*, **39**, 129–134.

Verbeek, M. (2000), *A Guide to Modern Econometrics*, Wiley, New York.

Vilcassim, N. J. and D. C. Jain (1991), Modeling Purchase-Timing and Brand-Switching Behavior Incorporating Explanatory Variables and Unobserved Heterogeneity, *Journal of Marketing Research*, **28**, 29–41.

Wedel, M. and W. A. Kamakura (1999), *Market Segmentation: Conceptual and Methodological Foundations*, International Series in Quantitative Marketing, Kluwer Academic Publishers, Boston.

White, H. (1980), A Heteroskedasticity-Consistent Covariance Matrix Estimator and a Direct Test for Heteroskedasticity, *Econometrica*, **48**, 817–828.

Windmeijer, F. A. G. (1995), Goodness-of-Fit Measures in Binary Response Models, *Econometric Reviews*, **14**, 101–116.

Wooldridge, J. M. (2000), *Introductory Econometrics: A Modern Approach*, South-Western College, Cincinnati.

Zemanek, J. E. (1995), How Salespersons Use of a Power Base can Affect Customers' Satisfaction in a Social System – An Empirical Examination, *Psychological Reports*, **76**, 211–217.

Author index

Subject index